D0793486

Erasmus' Vision of the Church

Habent sua fata libelli

Volume XXXIII
of
Sixteenth Century Essays & Studies
Charles G. Nauert, Jr., General Editor

Cover and title page by Teresa Wheeler, NMSU designer
Book design by Tim Rolands, typesetting by Gwen Blotevogel
Set in Centaur and Galliard
Manufactured by Edwards Brothers, Ann Arbor, Michigan

ERASMUS' VISION of the CHURCH

HILMAR M. PABEL
editor

foreword by
ERIKA RUMMEL

SIXTEENTH CENTURY JOURNAL PUBLISHERS, INC.
Volume XXXIII
1995

This book has been brought to publication with the
generous support of
Truman State University, Kirksville, Missouri

Library of Congress Cataloging-in-Publication Information

Erasmus' vision of the Church / Hilmar M. Pabel, editor : with a foreword by Erika Rummel.
      p. cm. — (Sixteenth century essays & studies : v. 33)
      Includes bibliographical references and index.
      ISBN 0-940474-35-2 (alk. paper)
1. Erasmus, Desiderius, d. 1536—Contributions in doctrine of the
church—Congresses. 2. Church—History of doctrines—16th century—Congresses. 3. Catholic Church—Doctrines—History—16th
century—Congresses. I. Pabel, Hilmar M., 1964– . II. Series.
BX1746.E68   1995
262.´0092—dc20   95-37531
                                                            CIP

DEDICATION

~

THE ESSAYS IN THIS BOOK are based on papers given at a conference in April 1992 to mark the five hundredth anniversary of Erasmus' ordination to the priesthood. The conference, which took place at the Warburg Institute in London, was organized by Richard L. DeMolen, the founder of the Erasmus of Rotterdam Society and its moving spirit during the first thirteen years of its existence. DeMolen established the Erasmus Society in January of 1980 at Oxon Hill, Maryland. His purpose was to honor the Dutch scholar, whose dedication to humanism, patristics, and Scripture he admired and shared. His interest in Erasmus was kindled by Albert Hyma, professor of history at the University of Michigan, where he was an undergraduate in the 1960s. In 1969, when DeMolen was assistant professor of history at Ithaca College, he organized a symposium to commemorate the five hundredth anniversary of Erasmus' birth. The appeal of Erasmus persisted, and DeMolen devoted much of his scholarship to him in the decades that followed. In his organization of the Erasmus Society, DeMolen had the active support of prominent Erasmians: Roland H. Bainton served as first president of the Society; Margaret Mann Phillips and Jean-Claude Margolin were Bainton's successors; and Léon-E. Halkin and Clarence H. Miller are providing ongoing leadership.

On DeMolen's initiative, the Erasmus Society undertook the publication of an annual *Yearbook* whose aim is to promote Erasmus scholarship. He also led the drive to establish three lecture series that are now held annually in

London at the Warburg Institute, in Leiden at the Sir Thomas Browne Institute, and in Toronto at the Centre for Renaissance and Reformation Studies (formerly in Washington at the Folger Library and at the Royal Netherlands Embassy). In the beginning DeMolen's home served as the Society's office and library. For many years he personally served as editor of the *Yearbook*, librarian, director of public relations, fund-raiser, and accountant. He regularly attended and chaired the Society's lectures and as an affable host promoted scholarly relations in an atmosphere of conviviality. In September 1993, DeMolen became a postulant with the Barnabite Fathers. He resigned his many functions at the Society to devote himself to spiritual concerns and a life of ministry. It is eloquent testimony to DeMolen's energy and dedication that the tasks he performed single-handedly have now been taken over by three people: Jane Phillips, editor of the *Yearbook* since 1993, Erika Rummel and Richard Graham, secretary and treasurer, respectively, since 1994.

Richard DeMolen remains an active supporter and a generous patron of the Society. In dedicating this book to the founder of the Society, we express our appreciation for his service and pay tribute to his achievements.

CONTENTS

~

FOREWORD

~

THE ESSAYS IN THIS COLLECTION provide a composite picture of Erasmus' ecclesiology. James Tracy leads into the subject by asking the fundamental question: can we hope to understand Erasmus' meaning, given the rhetorical makeup of his writings and the complexity and fluidity of the concepts involved? He answers in the affirmative, suggesting approaches to overcome the difficulty of discovering the authorial meaning. Tracy's introductory essay is followed by four essays that examine various aspects of Erasmus' vision of the church. They deal with the notion of piety (Erika Rummel); the elements of concord and consensus as touchstones of the true church (Hilmar Pabel); the perceived latitudinarianism of the early church (Irena Backus); and the ideal of priesthood (Germain Marc'hadour).

In his essay "Erasmus among the Postmodernists: *Dissimulatio, Bonae Literae*, and *Docta Pietas* Revisited," James Tracy views Erasmus' writings against the foil of contemporary literary theories. The humanists' call *ad fontes* and their belief that the admired past could be recaptured through the study of ancient authors invites comparison, on the one hand, with Jacques Derrida's deconstructionism and, on the other, with Hans-Georg Gadamer's theory of the hermeneutic circle. In view of the challenging questions raised by Derrida and Gadamer and the difficulties caused by glaring inconsistencies in Erasmus' writings, Tracy wonders aloud: "Can such a man be understood?"

He suggests constructing a perspective in which what Erasmus says "makes sense." This can be done by examining the editing process to which he subjected his writings. Additions, deletions, and the very decision to publish or withhold what he had jotted down for his private use or communicated in letters to personal friends may serve as a guidepost for reading Erasmian texts in a way that "makes sense." Turning to the specific task of interpreting the terms *bonae literae* and *docta pietas* in Erasmus' writings, Tracy places the two ideals in the context of the humanistic endeavor to achieve a cultural synthesis between classical and Christian values. For Erasmus *bonae literae* represented the source of moral education, intellectual training, and aesthetic sensibilities; *docta pietas* crowned these achievements by adding a pedagogy of the soul. Just as *bonae literae* represented a desirable alternative to logic, the central subject of the scholastic curriculum, *docta pietas* counteracted the useless speculation and legalism associated with scholastic theology.

Here Tracy pauses to consider the Marxist school of thought which challenges the ideal of harmonizing disparate cultures, labeling such efforts an attempt to conceal social antagonisms under the illusionary cover of harmony. He refers us more particularly to Pierre Bourdieu's argument that cultural preferences serve as markers of social class and the application (by Anthony Grafton and Lisa Jardine) of this argument to the cultural ideals promoted by Renaissance humanists. Tracy further examines Grafton and Jardine's claim that the connection between *bonae literae* and *pietas* was an "intellectual sleight of hand" and that Erasmus could offer no method for progressing from classical learning to piety. Tracy challenges this claim, noting that humanist philology played an ancillary role in establishing the literal sense of the scriptural text, a necessary step to a spiritually fruitful reading.

But does it follow that a discerning and meditative perusal of the text will make the reader pious? Obviously we have no yardstick to measure the success of such a "method." Instead, Tracy suggests that we consider the degree to which the conjunction of *bonae literae* and *docta pietas* had meaning to Erasmus' contemporaries and represented a tension genuinely felt by them. He argues that the idea of the civilizing effect of a humanistic education was widely accepted. Reading *bonae literae* was thought to give the youthful reader a sense of responsibility, to cultivate in the child a sense of what was shameful and what was decorous. The ideal of *docta pietas* is an extension of these notions, or rather, it represents "an effort to build a bridge between what we might now call acculturation in shame and acculturation in guilt."

Tracy completes his study of the relationship between humanistic pedagogy and the inhibition of undesirable behavior with a comparison between three contemporary educational tracts: Erasmus' *De pueris instituendis*, Luther's *Eine Predigt, daß man Kinder zur Schule halten sollte*, and della Casa's *Galateo*. He notes that Luther plays on the reader's guilt and fear; della Casa appeals to the practical implications of self-esteem; and Erasmus rests his pedagogical efforts on a strong belief in the malleability of human nature joined with a plea for gentle Christian nurture. Tracy concludes that the Erasmian ideal of *docta pietas* was no intellectual sleight of hand but a viable response to the cultural tensions felt by his contemporaries.

In my own essay, "*Monachatus non est pietas*: Interpretations and Misinterpretations of a Dictum," I adopt a philological or—as Erasmus' Scholastic critics would have said contemptuously—a "grammatical" approach to an Erasmian text. The phrase *monachatus non est pietas*, which appeared in the preface to the *Enchiridion*, shocked many readers. But were the words per se radical enough to warrant such a reaction or did readers invest them with a radical meaning because of their own cultural affiliations?

Examining Erasmus' use of the term *pietas* sheds light on this question. In his writings, *pietas* encompasses four aspects: love of God and charity toward our neighbor; the monastic ideal of otherworldliness; *docta pietas*, the fusion of piety and learning; and the inner devotion complementing the observance of rites. These concepts were traditional and in themselves unexceptional. It was Erasmus' polemical use of these concepts that aroused opposition and caused controversy. He frequently coupled praise of piety with criticism of the church. He routinely contrasted *docta pietas* with the dialectical quibbles of scholastic theologians; inner devotion with the superstitious observance of rules and regulations among the members of religious orders; otherworldliness with the greed and corruption of representatives of the church.

Erasmus' attitude toward monasticism was shaped by his personal experience as well as the communal experience of the Reformation. He had been obliged by his guardians to enter a monastery against his will and, although he never renounced his vows, he felt that he was not suited for the monastic life and eventually obtained a papal dispensation that allowed him to live the life of a secular priest. His attitude toward monasticism underwent several distinct phases. After an initial period of determined optimism, he went through a period of negativism in which he sought release from his obligations. In the wake of the Reformation, however, his attitude softened, as he was watching the dissolution of monasteries and the resulting social upheaval. "I don't see anyone improved.... I find everyone worse," he observed. He went as far as expressing regret over championing spiritual freedom in his books: "I wished for a little curtailment of ceremonies and a great increase in piety," he wrote, "but now, instead of spiritual freedom we have uncontrolled carnal license."

A better understanding of the controversial phrase *Monachatus non est pietas* (literally "Monasticism is not piety") is gained by examining in more detail the outraged responses of two critics, the Spanish Franciscan Luis Carvajal and the Louvain Dominican Eustachius Sichem. Carvajal objected to the Erasmian phrase as an improper definition. His insistence on a definition conforming to dialectical rules appears out of place in dealing with a rhetorical composition such as the *Enchiridion*, but the principle behind Carvajal's objection was strongly supported by his fellow theologians. It is expressed in unequivocal terms by a member of the committee examining Erasmus' works for the Spanish Inquisition. "In theological matters," the examiner noted, "one must write and speak theologically." Such criticism is characteristic of the debate between humanists and theologians concerning the methodology and the professional training required from anyone dealing with *res sacrae*. Sichem objected to Erasmus' provocative phrase on different grounds. He linked the Erasmian words "Monasticism is not piety" to the Lutheran statement "Monasticism is impiety." Although this conversion did not follow logical rules, Sichem postulated a subtle emotional connection. Luther, he said, had merely verbalized Erasmus' "tacit message." In the charged atmosphere of the Reformation, then, Erasmus' statement was given a more radical meaning than it had per se. At the same time, the explanatory phrase appended to it was ignored. The full statement read: "Monasticism is not piety, but a way of life which may or may not be beneficial to the person in pursuit of piety." In this form the statement hardly justifies Carvajal's and Sichem's outrage or the hackneyed claim that "Erasmus laid the egg and Luther hatched the chicken."

In "The Peaceful People of Christ," Hilmar Pabel examines Erasmus' irenic ecclesiology, establishing the idea of concord and consensus as integral to his notion of the church. Erasmus' pacifism has been studied extensively in the context of his political ideas. In this essay Pabel examines pacifism as a cornerstone of Erasmus' religious beliefs. His irenic ecclesiology is rooted in the Pauline concept of the church as the body of Christ and the believer as a member of Christ's body. The "*Sakramentengemeinschaft*" links Christians to each other and to God. Through baptism they are grafted onto the body of Christ; through the eucharistic sacrifice they become "one spirit with the spirit of Christ." In describing the Christian commonwealth in the 1518 preface to his *Enchiridion*, Erasmus uses the image of Christ seated in the center, surrounded by three concentric circles containing clergy, secular princes, and common people respectively. Although a spatial hierarchy—which places the clergy closest to Christ and the common people farthest away—is maintained, it is significant that the church embraces, not merely the anointed, but the entire people of Christ. Indeed, this inclusive definition of the church is echoed in a number of Erasmus' works: the *Ratio*, the adage *Sileni Alcibiadis*, and *Julius Exclusus* (the last one is of uncertain authorship, but certainly breathes the Erasmian spirit).

Pabel demonstrates that Erasmus' irenic ecclesiology informed and ultimately determined his attitude toward the Reformation. From 1520 on, Erasmus frequently asserts his unwillingness to be "torn away from the society of the Catholic Church." The formation of new churches was irreconcilable with the notion of the Christian people as a people of concord. He urged that doctrinal differences be settled by a process of arbitration or by a general council. It follows that his *Diatribe on Free Will* cannot be construed as a declaration of war on Luther. Rather, it was an effort to appease the Reformer with "a more accommodating view," and with a rhetorical strategy that stressed an inclusive rather than disjunctive mode of reasoning. Pabel argues that Erasmus was not adogmatic, as claimed by some scholars, but disapproved of dogmatism and the multiplication of articles of faith which carried with them the danger of dissent.

In Erasmus' view, consensus was the sign of the true church. Its body of doctrine was corroborated by the agreement of all Christians or a majority of Christians, and over an extended period of time, yet it was not merely an agreement between humans sanctioned by tradition. Christ himself was the guarantor of the consensus. Erasmus used this touchstone also in judging the validity of the doctrines promoted by the Reformers. Noting that they were unable to reach consensus among themselves, he concluded that they did not have the truth on their side. In two late works, *De sarcienda ecclesiae concordia* and *De puritate tabernaculi*, he calls for a restoration of unity through spiritual renewal, prayer, and mutual forbearance until "the healing relief of the synod will work for peace." In the *Ecclesiastes*, his last major work, he closely links the church to the Trinity, the archetype of concord: "Through faith and charity the members of Christ are taken up … into the unity of the Trinity." Where concord is absent, sin is present. The purity of the tabernacle, that is, the church, is assured only if its members are united in spirit, *concordes in veritate atque unanimes.*

In "Erasmus and the Spirituality of the Early Church" Irena Backus discusses Erasmus' attitude toward the Church Fathers. Erasmus' motives for initiating, producing, and promoting the edition of patristic texts have been variously interpreted by modern historians. Some regard his efforts as a token of his admiration for the Fathers; others have cited practical reasons, claiming that Erasmus mined patristic writings for proof texts, using them to shore up his own position in polemics. Others again claim that he supported Froben's commercial interests and satisfied the demands of the market. Backus searches for clues to Erasmus' motives in the prefaces to his various editions and translations of the Fathers and examines the qualities he attributed to each of them. It goes without saying that the prefaces fulfill a rhetorical rather than a historiographical function.

Jerome is a case in point. Erasmus depicts him as a Renaissance man, replacing the medieval myth of the perfect monk, ascetic, and miracle worker with another construct: that of the scholarly gentleman. Given the rhetorical character of the prefaces, the qualities ascribed to Jerome and other Church Fathers represent Erasmus' ideals rather than actual traits, or at any rate an idealized version of such traits. Backus' examination reveals certain recurrent and telltale themes in the prefaces. In some cases, moreover, Erasmus alludes to Reformation controversies and uses incidents in the lives of the Church Fathers in a programmatic manner. For example, the remark that Cyprian refrained from using the threat of excommunication was pregnant with meaning on the eve of Luther's condemnation. There was special relevance also in Erasmus' praise of Ambrose's conciliatory spirit. It gave him an opportunity to note that his own time stood in need of a man "who can bring tranquillity and peace ... to this wretched world in upheaval."

Erasmus regularly comments on the rhetorical qualities of the patristic work under discussion. Although not uncritical of the Fathers, Erasmus clearly indicates their superiority to the medieval theologians in both style and method of argumentation. He contrasts the ardent spirit pervading Cyprian's speech with the arid dialectics embraced by medieval theologians. He lauds Arnobius for using common speech and striving to make his commentary accessible to the people; he praises Chrysostom for being the perfect preacher moving the hearts of his audience. He commends Hilary for avoiding excessive speculation concerning the nature of the Trinity and finds in Augustine "a little philosophy, but not too much." Gregory of Nazianzus, by contrast, earns only moderate praise from Erasmus because he philosophizes about theological matters and writes in an obscure style. "He represents to Erasmus a schoolman *avant la lettre*," as Backus notes.

Most significantly, in Backus' view, Erasmus consistently discusses the attitude of the Church Fathers to heresy and uses the occasion to stress the fluidity of doctrine characterizing the early church. Cyprian is the apostle of tolerance; Ambrose combines authority with gentleness; Chrysostom is conciliatory in his exegesis of controversial passages. In this context Backus draws our attention to Luther's well-publicized exchange with Nicholas Amsdorf, which touches on Erasmus' understanding of the Fathers. According to Luther, Erasmus focuses on latitudinarianism to the extent of leaving the reader with the impression "that there never was any fixed dogma in the Christian religion." In his apologia, *Purgatio adversus Lutherum*, Erasmus in turn reproaches Luther for depicting the Fathers in an anachronistic fashion as the representatives of a fully developed doctrine. He reasserts his own position: not all doctrines are founded on the Bible. Some of them evolved gradually. It was for this reason that Hilary, for example, refrained from calling the Holy Spirit "God." He did not express heterodox opinions, but "with a certain religious awe awaited the authoritative decision of the church." It was their nondoctrinaire attitude, Backus claims, that particularly commended patristic writings to Erasmus and excited his desire to make their writings available to the public.

In the concluding essay, "Erasmus as Priest: Holy Orders in His Vision and Practice," Germain Marc'hadour puts Erasmus' sacerdotal career and his remarks on the nature of the priesthood in perspective. In an age when the clergy's ignorance and lack of preparation was universally lamented, Erasmus represents a minority of well-educated and idealistic priests. The Catholic priest is essentially a minister of the Eucharist. Although Erasmus was regarded by some as sympathetic to Oecolampadius' heterodox interpretation of the Eucharist, Marc'hadour is convinced of Erasmus' orthodoxy in this respect, noting that he stated in 1530: "I have never doubted the real presence of the Lord's body." Marc'hadour suggests, however, that Erasmus, following the pre-Tridentine custom, attended mass as one of the congregation more often than as a celebrant. It is clear, moreover, that Erasmus preferred scholarly to pastoral tasks. His scruples on that count were calmed by Archbishop Warham who reassured him: "Instead of preaching to one tiny rural village, you teach all the pastors through your books."

Erasmus portrayed the ideal of priesthood in his biographical sketches of Jehan Vitrier and John Colet. St. Paul provided the underpinning for Vitrier's preaching, and he was able to infuse his listeners with a love of God. Colet, too, relied on the Scriptures for inspiration and was a champion of Christian education. In his biography of Thomas More, Erasmus presents another essential feature of the good priest: the ability to lead a celibate life. Unlike many of his contemporaries, who entered the priesthood to obtain material comforts or took vows rashly without considering their vocation, More remained a layman because he "could not do without a wife." While sexual misconduct was a highly visible vice, it was by no means the most serious in Erasmus' eyes. He was inclined to pardon priests for sexual transgressions more readily than for pride, ambition, greed, or slander.

Marc'hadour raises the question whether Erasmus was a "pious" priest. Given the complex nature of the term, the answer must be qualified. No doubt, Erasmus pursued the lofty ideal of *docta pietas*. Some of his actions, however, bear the stamp of a more conventional piety. In spite of his frequent, and often biting, criticism of external rites, he went on pilgrimages, read his breviary, duly celebrated feast days, and went through the trouble of obtaining papal dispensations to free himself from certain obligations.

The discrepancy between his scathing criticism of legalism and his own compliance with rules and regulations led critics to accuse Erasmus of hypocrisy. Marc'hadour discusses this charge under the heading of *prudens ac pia dispensatio*, the prudent husbanding of the truth, a quality Erasmus praised in others and used in defense of his own conduct. He commended Vitrier's circumspect actions and his willingness to be accommodating, lest he cause scandal. Similarly, he praises Colet for avoiding anything giving offense or providing a stumbling block to his weaker brethren. Marc'hadour cites a number of passages pinpointing Erasmus' position on the need for truthfulness: "A Christian, I admit, ought to be free of all pretense, [but there are occasions] when it is right for the truth to remain unspoken." In defense of his approach to husbanding the truth, which he terms "evangelical prudence," Erasmus cites the examples of Paul and of Christ himself, who withheld some truths to accommodate the feelings of the uninitiated. Erasmus claims that, far from being a hypocrite, he erred on the opposite side, being too outspoken in his early works. In 1530, accordingly, he acknowledged that the turbulent times required a peacemaker and promised that he would take care henceforth to "give no offense, especially in devotional writings."

   Collectively, the five essays elucidate key elements in Erasmus' vision of the church: his concept of *pietas* as spiritual and intellectual virtue; his emphasis on concord as an essential quality of Christianity and on consensus as a criterion of religious truth; his views on modern doctrinalism as opposed to manifestations of tolerance in the early church; and the significance of "evangelical prudence" in dispensing the truth.

ERIKA RUMMEL

ERASMUS.

Acknowledgments

~

The contributors acknowledge the assistance and encouragement they received in preparation of their chapters in this book.

James D. Tracy specifically acknowledges the helpful criticism of an early draft by colleagues at the University of Minnesota, professor Joel Weinsheimer of the English Department and professor Susan Noakes of the French Department.

Erika Rummel gratefully acknowledges the travel grant from the Social Sciences and Humanities Research Council of Canada which enabled her to attend the conference at which her paper was presented.

Hilmar M. Pabel thanks the contributors to this volume for offering suggestions to improve his contribution, and he is grateful to the Centre for Reformation and Renaissance Studies (CRRS) at Victoria University in the University of Toronto. Having received a Senior Fellowship from the Centre, he was able to consult its admirable and extensive collection of Erasmiania as he carried out his revisions. A grant from the Social Sciences and Humanities Research Council of Canada made possible his research at CRRS.

Germain Marc'hadour thanks Peter Milward, S.J., of Sophia University, Tokyo, for a critical reading of his initial typescript, and Richard DeMolen, by whose invitation he addressed the subject of his chapter.

ABBREVIATIONS

~

Allen   *Opus epistolarum Des. Erasmi Roterodami*, ed. P. S. Allen, H. M. Allen, and H. W. Garrod, 12 vols. (Oxford: Clarendon Press, 1906–1958). Correspondence is cited by volume, epistle, and line nos.

ASD   *Opera Omnia Desiderii Erasmi Roterodami*, ed. C. Reedijk et al., (Amsterdam: North Holland Publishing Company, 1969–).

CW   *Complete Works of Sir Thomas More* (New Haven: Yale University Press, 1963–).

CWE   *Collected Works of Erasmus* (Toronto: University of Toronto Press, 1974–). Correspondence is cited by volume, epistle, and line nos.

Godin   Desiderius Erasmus. *Vies de Jean Vitrier et de John Colet*, ed. André Godin (Angers: Editions Moreana, 1982).

Holborn   *Desiderius Erasmus Roterodamus*: *Ausgewählte Werke*, ed. Hajo Holborn and Annemarie Holborn (Munich: C. H. Beck'she Verlagsbuchhandlung, 1933).

LB   *Desiderii Erasmi Roterodami Opera Omnia*, ed. J. Leclerc, 10 vols. (Leiden: 1703–1706).

Lupton   Desiderius Erasmus. *The Lives of Jehan Vitrier, Warden of the Franciscan Convent of Saint-Omer, and John Colet, Dean of St. Paul's*, trans. J. H. Lupton (London: G. Bell and Sons, 1883).

THE CONTRIBUTORS

~

IRENA BACKUS is professeur titulaire at the Institut d'Histoire de la Réformation, Université de Genève. She has served as the general editor of the collection *Reception of the Church Fathers in the West*. In addition to her research for a critical edition of Erasmus' *Paraphrase of the Gospel of John* for ASD, she has lectured and written about the reception of the Church Fathers, the Apocrypha, and the New Testament during the fourteenth through the sixteenth centuries and the history of Biblical exegesis in the sixteenth century. Her recent publications include *The Disputations of Baden (1526) and Berne (1528): Neutralizing the Early Church,* Studies in Reformed Theology and History 1 (1993), *La Patristique et les guerres de religion en France: Etude de l'activité littéraire de Jacques de Billy (1535–81) O.S.B. d'après le MS. Sens 167 et les sources imprimées.* Moyen Age et Temps modernes, 28 (1994), and numerous articles and reviews.

GERMAIN MARC'HADOUR is directeur du Moreanum, Centre de recherche et de publication sur l'univers de Thomas More. His recent research covers a biography of Thomas More, the impact of Pico della Mirandola on Europe, and a translation of Latomus' Latin treatise against Tyndale. Recent publications include the preface to the Chinese translation of R. W. Chambers, *Thomas More* (1993), the introduction to *Tutti Gli Epigrammi* (1994), an

Italian edition of More's *Epigrammata,* articles and chapters in journals and festschrifts in seven countries. He has served as editor of both the French-English *Lexique chrétien: Permanences et avatars* for the Centre de Linguistique et Littérature Religieuses and the well-known journal *Moreana.*

*H*ILMAR M. PABEL is assistant professor of history at Simon Fraser University. His recent research includes a book manuscript on Erasmus' understanding of prayer. He has authored numerous articles and book reviews, and he has worked as a senior fellow at the Centre for Reformation and Renaissance Studies, Victoria University, University of Toronto.

*E*RIKA RUMMEL is associate professor of history at Wilfrid Laurier University. She is the secretary of the Erasmus of Rotterdam Society, a recipient of both the Harold J. Grimm Prize of the Sixteenth Centuries Studies Conference and the Killam Fellowship. She served as convenor of the 30th Conference on Editorial Problems: Editing Texts in the Age of Erasmus. Her recent research is focused on a biography of Cardinal Ximenes de Cisneros, the conflict between Renaissance humanists and scholastics, and Reformation satire. She served as coeditor (with J. Glomski) of *Early Editions of Erasmus at the Centre for Reformation and Renaissance Studies* (Toronto, 1994). She is a member of the editorial board of the Collected Works of Erasmus. Her recent publications include articles, reviews, and *Scheming Papists and Lutheran Fools: Five Reformation Satires* (1993).

*J*AMES D. TRACY is professor of history at the University of Minnesota and a recent fellow of the Netherlands Institute for Advanced Studies. His current research is focused on the finances of the province of Holland during the sixteenth-century revolt. In addition to writing numerous articles and reviews, Tracy serves as coeditor (with Thomas A. Brady, Jr., and Heiko A. Oberman) of *Handbook of European History, 1400–1600,* vols. 1 and 2 (1994–1995).

~

James D. Tracy

Erasmus
among the Postmodernists
Dissimulatio, Bonae Literae, and *Docta Pietas*
Revisited

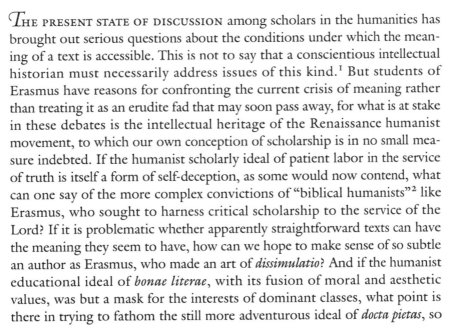

The present state of discussion among scholars in the humanities has brought out serious questions about the conditions under which the meaning of a text is accessible. This is not to say that a conscientious intellectual historian must necessarily address issues of this kind.[1] But students of Erasmus have reasons for confronting the current crisis of meaning rather than treating it as an erudite fad that may soon pass away, for what is at stake in these debates is the intellectual heritage of the Renaissance humanist movement, to which our own conception of scholarship is in no small measure indebted. If the humanist scholarly ideal of patient labor in the service of truth is itself a form of self-deception, as some would now contend, what can one say of the more complex convictions of "biblical humanists"[2] like Erasmus, who sought to harness critical scholarship to the service of the Lord? If it is problematic whether apparently straightforward texts can have the meaning they seem to have, how can we hope to make sense of so subtle an author as Erasmus, who made an art of *dissimulatio*? And if the humanist educational ideal of *bonae literae*, with its fusion of moral and aesthetic values, was but a mask for the interests of dominant classes, what point is there in trying to fathom the still more adventurous ideal of *docta pietas*, so

[1] See the preface to Alan Charles Kors, *Atheism in France, 1650–1729* (Princeton: Princeton University Press, 1990).
[2] Cornelis Augustijn, "In the World of the Biblical Humanists," chap. 9 of *Erasmus: His Life, Works, and Influence*, trans. J. C. Grayson (Toronto: University of Toronto Press, 1991).

characteristic of Erasmus? Hence those of us who find Erasmus' thought worth the labor of trying to understand better must now and then address questions of this kind, if only to bring out more clearly the reasons why we pay him the courtesy[3] of taking his convictions seriously. For the sake of convenience, one may distinguish between two sorts of postmodernist challenges, one that calls into question the integrity of Erasmian texts, and another that calls into question the intellectual coherence of the educational and religious ideals he propounded. Accordingly, the first part of this essay ("*Dissimulatio* and the meaning of Erasmian texts"), focussing on his practice of *dissimulatio*, will discuss ways of determining the meaning of Erasmian texts. The second part ("*Bonae Literae* and *Docta Pietas* in Their Historical Setting") will consider ways of vindicating the cultural ideal of harmonizing disparate values to create a richer whole, as in the Erasmian norms of *bonae literae* and *docta pietas*.

DISSIMULATIO AND THE MEANING OF ERASMIAN TEXTS

FROM HUMANISM TO HERMENEUTICS

In the wake of P. O. Kristeller's work, scholars have generally agreed that the common goal of Renaissance humanists was the cultivation of Latin eloquence.[4] But rhetoric in our day has the connotation of mere ornamentation, and if modern scholars feel a kinship with the humanists, it has less to do with the art of oratory than with the art of grammar, that is, the interpretation and clarification of texts by the great humanist philologists—notably Lorenzo Valla and Erasmus himself.[5] To highlight their own critical acumen, at the expense of all those "barbarous" centuries of scholastic erudition, humanist scholars made a sharp distinction between the clarity of an admired original text and the confusion of intervening translations or interpretations. This con-

---

[3] This phrase I borrow from George Steiner, *Real Presences: Is There Anything in What We Say?* (Chicago: University of Chicago Press, 1989). See also below, 9 n. 29.

[4] For the best general survey, Albert Rabil, Jr., ed., *Renaissance Humanism: Foundations, Forms and Legacy*, 3 vols. (Philadelphia: University of Pennsylvania Press, 1988), esp. John Monfasani, "Humanism and Rhetoric," 3: 171–235. Kristeller's characterization of the humanist movement as a phase in the rhetorical tradition of western culture has been widely accepted. See P. O. Kristeller, "The Humanist Movement," in his *Renaissance Thought* (New York: Harper, 1961), 3–23 and Charles G. Nauert, Jr., "Renaissance Humanism: An Emergent Consensus and Its Critics," *Indiana Social Studies Quarterly* 33 (1980): 5–20.

[5] See the classic study by Richard McKeon, "Renaissance and Method in Philosophy," *Studies in the History of Ideas* 3 (1933): 33–101.

trast often finds expression in a metaphor (borrowed from the Church Fathers) that may conveniently be illustrated by two quotations from Erasmus' textbook on theology, the 1519 *Ratio verae theologiae*:[6]

> The particular purpose of theologians is wisely to expound divine scriptures, to explain faith rather than frivolous questions. . . . To this end, let the novice theologian be given a brief compendium of doctrine, especially from the Gospel springs (*ex evangelicis fontibus*), then from the apostolic Epistles, so that he may have a fixed goal against which to compare other things he reads.

Human laws must be measured against the Gospels in the same way:

> If something is to be done or decreed by human laws that degenerates somewhat from the decrees of Christ, beware lest you mix the most pure spring (*fons*) of Christian philosophy with the stagnant waters (*lacunis*) of law. For human laws ought to find their model in [Christian philosophy]. The sparks [of wisdom] in human laws are taken from this one light, but the brilliance of eternal truth shines one way in iron, another way in a light clean mirror; one way in a dirty pond (*lacuna*), another way in the most limpid spring (*fonte*).

Thus the original text, in this case the Gospels, is a living spring (*fons*), while later interpretations, in this case human laws, are but stagnant water (*lacuna* = little lake, or pond).[7]

Nowadays of course one would not make such a sharp distinction between pure text and impure interpretations. But the humanists were very much a part of the culture in which they lived, and the dichotomy between *fons* and *lacuna* may be seen as a variant of one of the guiding assumptions of late medieval and Renaissance thought, namely, that specific evils of the present life could be overcome by direct appropriation and emulation of an idealized pattern from the past. In this sense, humanists who believed that Latin culture could be revived by returning to the pure usage of a Cicero or a Sallust[8] shared common ground with a very disparate company: Observant Franciscans seeking to revive the true poverty of Christ and the Apostles, Machiavelli calling upon Florence's rulers to imitate the steely political will of

---

[6] Werner Welzig, ed., *Erasmus von Rotterdam: Ausgewählte Schriften*, 8 vols. (Darmstadt: Wissenschaftliche Buchgesellschaft, 1967–1980), 3:170, 198–200.

[7] Dietrich Harth, *Philologie und praktische Philosophie: Untersuchungen zum Sprach- und Traditionsverständnis des Erasmus von Rotterdam* (Munich: W. Fink, 1970), 144–45. Cf. Augustijn, *Erasmus*, 105.

[8] The crucial work, of which the young Erasmus made a precis, was the *Elegantiarum Linguae Latinae Libri VI* of Lorenzo Valla, on which see Hanna-Barbara Gerl, *Rhetorik als Philosophie: Lorenzo Valla* (Munich: W. Fink, 1974), 231–50.

the Roman Republic, or Calvin striving to recreate the primitive church in Geneva. In light of this persistent hope for the rebirth of an admired past, it has been suggested that one cannot speak of a modern historical conscious- ness until thinkers like Francesco Guicciardini (d. 1540) were able to see that no age in the past was worthy of unqualified admiration.[9]

In a different sense, however, the critical self-understanding of modern historians may have perpetuated something akin to the naïve humanist belief in the possibility of immediate contact with the *fontes* of truth in the past. The notion of what are called in English "primary sources"—documents of the period being studied, as distinct from later treatments—prolongs the human- ist metaphor just illustrated. The point may not be immediately clear in English—many English speakers are not aware that the French word *source* means a spring—but it is in other European languages, in which the same word is used for fountains of water and for primary sources: *fonti* in Italian, *Quellen* in German, *bronnen* in Dutch, and *sources* in French. Moreover, just as the humanists quite understandably thought they had an intuitive grasp of Greek texts that had previously been known only in translation, the historian who takes up a document covered with the dust of centuries, and finds in it the contours of a personality long dead, feels an obscure thrill. Leopold von Ranke could not begin his famous *History of Germany in the Age of the Refor- mation* without a word about what it was like to take in hand the correspon- dence of Emperor Charles V at the archives in Brussels:

> True, they are dead papers, but they are the remnants of a life, whose spirit now and then breathes forth from them. For me—in a preface, one has a duty to speak about oneself, which one would otherwise rather not do—they still hold a special interest.

The experience Ranke describes here will be familiar to every historian who has ever worked in an archive.[10]

Thus we modern scholars are heirs not only of the humanists' philolog- ical skills but also, it seems, of unconscious assumptions that follow as a pen- umbra in philology's train. However it is formulated, it is precisely the notion that a reader can have immediate contact with a past author that has in recent

[9] Federico Chabod, "The Concept of the Renaissance," in his *Machiavelli and the Renaissance*, trans. David Moore (Cambridge: Harvard University Press, 1965), 162–74, 191–200; cf. Francesco di Caprariis, "Conversione alla Storia," part 2 of *Francesco Guicciardini: Dalla Politica alla Storia* (Bari: Laterza, 1950).

[10] Leopold von Ranke, "Vorrede," in *Deutsche Geschichte im Zeitalter der Reformation*, ed. Willy Andreas, 2 vols. (Wiesbaden and Berlin: Vollmer, 1957), 1:2. I too have had the pleasure of working at the Algemeen Rijksarchief / Archives Généraux du Royaume.

decades evoked critical scrutiny. There is, of course, good reason to reject the idea that one can, as it were, overleap the centuries that separate us from a given text.[11] But the postmodernist critique of this form of intellectual naïveté goes much farther, often to the point of denying the very possibility of sensing an authorial presence in the text; this at least is the argument made by Jacques Derrida in his *De la grammatologie*. At a practical level, Derrida contends that even when an author's intended meaning seems clear from his own statements, there will be fissures or breaks in the text which betray or undermine this explicit intent. By way of illustration, he turns to *Les Tristes Tropiques*, a work of the noted anthropologist Claude Lévi-Strauss. The author's stated purpose is to undermine the premises of Western ethnocentrism, in part by extolling the culture of the Amazonian Nambikwara and other peoples who lack the art of writing. But in Derrida's view Lévi-Strauss betrays his own ethnocentricity by failing to see the significance of the fact that the supposedly "nonwriting" Nambikwara have a word for "drawing lines." In other words, their culture, like all others, contains the possibility of writing, that is, a language system which is anterior both to speech and to writing.[12]

To say that authors contradict themselves is not to say anything new or startling. But Derrida contends that there is no logical reason not to treat self-contradiction as the norm, rather than as the exception to a presumed consistency. If we as readers are conditioned to look for a *persona* or presence in the text that might permit us to reconcile inconsistencies, it is only because of unexamined premises tracing to what Derrida sees as the fundamental postulate of occidental metaphysics and theology, that is, the idea of the *logos,* taken in both its Greek and Hebraic senses: "the [verbal] sign and the divinity have the same time and place of birth." For Derrida the very notion of being is intimately connected with human speech: "the idea of being ... manifests itself in the voice." Thus for the "logocentric" worldview that Derrida seeks to undermine, speech must be prior to writing, in the same way that the intuition of present being must take precedence over any derivative account of such an experience.[13] But Derrida, citing the pioneering linguist Ferdinand de

[11] See David Harlan, "Intellectual History and the Return of Literature,"*American Historical Review* 94 (1989): 600, for a critique of contemporary scholars who "argue that meanings are accessible ... if the critics or historians will only cut through the layers of interpretation that stand between the naked text and their inquiring minds."

[12] Jacques Derrida, *De la grammatologie* (Paris: Editions de Minuit, 1967), 124–25, 156–90. The English translation by Gayatri Chakravorty, *Of Grammatology* (Baltimore: Johns Hopkins University Press, 1976), is uneven.

[13] Derrida, *De la grammatologie*, 17–34. One might think that the Gospel of John would be central for any discussion of "the *logos* doctrine" in Western thought, but Derrida does not even mention the Christian doctrine of the Incarnation.

Saussure, argues that human beings are endowed with a system of linguistic differentiation that is logically prior to speech no less than to writing. Saussure's notion of language as a system highlights the importance of the common linguistic stock (*langue,* as he called it) at the expense of that slice of actually used language (*parole*) which is proper to each speaker or writer.[14] Taking Saussure a step farther, Derrida maintains that words in a text refer only to other elements in the system of linguistic signifiers, not to anything outside the system: "there is no ground of nonsignification ... that one can understand as the intuition of a present truth." It is because language refers only to itself that there can be no such thing as the presence of an author within or behind the text, or a presence of being outside the text.[15]

This is an argument fraught with implications, and worthy of response at many different levels. From the standpoint of intellectual history, it seems clear that the modern conception of responsible personhood does indeed have deep roots in the Western past, even if scholars have yet to sort out the relative importance of the contributions of Greek philosophers,[16] or of the Hebrew prophets,[17] or of Christian doctrine[18] and Christian preaching.[19] But Derrida's critique is more philosophical than historical. Indeed, Alan Megill stresses the indebtedness of Derrida and other postmodernist critics to a late-nineteenth-century crisis of intellect in Western thought, epitomized by the "aesthetic nihilism" in which Nietzsche proclaimed not only that there is no God, but that "there is no *true world,*" and hence that everything is a "*perspectival appearance* whose origin lies in us."[20] Yet one may have doubts about whether Derrida really is a proponent of the intellectual nihilism that his conception of

---

[14] The most recent treatment is David Holdcroft, *Saussure: Signs, System, and Arbitrariness* (Cambridge: Cambridge University Press, 1991). Holdcroft (39–40) accepts Derrida's critique of Saussure for his inconsistency in holding to the traditional primacy of speech over writing.

[15] Derrida, *De la grammatologie,* 64–103, 124–25, 214–15.

[16] Werner Jaeger, *Paideia: The Ideal of Greek Culture,* 3 vols. (Oxford: Blackwell, 1939–1944).

[17] Thorleif Boman, *Hebrew Thought Compared with Greek* (Philadelphia: Westminister Press, 1960).

[18] See Charles Norris Cochrane, *Christianity and Classical Culture* (1940, 1944; reprint, New York: Oxford University Press, 1957), 236–39, 449–51, on the historical importance of the orthodox doctrine of the Trinity.

[19] On the theme of *culpabilisation,* for which there is no good English word, see Jean Delumeau, *Le péché et la peur: Culpabilisation en occident* (Paris: Fayard, 1983), trans. Eric Nicholson, *Sin and Fear: The Creation of a Guilt Culture in the West* (New York: St. Martin's, 1990).

[20] Alan Megill, "Nietzsche and the Aesthetic," chap. 1 of *Prophets of Extremity* (Berkeley: University of California Press, 1987). For the quotation, see 34. Steiner, *Real Presen-ces,* 93–101, sees the late-nineteenth-century negation of traditional ontology best represented in Rimbaud's dissolution of the self, his "pulverization of psychic cohesion into charged fragments of centrifugal and transient energy."

language entails. He seems to use the deconstructive method as an ideological weapon, targeting meanings by which more "progressive" ideas are obstructed, as in the case of his critique of the ethnocentricity of Lévi-Strauss. In this sense there is an implicit, sometimes explicit alliance between deconstructionism and Marxism.[21] Whether a text has meaning only or mainly insofar as it advances class interests is a serious question (see the second part of this essay), but it is not the question to be asked if one takes *De la grammatologie* seriously, that is, the question of whether a text can have any meaning at all, apart from the endless self-referential play of language. In a deeply reflective essay, George Steiner argues that one can overcome arguments of this sort only from a context of personal faith—faith in the presence of an "other" in the work of art, faith in the possibility of communion between human beings, and, ultimately, faith in God.[22] In an indirect way, this line of reasoning honors the memory of Erasmus, since his own faith was tinged with fideism.[23] But it may also be wanting in respect for the ideal of a scholarship willing to test its conclusions in the public forum of reasoned debate, an ideal to which Erasmus himself contributed a great deal. For an intellectually compelling explanation of how it is that one does indeed find meaning in a text, Derrida notwithstanding, one may look to the German exponent of philosophical hermeneutics, Hans-Georg Gadamer.

Gadamer's hermeneutic reverses the assumptions of the humanist *fons/ lacuna* metaphor: one can understand a text not because a stripping away of intervening interpretations gives access to the original meaning, but because these intervening interpretations are themselves stepping-stones back to the text.[24] In Gadamer's view, what he calls the "situation" of the interpreter, properly understood, precludes any possibility of "immediate" contact with the author or text to be interpreted. Following the Heidegger of *Being and*

---

[21] Michael Ryan, *Marxism and Deconstruction* (Baltimore: Johns Hopkins University Press, 1983), esp. xii–xv (author's report of an interview with Derrida). On the affinities between left-wing politics and "the prospect of interpretative nihilism," see also the author's account of his interview with Stanley Fish in Dinesh D'Souza, *Illiberal Education* (New York: Free Press, 1991), 173–76.

[22] Steiner, *Real Presences*, is perhaps unduly pessimistic in thinking that a deconstructive "logic of nullity and nihilism" cannot be refuted "on its own terms and planes of argument" (57–82, 90–134).

[23] Richard Popkin, *Skepticism from Erasmus to Descartes* (Assen: Van Gorcum, 1960), 3–7.

[24] Hans-Georg Gadamer, *Truth and Method*, trans. Joel Weinsheimer and Donald G. Marshall, 2d rev. ed. (New York: Crossroad, 1989), 297: "The important thing is to recognize temporal distance as a positive and productive condition enabling understanding. It is not a yawning abyss but is filled with the continuity of custom and tradition, in the light of which everything handed down presents itself to us."

Time (1927), Gadamer recasts the traditional notion of the "hermeneutic circle" by referring it to a reciprocal relationship between interpreter and text. The mind of the interpreter is never a blank slate, prepared to take in the text as if objectively. Rather, "interpretation begins with fore-conceptions" of a work's meaning[25] that enable an interpreter to understand the text. Moreover, these "fore-conceptions" are not fully under the interpreter's control: "The anticipation of meaning that governs our understanding of a text is not an act of subjectivity, but proceeds from the commonalty that binds us to the tradition."[26] Thus the interpreter's reading of a text cannot be immediate; it is necessarily mediated by the whole history of readings that lies between the interpretative present and the past of the text. Tradition can of course provide misleading interpretations, but if "a person trying to understand a text is prepared for it to tell him something," he can be "pulled up short" when it contradicts his expectations, and this experience will permit him to replace his "fore-projection" of the meaning with another that is "more suitable."[27] Finally, understanding a text for Gadamer means to understand the "world" or "horizon" of thought within which it was produced:

> When we try to understand a text, we do not transpose ourselves into the author's mind, but, if one wants to use this terminology, we try to transpose ourselves into the perspective within which he formed his views. But this simply means that we try to understand how what he is saying could be right.[28]

This last point is of particular importance: it is a condition of our understanding that we presume an author has something to say that is worth our effort to understand.[29] The terminus of such an effort on our part is an understand-

---

[25] More commonly, the fact that one cannot understand the parts of a work without grasping the whole, or vice versa, has given rise to the notion of a "hermeneutic circle." See Gadamer, *Truth and Method*, 190–92, 265–67, 300–2. These" fore-conceptions" Gadamer calls "prejudices," using the term in a neutral sense it has not had since the Enlightenment. His reference is to German legal terminology in which a *Vorurteil* (prejudgment) was a "provisional legal verdict before the final judgment is reached."

[26] Ibid., 269–77, 293; cf. 295: "The prejudices and foremeanings that occupy the interpreter's consciousness are not at his free disposal."

[27] Ibid., 297, cf. 267–69: "This kind of sensitivity involves neither 'neutrality' with respect to content, nor the extinction of one's self, but the foregrounding and appropriation of one's own bias, so that the text can present itself in all its otherness, and thus assert its own truth against one's own foremeanings."

[28] Ibid., 292, 302–7.

[29] Cf. Steiner's description of how art repays the "courtesy" of informed and attentive listening: *Real Presences*, 3, 11–19, 84–85, 141–56. Steiner's argument is reminiscent of Gadamer here and at other points, although he is critical of the phenomenological tradition in which Gadamer stands. See his comment on Edmund Husserl (133).

ing of the author that is indirect yet nonetheless genuine; it discloses not his inner thoughts, but a "perspective" from which his views would make sense.

DISSIMULATIO IN THE WRITINGS OF ERASMUS

The issues raised by Derrida and Gadamer may seem remote from the study of Erasmus, but in fact they are just beneath the surface of normal scholarly discussion. For example, what Derrida calls the *logos* doctrine entails a synthesis between Greek philosophy and biblical religion. But it cannot be doubted that Erasmus devoted most of his life to a refashioning of the Christian-classical synthesis undertaken first by the Fathers of the church, and later by the scholastics.[30] If, following Derrida, one understands this great work of harmonization as the source of a false consciousness of personhood, then Erasmus' vision of *docta pietas* (learned piety) will be one of history's byways, a mere gloss on a fatally flawed assumption.[31] Conversely, if one regards the Christian-classical synthesis as the matrix from which emerged modern ideas of the dignity of the individual, whose long-term viability in isolation from their historical roots may even be open to doubt, Erasmus' lifework becomes an example of that critical rethinking of roots upon which the continuity of a civilization depends.

More concretely, every student of Erasmus has had to struggle with what Derrida might call "fissures" in his writings.[32] Thus the same Erasmus who in one of his polemical writings defended the Catholic doctrine of the real presence of Christ in the Eucharist could also write, apparently to a wavering Catholic, that one need not have "scruples" about adoring the consecrated host, since Christ's "divine nature is present everywhere."[33] The *Praise of Folly* (*Moriae Encomium*, 1511) stands out among Erasmus' works because his habitual moral earnestness is transcended by a vision of life as a divine comedy; yet as M. A. Screech points out, the original tone of the work seems inconsistent with the many additions Erasmus made for the revised edition of 1514, in

---

[30] Augustijn, *Erasmus*, 105–6: "This coupling of classic culture and theology was what Erasmus found in the Fathers of the church ... in these old masters, the synthesis he needed would be found."

[31] The link Erasmus makes between piety and learning is treated with great skepticism in Anthony Grafton and Lisa Jardine, *From Humanism to the Humanities* (Cambridge: Harvard University Press, 1986), 123–44, a work discussed below.

[32] Augustijn, *Erasmus*, 3: "There is something hard to fathom in Erasmus, and every biography must take this into account. The elusiveness is not the fault of the sources, for Erasmus wrote a great deal."

[33] *Detectio praestigiarum cujusdam libelli germanice scripti* (Basel, 1526) = LB 10: 1557–1571; Erasmus to (unknown) [August 1533], Allen 10: Ep. 2853, lines 46–58.

which he greatly expands the first edition's sharp attack on popes, bishops, and monks.[34] Erasmus is often celebrated for his pacifist leanings and for his advocacy of limited toleration for Protestant dissenters; less well known is his hatred of Jews which coexisted with these noble sentiments, as when he gives as one of the reasons for not making war against France the fact that France alone, of all Christian countries, is "not corrupted by commerce with Jews."[35] These problems of consistency are in Erasmus' case compounded by the fact that he found warrant in Scripture for considering it a writer's prerogative to "dissimulate," that is, to conceal his meaning from all but the cleverest of readers. *Simulatio* (or *dissimulatio*) in conventional usage could mean nothing more than a tactful suppression of minor differences, but it could also mean outright deception. A *locus classicus* for discussion of dissimulation in the Christian tradition occurs at Gal. 2:11–14, where Paul recounts how he rebuked Peter for seeming to acquiesce to the demands of zealously Jewish Christians. For Saint Jerome (and the Greek Fathers), both Peter's behavior and Paul's rebuke were "simulated," that is, worked out by prearrangement, so as to bring out the principle that Gentile Christians were not subject to Jewish dietary laws. But, in the view of Saint Augustine, Peter had been guilty of a *prava simulatio*, and Paul's rebuke was genuine, not simulated. Augustine was followed by Saint Thomas Aquinas, and by all sixteenth-century exegetes, with one exception; as Peter Bietenholtz points out, only Erasmus maintained, with Jerome, "the legitimate dissimulation of Peter and Paul."[36] Elsewhere, Erasmus followed Jerome again in pointing out that Saint Paul employed "a certain pious artfulness" in reminding the Athenians of their shrine to the "unknown god," when in fact the dedication was "to unknown gods." Moreover, for Erasmus, Christ himself in the Gospels "dissimulates his divinity" whenever he gives way to hunger, tears, or anger. In a different setting, when he found his admired Saint Jerome accepting as genuine the correspondence between Saint Paul and Seneca, he assumed that Jerome must have

---

[34] M. A. Screech, *Ecstasy and the Praise of Folly* (London: Duckworth, 1980). Additions from the 1514 edition are marked by the sigillum "C" in Clarence H. Miller, ed., *Moriae Encomium*, in ASD 4–3, e.g. the attack on scholasticism, ASD 4–3:148–54; Augustijn, *Erasmus*, 63–65.

[35] *Querela Pacis*, LB 4:633E–F. For Erasmus' "deep and boundless hatred of Jews," see Guido Kisch, *Erasmus' Stellung zu Juden und Judentum* (Tübingen: J. C. B Mohr [Paul Siebeck], 1969); for the "virulent theological anti-Judaism" betrayed by his characterization of legalistic Christianity as "Judaism," see Heiko A. Oberman, *The Roots of Antisemitism in the Age of Renaissance and Reformation*, trans. James I. Porter (Philadelphia: Fortress, 1984), 38–41.

[36] Peter G. Bietenholtz, *"Simulatio*: Erasme et les interprétations controversées de Galates 2:11–14," in *Actes du Colloque international Erasme*, ed. Jacques Chomarat, André Godin, and Jean-Claude Margolin (Geneva: Droz, 1990), 161–69.

recognized the letters as spurious, and treated them as authentic only to commend to Christian readers the writings of the pagan Seneca.[37]

Erasmus found further support for this conception of an author's prerogative in classical sources. For example, Quintilian, his favorite among the
Latin rhetoricians, described a Greek figure of speech (*emphasis*) by which one
might convey one meaning "in" or "through" another. One would expect
Erasmus himself to do as he thought Jerome had done, and Quintilian had
recommended. In fact, as Jacques Chomarat observes, Erasmus had a number
of techniques for saying one thing while suggesting something else. At the
simplest level, he no doubt expected learned readers (but not others) to recognize and appreciate unacknowledged allusions of phraseology to well-known
classical texts. Erasmus also had a habit of disavowing the more provocative
assertions of characters in his *Colloquia*, in a way that was, to quote Chomarat,
"true according to the letter, but not according to the spirit." Finally, Chomarat finds that, in many of Erasmus' letters, "without speaking untruths, he
nonetheless says something other than the truth."[38] *Dissimulatio* stretched a bit
further becomes the Platonic lie, and this too was an idea that Erasmus found
at least tempting. On one occasion he mused that in order to rein in the popular tumults of the early 1520s, it might be permissible to speak of the pope as
if he were infallible (a doctrine Erasmus himself rejected), "provided we admit
the Platonic lie, by which a wise man can deceive the people for their own
good."[39]

Thus, for the works of Erasmus, the frail reed of authorial meaning,
bruised by the critique of Derrida and others, seems at times split into gossa-
mer filaments of innuendo and suggestion. Can such a man be understood?
How can one recreate a perspective from which what he says would make
sense, if it is not clear what he is saying? Surely the most promising approach
is to remove at least some of the ambiguity by measuring what Erasmus says
against what he has previously said, or no longer wishes to say—to look over
Erasmus' shoulder[40] as he read and edited his own writings. Thanks to the

---

[37] Note on Acts 17:23 in the 1519 *Novum Testamentum: Erasmus' Annotations on the New Testament: Acts—Romans—I and II Corinthians*, ed. Anne Reeve and M. A. Screech (Leiden: E. J. Brill,
1990), 311; *Appendix respondens ad quaedam antapologiae Petri Sutoris*, LB 10:806 A–D; Allen 2: Ep.
325, lines 65–75.
[38] Jacques Chomarat, *Grammaire et rhétorique chez Erasme*, 2 vols. (Paris: Société d'Edition
"Les belles lettres," 1981), 2:778–79, 803–15, 923–29, 1044–47. For Quintilian on *emphasis*, see *Institutionis oratoris libri XII*, 7.3.83–86; 9.2.64.
[39] James D. Tracy, *Erasmus: The Growth of a Mind* (Geneva: Droz, 1972), 208, 193.
[40] Cf. Erika Rummel's comment on successive editions of the *Adnotationes* to the New Testament: "They allow a glimpse behind the scenes. We see Erasmus in his workshop, adding, delet-
ing, revising." Rummel, *Erasmus' Annotations on the New Testament: From Philologist to Theologian*
(Toronto: University of Toronto Press, 1986), 25–26.

labor of our predecessors,[41] Erasmus scholars of this generation are able to see at a glance the differences between an added passage and the surrounding text; by taking into account concerns that are evident in Erasmus' correspondence at the time of the addition, it is often possible to reconstruct a "perspective" (in Gadamer's terminology) in which the added language "makes sense." For example, the passages added for the 1514 edition of *Moriae encomium*, published at Strasbourg, date from Erasmus' triumphal progress up the Rhine to Basel, when he was lionized as a hero of learning and of religious reform;[42] the lines just quoted about papal infallibility and the Platonic lie date from a revision of the *Ratio verae theologiae* (June 1522) at a time when Erasmus' letters express deep pessimism about the possibility of a peaceful reform of the church.

THE EPISTOLAE ERASMUS HIMSELF DID NOT PUBLISH

For purposes of looking over Erasmus' shoulder, the choices he made about withholding letters from publication are perhaps even more interesting than his revisions of his writings. Between 1517 and 1531 Erasmus authorized six major editions of his *Epistolae*, and the process by which these collections were assembled has recently been clarified by Léon Halkin.[43] By 1509 at the latest, Erasmus had servant-pupils working as amanuenses, either to make copies of his letters in a letter-book, or to write out a clean copy for dispatch while he kept the draft for his files.[44] The editing of authorized volumes of *Epistolae* would sometimes be assigned to a trusted friend, on whom Erasmus could then place the blame for the appearance in print of letters that might better have been suppressed. Halkin rightly takes his protestations of innocence in such cases with a grain of salt.[45]

Halkin's belief that Erasmus in fact edited his own correspondence is confirmed by comparing the letters published in authorized editions with others that appeared only after his death. The terminus ad quem for this comparison is Allen's Letter 2508 (June 1531), the final item in the last major collection published by Erasmus, the *Epistolae Floridae* of August 1531. Up to this

---

[41] Of particular importance are Allen, ASD, and the critical apparatus of CWE.

[42] James D. Tracy, "Erasmus Becomes a German," *Renaissance Quarterly* 21 (1968): 281–88.

[43] Léon-E. Halkin, *Erasmus ex Erasmo: Erasme éditeur de sa correspondance* (Aubel, Belgium: P. M. Gason, 1983). The six key editions correspond to the letters C, D, E, F, H, and J in the "Brief Table of Editions" which is prefaced to each volume of Allen.

[44] Allen 1: Appendix 8: 603–9, and Appendix 13: 3.630–34; Halkin, *Erasmus ex Erasmo*, 24. For a 1553 woodcut showing Erasmus at work with Gilbert Cousin, his amanuensis from 1530 to 1535, see Allen 9, opposite to 44.

[45] Halkin, *Erasmus ex Erasmo*, 37–38, 46–48, 58–60, 70, 98, 110, 149.

point, Allen has 1,674 letters by Erasmus to 529 correspondents, including 480 not published until after his death, to 199 of the correspondents. An analysis of who received the unpublished letters creates a strong presumption that the fact of nonpublication resulted not from random circumstance, but from a conscious decision on Erasmus' part. The following table groups the thirty correspondents who received at least ten letters from Erasmus, published or unpublished, up until June 1531.

Erasmus' Most Frequent Correspondents

Correspondent[A]	No. of Letters from Erasmus	No. Unpublished	Percentage Unpublished
Boniface Amerbach	40	30	75%
Willibald Pirckheimer	40	26	65%
Andrea Ammonio	31	0	—
Maarten Lips	29	23	79%
Guillaume Budé	27	0	—
Pieter Gillis	25	3	12%
Thomas More	25	9	36%
Erasmus Schets	22	21	95%
Duke George of Saxony	21	4	19%
Jacob Batt	20	1	5%
Archbishop William Warham	19	3	16%
Pierre Barbier	16	5	31%
Wm. Blount, Lord Mountjoy	16	2	12%
John Colet	16	0	—
Cornelis Gerard	14	11	78%
Richard Pace	14	3	21%
Servatius Roger	14	13	93%

Continued on next page

ERASMUS' MOST FREQUENT CORRESPONDENTS (CONTINUED)

Correspondent[a]	No. of Letters from Erasmus	No. Unpublished	Percentage Unpublished
Germain de Brie	13	0	—
Bishop John Fisher	13	6	47%
Cardinal Thomas Wolsey	13	2	16%
Cardinal Lorenzo Campeggio	12	3	25%
John Choler	12	5	42%
Philip Melanchthon	11	7	63%
Ludwig Baer	10	5	50%
Cardinal Bernhard von Cles	10	1	10%
Gerard Geldenhouwer	10	0	—
Marcus Laurinus	10	6	60%
Bishop Cuthbert Tunstall	10	5	50%
Johann von Vlatten	10	3	30%
Ulrich Zasius	10	4	40%

a. A short biographical sketch of each correspondent is in *Contemporaries of Erasmus: A Biographical Register of the Renaissance and Reformation*, 3 vols., ed. Peter G. Bietenholz and Thomas B. Deutscher (Toronto: University of Toronto Press, 1985–1987).

In cases where frequent correspondents received almost no unpublished letters, there are obvious explanations. That there were no unpublished letters to Budé or Brie is not surprising, since Erasmus' relations with French humanists were always wary, and were not improved by his literary quarrel with one of their number, the celebrated Jacques Lefèvre d'Etaples.[46] Ammonio (d. 1517), Colet (d. 1519), and Batt (d. 1502) were all trusted friends, but

[46] Laurel Carrington, "The Writer and His Style: Erasmus' Clash with Guillaume Budé," *Erasmus of Rotterdam Society Yearbook* 10 (1990): 61–84; John B. Payne, "Erasmus and Lefèvre d'Etaples as Interpreters of Paul," *Archiv für Reformationsgeschichte* 65 (1974): 54–83. Three of Erasmus' four letters to Lefèvre were published, as well as all of his five letters to Nicholas Bérault, another French humanist.

Erasmus' correspondence with them precedes the period (beginning in 1517) from which most of the unpublished letters date. By contrast, if Erasmus published few of the letters to Servatius Roger and Cornelis Gerard, friends from his years as a monk of the Augustinian Canons Regular, it was because he was cautious about allowing material from this early period in his life to surface.[47] As for other correspondents who received letters that Erasmus usually did not publish, Erasmus Schets, head of Antwerp's greatest merchant-banking house, was also Erasmus of Rotterdam's personal banker. The humanist's financial arrangements were not for publication, as may be seen also in the letters to Barbier, who had arranged for Erasmus a pension funded by a canonry in Kortrijk.[48] (For the most part, he was equally careful to keep his dealings with printers screened from the public eye.[49]) In other cases a high percentage of unpublished letters indicates Erasmus' friendship and confidence in a particular correspondent. Boniface Amerbach, humanist and professor of law at the University of Basel, handled Erasmus' affairs in the city, shared his views of the religious controversy, and was named legal heir in his last will (1536). Maarten Lips, a humanist among the Augustinian Canons Regular at Saint Maartensdal in Leuven, was one of Erasmus' principal informants about affairs at the university, where conservative theologians kept up their campaign against the *Collegium Trilingue* (with professorships in Greek, Hebrew, and Latin), an institution that more than any other embodied his ideals.[50] Erasmus never met Pirckheimer, the patrician humanist of Nuremberg, but the affinity between these two men is apparent from the abundant correspondence that has survived. As for younger humanists who embraced the cause of the Reformers, it is to be expected that Erasmus might withhold from publication some of his letters to Melanchthon, for whom he always had kind words, but not to Geldenhouwer, against whom he was later to write a polemical treatise.[51] Erasmus had numerous contacts at the Roman curia, including the influential Cardinal Campeggio, but the only curialist to whom he wrote only letters (six)

[47] Of his letters to other fellow monks from this period, Erasmus did publish two of the five to Willem Hermans, but none of the five to Franciscus Theodoricus or to Claes Warnerszoon.

[48] To Jan de Hondt, holder of the canonry to whose income this pension was assigned, there were seven letters, six of them unpublished.

[49] Four of Erasmus' five letters to Johann Froben in Basel were unpublished, as were all nine of his letters to Aldo Manuzio and his successor at the Aldine press in Venice, Andrea Torresani of Asola.

[50] See also Erasmus' eight letters (seven unpublished) to Conrad Goclenius, Professor of Latin at the *Trilingue*; Henri de Vocht, *History of the Foundation and Rise of the Collegium Trilingue Lovaniese: 1517–1550*, 4 vols. (Louvain: Librairie Universitaire, 1951–1955).

[51] *Epistola contra eos qui se falso iactant evangelicos* (1529), ASD 9–1:263–309.

that he did not publish was the lesser-known Cardinal Ennio Filonardi, who in 1535 lent his support to a proposal to raise Erasmus himself to the cardinalate.[52]

One finds even clearer evidence that Erasmus screened out letters that were not suitable for public consumption by comparing published and unpublished letters to the same correspondents, such as his two English friends, Thomas More and Cuthbert Tunstall. The published letters to More are not lacking in indiscretions; for example, Erasmus brags about how the dialogue *Julius exclusus e coelo* (*Pope Julius Excluded from Heaven*) was read and enjoyed by his patron at the Habsburg court in Brussels,[53] and denounces what he saw as the warmongering policies of the late Emperor Maximilian I.[54] But the unpublished letters are sometimes even more indiscreet: Erasmus attacks the leading figure at court, Guillaume de Chièvres, who had been mentor to the young Charles V;[55] he comments on the bad judgment shown in a recent book by his and More's mutual friend, the English humanist Richard Pace;[56] and he claims that the Netherlands government and its German allies had colluded to spare the lives of the Black Band, a mercenary company that had just cut a brutal swath across his native Holland.[57] Of particular interest are a letter of 1518 in which Erasmus encloses a copy of Martin Luther's Ninety-Five Theses, while denouncing as a mere "pretext" the pope's plans for a Crusade against the Turks,[58] and another of 1527 in which he explains, in response to More's query, that he has put off the second part of his response to Luther's latest blast because of difficulties in reconciling what he would like to say about free will with the teachings of Saint Paul and Saint Augustine.[59]

[52] Manfred Welti, "Ennio Filionardi," *Contemporaries of Erasmus*, 2:34–35; Ludwig Baer to Erasmus, Allen 11: Ep. 3011, lines 15–18.

[53] Allen 2: Ep. 543, lines 9–11. Erasmus' authorship of this anonymous satire (which I formerly doubted) is no longer contested: see J. K. McConica, "Erasmus and the *Julius*: A Humanist Reflects on the Church," in *The Pursuit of Holiness in Late Medieval and Renaissance Religion*, ed. Charles Trinkaus and Heiko A. Oberman (Leiden: E. J. Brill, 1974), 444–71.

[54] Allen 2: Epp. 543, lines 15–21, and 584, lines 22–33. Maximilian died on January 12, 1519, and these letters appeared in the *Farrago nova epistolarum* of October 1519. For the context see James D. Tracy, *The Politics of Erasmus: A Pacifist Intellectual and His Political Milieu* (Toronto: University of Toronto Press, 1978), 37–38, 92–94.

[55] Allen 3: Ep. 597, lines 4–16.

[56] Allen 3: Ep. 776, lines 1–15.

[57] Allen 3: Ep. 829, lines 8–17. See the references to the Black Band in Tracy, *Politics of Erasmus*.

[58] Allen 3: Ep. 785, lines 15–36.

[59] Allen 7: Ep. 1804, lines 75–95. Erasmus' *De libero arbitrio* (1524) provoked Luther's *De servo arbitrio* (1525). Erasmus' response to Luther's introduction, *Hyperaspistes I*, appeared in 1526, but his response to the rest of the book, *Hyperaspistes II*, was delayed for over a year. See James D. Tracy, "Two Erasmuses, Two Luthers: Erasmus' Strategy in Defense of *De Libero Arbitrio*," *Archiv für Reformationsgeschichte* 78 (1987): 37–60.

Differences between the published and unpublished letters to Tunstall are not as striking, but it is in an unpublished letter that Erasmus claims that the Habsburg government had deliberately launched against its own people the Black Band's recent campaign of destruction. This interpretation of events is utterly fantastic, but for Erasmus it was a secret to be whispered to a few; other than in this letter, he mentions it only in unpublished letters to More, and to an equally trusted friend, Beatus Rhenanus.[60]

As a final test of the distinctive character of the unpublished letters, one may usefully compare statements on the same topic that Erasmus makes in published and unpublished letters of roughly the same period. The appendix to this essay gives the Latin text for five passages dealing with the question of papal primacy in the church, including four from the years 1518 to 1521, when the perception that Erasmus had laid the egg that Luther was hatching was rapidly gaining ground. In the two published letters, Erasmus provides assurance of his loyalty to the church, for Cardinal Campeggio in Rome, and for Bishop Luigi Marliano of Tuy in Galicia, a member of Charles V's privy council in Castile. In both letters he uses the same phrase:[61] "it seems to me (*opinor*) the Roman church does not disagree with the Catholic church." On the face of it, it might seem that Erasmus is indulging here in understatement, stating the obvious in a nonassertive way. But the two unpublished letters from a few years earlier, to John Colet and to Luther's friend Johann Lang, make it clear that for Erasmus papal domination of the church was nothing less than "tyranny." Owing to cynical manipulation of popular credulity by papal politicians, it might soon be better to live under the Turk than among Christians; indeed the *monarchia* (absolute authority)[62] of the papacy was "the plague of Christendom." Worse yet, the princes, whose affair it was to correct such abuses, were in all likelihood "colluding" with the pope, in hopes of a share in the booty.[63] Hence Erasmus warned Lang that this "wound is better not touched openly." As if to say I-told-you-so, he complained years later in an

---

[60] To Tunstall, Allen 3: Epp. 643, lines 29–34, and 832, lines 12–28. Cf. Erasmus to Beatus Rhenanus, Allen 3: Ep. 628, lines 28–48.

[61] For a near analogue, see the published letter to the Basel Reformer Conrad Pellican, Allen 6: Ep. 1637, lines 59–61: "Scio quam levis sit apud vos conciliorum autoritas: ego vero nec Ecclesiam Romanam contemno, multo minus quum illa habet sibi consentientes omnes ecclesias." Here "nec" has the force of "not even."

[62] For the meaning of this term for Erasmus, see the references in Tracy, *Politics of Erasmus*.

[63] Erasmus was of course aware of the indulgence controversy (see the letter to More cited on 16 n. 57), but his fears about "collusion" between pope and princes have to do with his (and others') skepticism about papal plans for a Crusade against the Turks: Tracy, *Politics of Erasmus*, 109–14.

unpublished letter to the Strasbourg reformer Martin Bucer that papal tyranny could have been "broken" if only certain things had been "dissimulated."[64]

From the letters to Colet and Lang it is evident that Erasmus readily gave credence to a conspiratorial view of the papacy, parallel to his conspiratorial view of Habsburg rule in the Netherlands; it bears noting that in both respects he had much company among his contemporaries, learned as well as unlearned.[65] It may be difficult to imagine such a great scholar promoting such a naïve and simplistic conception of the world, but we know well enough from our own times that critical acumen affords no protection against the siren song of terrible simplicities. In fact, the only way in which these and a number of other unpublished letters make sense is on the assumption that political events in the Christian world resulted from the manipulations of evil schemers in the highest places. Erasmus' view of things was not totally hopeless, because he did believe that even papal tyranny could be "broken" by indirect means. How he thought that a reform of the church and of Christian society might still be accomplished is a topic that exceeds the limits of this discussion. What is important to note is that dissimulation was part of his strategy. One can see him practicing the dissimulation he preached in the published letters to Campeggio and Marliano. If these letters are read against the background of the unpublished letters, his comment about the Roman church and the Catholic church cannot be understood as a statement of the obvious. Rather, he should be read as professing allegiance to the Catholic church, while conceding that the Roman church, which is something quite different, "does not dissent" from the former. This interpretation is confirmed by verbal clues in both letters. To Campeggio, Erasmus says he would be "impious" to turn his back on the Catholic church, but only "ungrateful" to turn his back on Pope Leo X. In the letter to Marliano, "this church" from which not even death will separate Erasmus is the Catholic church, not the Roman church.

I hope by this example to have shown that Erasmus' unpublished letters can plausibly be used as a guide or baseline for reading published texts.[66] One

[64] To Bucer, Allen 9: Ep. 2615, lines 257–60.

[65] James D. Tracy, *Holland under Habsburg Rule, 1506–1566: The Formation of a Body Politic* (Berkeley: University of California Press, 1990), 65–74; Kurt Stadtwald, "'When O Rome Will You Cease to Hiss?' The Image of the Pope in the Politics of German Humanism" (Ph.D. diss., University of Minnesota, 1991).

[66] Karl Schaetti, *Erasmus von Rotterdam und die römische Kurie* (Basel: Helbing & Lichtenhahn, 1954), 75, misreads the passage he cites from Allen 4: Ep. 1183, lines 133–39. The "rock" on which Erasmus will stand is the Catholic church, not the papacy.

might be tempted to go further, and to presume that one can make a distinction between letters written with the intent of publication, and others intended only for the eyes of favored correspondents. Chomarat believes there are clear differences between the informal style of "familiar" letters to friends, and the measured periods of epistles that illustrate the "suasory" genre of rhetoric and are intended for a public audience. But the familiar style was for Erasmus very much a part of the conscious art of composition.[67] Moreover, if we understand ourselves as standing in the situation of the interpreter as Gadamer describes it, we must acknowledge that Erasmus made certain letters "public" only when he chose to publish them, and recognized others as "private" by choosing to withhold them. There remains the question of how to characterize Erasmus' practice of "dissimulation" in his correspondence. Chomarat's view has already been noted: "without speaking untruths, he nonetheless says something other than the truth." But statements made for the public record, if by definition lacking in candor, can have a truth of their own, especially if they involve some kind of public commitment on the author's part. In the case of Erasmus' published statements on the Roman church, only close friends could have divined the mental reservation conveyed by his carefully chosen words, but friend and foe alike would have understood him as saying he would not join in an open rebellion against papal authority. Thus by juxtaposing what he says in the unpublished letters with what he says in his published writings, it may be possible to construct a "perspective" in which it would have "made sense" for him to say what he did in both settings.

BONAE LITERAE AND DOCTA PIETAS IN THEIR HISTORICAL SETTING

INTELLECTUAL CULTURE, FROM HUMANISM TO THE FRANKFURT SCHOOL

In his discussion of the development of modern nations, Friedrich Meinecke states a rationale for political integration which can apply as well to the equally difficult process of harmonizing disparate values into a richer cultural whole:

---

[67] Chomarat, *Grammaire et rhétorique chez Erasme*, 2:1043–44; Erasmus, *De conscribendis epistolis* (Cambridge: Siberth, 1521), fol. i: "Scenicus quidam verborum apparatus, & affectata grandiloquentia, cum alibi vix ferri potest, tum ab epistolari familiaritate vehementer abhorret. Is enim debet esse epistolae character, tanquam cum amiculo in angulo susurres."

> In the more recent national state ... where the most widely differing individualities and social groups seize on the idea of the nation and project themselves into it, there is no end of doubt and struggle.... Whoever observes this struggle might well think that we are moving not closer to the goal of a complete national community, but farther away from it ... But it is not just unity in itself that appears to the modern sensibility as the highest value. It is rather a unity replete with life and energy, not just a harmonic chord as such but the richest possible harmonic chord.[68]

Humanists of the Renaissance era were striving to achieve a cultural synthesis at two different levels. On the one hand, they sought to recreate for their own times the classical ideal of education, itself a blend of aesthetic and moral values. On the other hand, they had to show how the literary and rhetorical culture of pagan antiquity could enhance Christian faith rather than undermine it, much as the Scholastics of earlier generations had to do for Aristotelian logic. Different humanists used different terminology in setting out these programmatic goals, but for Erasmus the terms *bonae literae* and *docta pietas* are of particular importance. *Bonae literae* did not have a purely secular or classical meaning for Erasmus; for example, he would often describe the Scholastic theologians who attacked his philological work on the New Testament as enemies of *bonae literae*. For present purposes, however, it will be convenient to use *bonae literae* to refer to that part of his educational program that was based on the classics, and *docta pietas* for his vision of the mature Christian life.

Humanist pedagogy, aiming at the formation of character no less than at the cultivation of intellect,[69] was invariably encapsulated in slogans that had a polemical edge. Thus, phrases like *bonae literae* or *literae humaniores* implied a contrast with the "thorny and contentious" *literae* of scholastic philosophers.[70] This rudimentary notion of "literature" presumed some connection between the cultivation of aesthetic sensibility and the moral improvement of the person whose habits of thought and speech were "formed" by good letters. Thus for Adriaan Barland, a Leuven professor and sometime editor of Erasmus' correspondence, books like the *Aeneid* "teach us to forget avarice, pride, and ambition; they despise war and discord, they invite us to peace."[71]

---

[68] Friedrich Meinecke, *Cosmopolitanism and the National State*, trans. Robert B. Kimber (Princeton: Princeton University Press, 1970), 16–17.

[69] See the introduction of Jean-Claude Margolin's edition of Erasmus' *Declamatio de pueris statim ac liberaliter instituendis* (Geneva: Droz, 1966).

[70] Harth, *Philologie und praktische Philosophie*, 97. Terms used by Erasmus include: "purgatiores illae ac germanae literae" (Allen 2: Ep. 541, lines 3–35); "optimas literas" (Allen 2: Ep. 566, lines 36–39); "bona studia" (Allen 3: Ep. 597, lines 62–63); and "bonae literae" (Allen 3: Ep. 620, line 19).

[71] Adriaan Barland, *Enarrationes in quattuor primos libros Aeneidos* (Antwerp: Hillen, 1544), sig. Bi–ii; C. G. van Leijenhorst, "Adrianus Barlandus," *Contemporaries of Erasmus*, 1: 95–96.

For Erasmus, there was also a pedagogy of the soul, a formation of spiritual character. For an explanation of what he understood by *docta pietas*, one may turn to his preface to the celebrated 1518 edition of his manual of piety, the *Enchiridion militis christiani*. At the outset, Erasmus praised Alsatian abbot Paul Volz, the addressee of this letter, as a man of "pious learning and learned piety" (*pia doctrina et docta pietate*).[72] The body of the letter goes on to show how genuine learning can foster genuine piety through service to others.[73] In order to "inflame" others with the love of Christ, one must rediscover the "genuine theology" of the ancient church, which vanquished the proud wisdom of the philosophers. To overcome the obscurity of Scripture, "men both pious and learned" can make "a compendium of the philosophy of Christ, drawn from the purest fountains (*ex purissimis fontibus*) of the Evangelists and Apostles, and from the best interpreters." In this corrupt age, only men of discernment can "rekindle the sparks" of Christ's teaching, now buried beneath the embers of human opinion, so that the "celestial philosophy of Christ" not be "contaminated by human decrees." Finally, just as there are stages of piety, so that men can be led from the lower to the higher, there is also a need for rules or precepts of spiritual growth, such as those Erasmus has offered in his *Enchiridion*. Thus just as *bonae literae* stand opposed to the disciplines of the Scholastic curriculum, *docta pietas* is set off against what Erasmus saw as the useless complexities of scholastic theology, and the ceremonialism of monastic religion. In Georges Chantraine's view, Erasmus' vision of the harmony between faith and reason also has an aesthetic dimension, for the beauty of creation is mirrored in the beauty of a moral order in which knowledge is at the service of Christian love.[74]

Erasmus' devotional writings were reprinted all through the sixteenth century,[75] but, as his name had become suspect to each of the warring confessional camps, Europe's continuing demand for manuals of piety was more often met by works of a Protestant or uncontestably Catholic (that is, Post-

---

[72] Allen 3: Ep. 858, lines 4–5. See the analysis of this important letter by Georges Chantraine, *"Mystère" et "Philosophie du Christ" selon Erasme* (Gembloux: Editions J. Duculot, 1971), 101–52, and, on the 1518 edition of the *Enchiridion* (first printed 1503), see Augustijn, *Erasmus*, 44.

[73] Erasmus does not claim in this letter that he himself has become a better Christian through urging others to piety: "Verum illud rursus saepenumero male habet animum meum quod olim amicus quidam eruditus salsissime dixit, ludens quidem ille, sed utinam non perinde vere ac salse: in libello plus conspici sanctimoniae quam in libelli auctore." Allen 3: Ep. 858, lines 8–12.

[74] Allen 3: Ep. 858, lines 65–67, 103–9; 164–75, 223–31; 292–304, 360–75. Chantraine, *"Mystère" et "Philosophie du Christ,"* 54–55, 104.

[75] For example by 1600 there had been fifteen editions of the *Enchiridion* in Dutch: Augustijn, *Erasmus*, 44. For Erasmus' reputation, see Bruce Mansfield, *Erasmus: Phoenix of His Age* (Toronto: University of Toronto Press, 1979).

Tridentine) inspiration. The ideal of *bonae literae*, taken in a more restricted sense, was destined for a brighter future. The French expression *belles lettres*, first attested in 1691 and sometimes used as a synonym for *lettres humaines*, shows the prolongation of this idea into later centuries.[76] By the nineteenth century, the notion of literature, embodying both moral and aesthetic values, was caught up in a larger understanding of "culture," that is, "the training, development, and refinement of mind, tastes, and manners."[77] In a treatment that remains influential, Raymond Williams shows how the ideal of a broad "culture of the intellect" (John Henry Newman) developed among English thinkers who were appalled by the way the "organic" society of the past was being destroyed before their eyes by a nascent industrial capitalism. As an antidote to the dehumanization they saw around them, men like Samuel Coleridge and Matthew Arnold put forward an ideal of culture, including "a view of the humanizing effects of literature" which a Renaissance humanist like Thomas More could well have recognized.[78] Even for those who may disagree with its conservative political implications, Williams finds that this tradition has in some of its exponents (e.g. Newman, Coleridge) a certain integrity, which he contrasts with Matthew Arnold's narrowing of the concept of culture so as to exclude science and politics, and with the pure aestheticism of a Walter Pater or an Oscar Wilde.[79] Williams himself, working from a British Marxist perspective, struggles to envision a way in which the values embodied in this nineteenth-century idea of "culture of the intellect" can be salvaged for the democratic, egalitarian society of the twentieth century, a task made more difficult by the fact that conventional methods for the "diffusion of culture" among the masses of people have had a "dominative" character.[80]

Some other varieties of Marxist thought have been less willing to see in the concept of culture of the intellect anything worth salvaging. Indeed, insofar as the notion of a cultivation of the intellect that also has a moral purpose still commands respect in the late twentieth century, one may say that the

---

[76] *Trésor de la langue française* (Paris: Champion, 1971–), 4:370.

[77] The definition is Wordsworth's. See *Oxford English Dictionary*, 4:121–22, and *Trésor de la langue française*, 6:616–18. W. H. Bruford, *Culture and Society in Classical Weimar* (Cambridge: Cambridge University Press, 1975), 8, suggests that Samuel Pufendorf (1686) was the first to use the Latin word *cultura* in this broad sense. For the development of the related German concept of "Bildung," see Gadamer, *Truth and Method*, 9–18.

[78] Raymond Williams, *Culture and Society: 1780–1950* (1958; reprint, New York: Columbia University Press, 1983), esp. 20–25. Robert Southey made Thomas More one of the speakers in his *Colloquies on the Progress and Prospects of Society* (London: John Murray, 1829).

[79] Williams, *Culture and Society*, 61–62, 111, 115–18, 126–27, 167–70.

[80] Ibid., 238, 319–29.

principal challenge to this ideal of harmony of disparate values comes from a Marxist vantage point, and in particular from the premise that class conflict is the organizing principle of human society.[81] The Institute of Social Research, founded in Frankfurt in 1923 for the development of Marxist philosophy and later moved to New York to escape Nazi persecution, has been of special importance for the critique of high culture. The task of what founding members of the Frankfurt School called "the critical theory of society" was to educate progressive social forces by exposing the ideological superstructure of the capitalist order for what it was, that is, a way of "concealing social antagonisms and replacing an understanding of these antagonisms with the illusion of harmony." As a means of explaining why their fellow countrymen allowed themselves to be manipulated by Hitler, members of the Institute revised Freudian psychology so as to understand the repressive superego not as a timeless component of the psyche, but rather as a time-specific response to a frustrating environment. In this analysis, National Socialist propaganda owed its appeal to a psychological mechanism that induced "the suppressed classes" to feel a sense of attachment to their masters; more importantly for cultural critique, this mechanism was reinforced by a self-defined high culture that brought people to bow down before the existing order: "The consumer really does worship the money that he has paid out for his ticket to the Toscanini concert."[82]

Among the many currents of contemporary cultural critique that are in some way indebted to the Frankfurt School, the critical sociology of Pierre Bourdieu is perhaps most germane to this discussion. Bourdieu's *Distinction*, based on survey research carried out in Paris in the 1960s, argues that fractions of classes are set off from one another not merely by their members' possession of the all-important economic capital but also by their possession

---

[81] Some of us are predisposed to credit the possibility of harmonizing differences in cultural ideals, or social conflicts, just as others incline to an agonistic view of society and culture. Cf. Alan Liu, "Local Transcendence: Cultural Criticism, Postmodernism, and the Romanticism of Detail," *Representations* 32 (Fall 1990): 97: "High postmodern cultural criticism is committed to the antitotalistic vision of culture as the 'or' or the 'versus' of the struggle itself. For high cultural critics, culture is a tragedy, an eternal agon."

[82] Phil Slater, *Origin and Significance of the Frankfurt School: A Marxist Perspective* (London: Routledge and K. Paul, 1977), 26–27, 37–41, 54, 94–117, 119–23. From his vantage point, Slater (xvi, 43–45) takes issue with later writers in the Frankfurt School tradition (notably Jürgen Habermas) who have either interpreted the original program of the Institute as critical of Marx himself, or who have moved away in their own thinking from a Marxist framework. For a different view, see Martin Jay, *The Dialectical Imagination: The Frankfurt School and the Institute of Social Research, 1923–1950* (Boston: Little, Brown, 1973).

of "cultural capital" (education). The crucial point is that "taste" or "cultural preference" functions as a "marker" by which members of a particular class fraction can recognize one another, and also proclaim their felt superiority to a fraction adjacent to their own in the "field" of class conflict. Thus because "teachers" (at the universities and elite secondary schools) are, in economic terms, a dominated fraction relative to "professionals" (lawyers and doctors), the former assert their collective identity by preferring Goya to Renoir, Franz Kafka to André Maurois, and rustic furniture to antiques: "The aristocratic asceticism of the teachers ... is opposed to the luxury tastes of the members of the professions."[83]

Bourdieu's book has much to offer, not least the author's effort to bring "culture ... back into culture," that is, to show connections between such things as "the elaborated taste for the most refined objects" and "the elementary taste for the flavors of food."[84] Yet Bourdieu's argument is guided less by this holistic view of human life and culture than by the premise that class conflict is the organizing principle of the social field. Thus he asserts that the shift over time from "authority" to "advertising" amounts to nothing more than a change in the mode of domination.[85] Just as Derrida never quite endorses the intellectual nihilism that deconstruction seems to imply, Bourdieu never quite says that aesthetic experience is merely a learned procedure by which we affirm our place in the pecking order of class fractions, rather than a going out of ourselves to encounter a work of art.[86] But if Bourdieu's cultural critique is to be taken seriously, it will be difficult to take seriously the ideas of one who, like Erasmus, stands at an early stage in the formation of the modern conception of high culture, which not only presumes the integrity of aesthetic experience but links it to moral development.

BONAE LITERAE, SOCIAL STATUS, AND THE PEDAGOGY OF SHAME

Without professing allegiance to any school of thought, Anthony Grafton and Lisa Jardine interpret the humanist educational program in ways that parallel Bourdieu's reduction of the cultural preferences of modern

---

[83] Pierre Bourdieu, *Distinction: A Social Critique of the Judgment of Taste* (Cambridge: Harvard University Press, 1984), 1–4, 23, 60, 114–15, 286 (quotation source), 287–93.

[84] Ibid., 1; cf. 173–74: "An old cabinet-maker's world view, the way he manages his budget, his time or his body, his use of language and choice of clothing are fully present in his ethic of scrupulous, impeccable craftmanship."

[85] Ibid., 154; cf. 165, 31.

[86] Bourdieu's discussion of "the world of ideas" as "objectified cultural capital" (ibid., 228) does not seem to allow for real autonomy of the former.

Parisians to stratagems of class conflict. The authors begin with a careful analysis of what some noted Italian humanists actually did in their lectures, finding little support for claims made in behalf of the character-forming value of *bonae literae*. On this basis, Grafton and Jardine argue that historians ought to pay more attention to the seemingly incidental advantages of a humanist education:

> It stamped the more prominent members of the new elite with an indelible seal of cultural authority. . . . [It] offered everyone a model of true culture as something given, absolute, to be mastered, not questioned—and thus fostered in all its initiates a properly servile attitude towards authority.[87]

Humanist culture did indeed serve as a "marker" of elite status in the sixteenth century; no one who has read Baldassare Castiglione's manual on how to get ahead at a princely court (*The Courtier*) can have any doubts on this score.[88] Thus the question is whether humanist culture can have had something like the aesthetic and moral value attributed to it by its proponents, in addition to or in spite of the fact that it served also to "stamp" the sons of noble and burgher families with a "seal of cultural authority."[89]

If Grafton and Jardine cannot take the ideal of *bonae literae* at face value, their chapter on Erasmus is even more skeptical about his *docta pietas*. If there really was a link between piety and learning, Erasmus, as a man of his time, must have had a *methodus* for connecting piety and learning.[90] But modern readers have found the *Enchiridion* "gummy and diffuse," and a perusal of his New Testament studies reveals only "the ultimate vagueness of the Christian humanists' claim that their art of reading and composition built on solid spiritual foundations." He might have been thinking of the *methodus* or humanist logic of Rudolph Agricola, a scholar from the Netherlands of the previous generation, but Agricola himself nowhere explains "how training in rhetoric on the ancient model is elevated into a spiritually enlightening *educatio*." Possibly Erasmus thought that the practice of humanist philological scholarship "will make the reader moral and wise in a direct way"; but in light of the fierce

[87] Grafton and Jardine, *From Humanism to the Humanities*, 23–24.
[88] See also Guillaume Budé's caustic remarks on how courtiers in France were spicing their flatteries with classical allusions: *De transitu Hellenismi ad Christianismum* (Paris: R. Estienne, 1535), 31–32.
[89] James D. Tracy, "From Humanism to the Humanities: A Critique of Grafton and Jardine," *Modern Language Quarterly* 51 (1990): 122–43.
[90] Cf. *Enchiridion*, LB 5: 21A: "Est autem omnino virtutis ars quaedam & disciplina." Erasmus' textbook on theology, the *Ratio verae theologiae*, was called *Methodus verae theologiae* in its first edition (1516).

quarrels among humanists—the celebrated *odium philologicum*—the absurdity of such a view needs little comment. According to Grafton and Jardine, then, one is left with the conclusion that there is no method of piety, and that piety and learning are connected only by a kind of "intellectual sleight of hand" in which the *persona* of Erasmus himself "validates the equation [that] 'competence in the ancient languages is equivalent to a preparation for Christian piety.'"[91]

The *Enchiridion*, with its labored comparisons and self-conscious erudition, is indeed tough going for twentieth-century readers, but the multiple editions and translations of the work suggest that sixteenth-century readers found it rather more interesting.[92] This work, first printed in 1503, was Erasmus' first major effort as a devotional writer, and, as in other genres, he got better as he went along.[93] But in Grafton and Jardine's discussion, the facts of the case are treated with stunning insouciance. The authors seem quite unaware of what the *Enchiridion* says repeatedly and of the modern scholarship that has confirmed Erasmus' point, namely, that his "art" or method for a spiritually fruitful reading of Scripture comes from the Fathers of the church, especially those who favored a figurative or allegorical interpretation.[94] For this purpose, Agricola's logic has no relevance whatever, and humanist philology has only an ancillary role, in that scholarship establishes the literal sense upon which spiritual reading builds.

The question that underlies this argument is not so easily dismissed: what evidence is there that one could indeed become a better person by meditative reflection on Scripture, as Erasmus recommended, or, in a different sense, by learning to appreciate great literature, as humanists in general recommended? But the problem with questions of this sort is that one can hardly imagine what form a satisfactory answer might take. If (following Gadamer) we accept that we cannot peer into the minds of persons long dead, we must accept *a fortiori* that we cannot peer into their souls. Civility towards others

---

[91] Grafton and Jardine, *From Humanism to the Humanities*, 123–49, cf. 65–66.

[92] Augustijn, *Erasmus*, 44–47, citing Heiko Oberman's characterization of the *Enchiridion* as "the dullest book in the history of piety," but then offering a plausible explanation of its appeal to contemporaries.

[93] By way of contrast with the *Enchiridion*, see the *Paraclesis* preface to his 1516 New Testament, and reprinted in Holborn.

[94] *Enchiridion*, LB 5: 8D, 19A–B, 29E, 30B, 53B–C; *Ratio verae theologiae*, LB 5: 75D–E, 79C–D, 80F, 81B–E, 83E, 121C–F, 125B–D, 131A–B, 132F. On the *Enchiridion*, see Alfons Auer, *Die vollkommene Frömmigkeit eines Christen* (Düsseldorf: Patmos, 1954), and the pertinent sections of André Godin, *Erasme, lecteur d'Origène* (Geneva: Droz, 1982); on the *Ratio verae theologiae*, see Chantraine, *"Mystère" et "Philosophie du Christ."*

might seem easier for the historian to assess than the quality of a person's religious life, but here too the difficulties seem insurmountable. Grafton and Jardine's efforts to find "proof of the pudding" in the lives of teachers who followed Erasmus' ideas do not inspire confidence.[95] There are good studies of Europe's humanistic *gymnasia*, some of which were founded during Erasmus' lifetime, but they cannot be expected to tell us whether or how far these schools succeeded in impressing on the young men of prominent families who attended them a lively and lasting sense of their responsibilities to God, and to their fellow citizens.[96]

If one is to gauge the soundness of cultural ideals like *bonae literae* or *docta pietas*, one can do so only in terms of their consistency. A philosopher or theologian would be primarily interested in internal consistency, that is, the degree to which the component parts of the ideal are brought into a harmonious relationship. A historian would focus more on external consistency, that is, the degree to which the ideal addresses genuine concerns of people of that era. The two kinds of consistency need not go together; thus a particular ideal can be logically cohesive but of little interest to contemporaries, or of great interest to contemporaries precisely because the integration of its component parts is less than completely successful. The balance of this essay will argue that both *bonae literae* and *docta pietas* had meaning for contemporaries precisely because each of these ideals sought to resolve tensions that readers would have felt in themselves, between cherished and yet seemingly incompatible values.

Bonae literae may be taken as a shorthand expression for the humanist theory of classical education, based especially on Quintilian's *Institutes of Oratory*, in which a teacher was to "draw out" (*e-ducare*) his (male)[97] pupils by appealing to their better instincts. By relying on persuasion rather than

---

[95] Grafton and Jardine, *From Humanism to the Humanities*, 149–57; e.g., 156–57, Nicolaus Clenardus, the Flemish humanist in Portugal, is said in his letters to "evidence no humanity whatever towards his African slaves—he appears to have regarded *them* as less than human" (emphasis in the original). But this indictment cannot fairly be made against a man who taught three illiterate Ethiopian boys to speak and write classical Latin and outlined a grammar of "Ethiopian" from materials provided by his cook: Clenardus, *De modo docendi pueros analphabetos* (Cologne, 1550), sig. B5, E4.

[96] Anton Schindling, *Humanistische Hochschule und Freie Reichsstadt* (Wiesbaden: Steiner, 1971), 397, limits himself to the comment that the humanist education provided by the town *gymnasium* "certainly contributed" to socializing Strasbourg's elite in the roles and responsibilities expected of them.

[97] For the difficult position of women humanists, see Margaret L. King, "Book-Lined Cells: Women and Humanism in the Early Italian Renaissance," in Rabil, *Renaissance Humanism*, I: 434–53.

coercion, and by fostering competition, he would build on that passion for honor and esteem—what Aristotle called greatness of spirit—that made noble youth strive to excel, and to avoid what is base and unworthy. But as Cicero pointed out, greatness of spirit by itself could degenerate into "savagery"; hence the teacher must also cultivate in his pupils the instincts that enabled men to live peaceably together in civilized society, such as *humanitas*. To achieve these objectives, boys were to be schooled in "good authors" whose works provided them with memorable *exempla* of admirable and shameful deeds, awakening in them that natural sense of beauty and decorum (*decus*) which, so Cicero and others argued, could readily be transferred to the sphere of moral judgment. Writing to one of the boys he tutored while studying in Paris, Erasmus summed up this tradition in a few lines:

> Unlike public honors, [*bonae literae*] do not come to those who are unworthy; they instruct a man in virtue, rather than calling him away from it; they alone calm our spirits, a remedy always at hand: indeed, without them we are not even men.[98]

In the classical authors this was quite literally an education for "noble" youth, and the aristocratic setting of Roman schooling was in effect replicated by some of the Italian humanists, those who tutored a select group of boys at princely courts.[99] But northern humanists generally had less contact with the aristocracy, and could not accept the premise that an education was mainly for the sons of the nobility. Erasmus rejected Quintilian's preference for private tutors in favor of a *schola publica*, that is, a school under civic or church authorities.[100] But grafting a humanist curriculum onto crowded town schools meant that harassed teachers had to boil the classics down to copybooks of worthy *sententiae* from the ancients, so as to impress at least these nuggets of wisdom firmly in the minds of their many charges.[101] Thus the disparity between what men like Erasmus had in mind and how *bonae literae* were actually taught in many classrooms may be seen as reflecting an inner tension in the humanist ideal, between the charm that "good authors" might have for the few whose sensibilities had been properly cultivated, and the moral training that was the stated aim of education in "public" schools.[102]

---

[98] Tracy, *Erasmus: The Growth of a Mind*, 57–71; Allen 1: Ep. 61, lines 88–95.

[99] W. H. Woodward, *Vittorino da Feltre and Other Humanist Educators* (1897; reprint, New York: Teachers College, Columbia University, 1964); Grafton and Jardine, *From Humanism to the Humanities*, chap. 1.

[100] *Declamatio de pueris instituendis*, 504D: "Oportet esse scholam aut publicam, aut nullam," with Margolin's explanation of "schola publica" at nn. 550, 625.

[101] On *sententiae* and copybooks, see the article cited on 25 n. 89.

[102] Margolin, *Declamatio de pueris instituendis*, 53–54: even though Erasmus in this work "freely accepted the system of common education, he has a secret, even explicitly avowed preference for educating the child at home, by a tutor."

This bipolarity between the aesthetic and the moral gave the humanist program a double-barreled appeal for prominent families, titled nobles, and burghers who wanted for their sons an education that might instill in them a sense of responsibility, while cultivating at the same time their *amour propre*. For a framework of analysis that suggests the historical importance of this tension, one may turn to the German sociologist Norbert Elias, whose *On the Civilizing Process*, though published in the 1930s, has reached a wider audience only in recent decades. Elias seeks to outline "structural changes in the mechanisms for controlling emotions," culminating in the eighteenth-century notion of "civilization," or politeness and refinement of life. His guiding hypothesis is that there was over the centuries "an advancement of the shame frontier," as more and more forms of behavior were stigmatized as impolite and therefore unacceptable. In this gradual change Elias gives Erasmus a pivotal role. His little treatise on manners for boys (*De civilitate morum puerilium*, 1530) effectively replaced the medieval aristocratic notion of "courtesy" with the classical ideal of "civility" as the norm of politeness. Since Erasmus often dealt with issues from a layman's point of view, his reinforcement of traditional sexual ethics in the popular *Colloquia* expressed, when measured by the standards of lay society in the Middle Ages, or even in his own day, a mighty push in the direction of that form of instinctual repression which the nineteenth century would justify by its morality.

For Elias, Erasmus' importance lay in his direct appeal to a reader's sense of shame; as he said of one of his *Colloquia* ("The Suitor and the Whore," in which a youth converts the girl from a wayward life and then marries her): "What could be said more efficaciously for instilling in the souls of youth a consciousness of shame?"[103] The point is that by cultivating in youth a sense of what is shameful or indecorous (cf. Cicero's concept of *decus*), one creates in them a "superego"[104] or mechanism for inhibiting undesirable behavior without infringing on their sense of self-worth. One could hardly imagine an educational program that would better suit this dual need than the one which Erasmus and other humanists borrowed from the classics. The ideal of *bonae literae* was indeed focused on the privileged, families who could afford the best for their sons, but in a very specific sense; it was a modern form of the ancient pedagogy whose premise was that privilege begets responsibility.

[103] Norbert Elias, *Über den Prozess der Zivilisation*, 2 vols. (Bern and Munich: Francke, 1969), 1: 1–16, 46–63, 65–73, 89–106, 231–39.

[104] Ibid., 2: esp. 313–35. Elias never mentions Freud, but the concept of "sociogenesis," to which vol. 2 is devoted, is an implicit critique of Freud's theory that morality arises from conflicts within the psyche; rather, Elias argues, respect for others (for which he appropriates the Freudian term, superego) must grow apace as society becomes more and more differentiated.

DOCTA PIETAS: BETWEEN SHAME CULTURE AND GUILT CULTURE

Erasmus' concept of *docta pietas* is likewise fraught with a certain inner tension, and here too the tension reflects a larger historical situation. For Erasmus, pagan wisdom had a place of honor next to divine revelation for the same reason that human nature had a necessary role in the economy of grace. This fundamental stance, whether in early writings like *Antibarbarorum liber* (1494/1495) or in mature works like the treatise against Luther (*De libero arbitrio*, 1524), represents a selective appropriation of the theological tradition with an emphasis on the Greek Fathers and their optimistic view of human nature as redeemed by Christ.[105] Prior to the fixation of Catholic doctrine on nature and grace at the Council of Trent, the tradition had a good deal of room for different views,[106] but even so, Erasmus seems at times to jump the traces. For example, the *Enchiridion* treats the desire to protect one's reputation as a valid motive for action, quite apart from religion: "If Christ be vile to you, at least abstain from shameful things for your own sake."[107] Erasmus always professed his adherence to the orthodox doctrine of original sin, but never found any of the biblical texts usually alleged in its favor to be convincing. All in all, he had some difficulty with those elements of Latin Christianity most closely associated with the powerful influence of Saint Augustine: a keen sense of one's own duplicity, and of the sinner's utter dependence on God's grace. Erasmus came to terms with Augustine's theology of sin and grace, if at all, only in the final stage of his controversy with Luther, in the *Hyperaspistes II* of 1527.[108]

To appreciate the significance of Erasmus' equivocations about the classical doctrine of sin, one must understand that he lived in the midst of a long period when the Christian sense of religious guilt was more intensely

[105] On the theology of the early works, see Ernst W. Kohls, *Die Theologie des Erasmus*, 2 vols. (Basel: Helbing & Lichtenhahn, 1966), which is less reliable than two older studies: Paul Mestwerdt, *Die Anfänge des Erasmus* (Leipzig: R. Haupt, 1917), and Otto Schottenloher, *Erasmus im Ringen um die humanistische Bildungsform* (Münster: Aschendorff, 1933). On *De libero arbitrio* see Georges Chantraine, *Erasme et Luther: Libre et serf arbitre?* (Paris: Lethielleux, 1981). There is no general study of Erasmus and the Greek Fathers, but see the superb work of Godin, *Erasme, lecteur d'Origène*.

[106] Harry McSorley, "Free Will, Unfree Will, and Neo-Semipelagianism in Late Scholasticism," chap. 7 of *Luther, Right or Wrong? An Ecumenical-Theological Study of Luther's Major Work, "The Bondage of the Will"* (New York: Newman Press, 1969), 183–215.

[107] Tracy, *Erasmus: The Growth of a Mind*, 104–7; for the quote, LB 5:51E.

[108] Charles Trinkaus, "Erasmus, Augustine, and the Nominalists," *Archiv für Reformationsgeschichte* 67 (1976):5–32; Tracy, "Two Erasmuses, Two Luthers," esp. 46–56. Charles Béné, *Erasme et Saint Augustin* (Geneva: Droz, 1969), takes a far more positive view of Erasmus' indebtedness to Augustine, but a comparison with Godin, *Erasme, lecteur d'Origène*, will show which of the two was more important for Erasmus' cherished opinions.

developed than ever before or since. According to Jean Delumeau's monumental study, *Sin and Fear*, as the pessimistic spirituality of the monastic tradition gained currency among devout layfolk, Christians of the fourteenth and fifteenth centuries showed clear signs of a heightened awareness of sin that was to endure, in both Protestant and Catholic forms, into the eighteenth century. Saint Thomas Aquinas (d. 1271) had not found it necessary to discuss the problem of scrupulosity, but in later centuries it was a familiar theme for spiritual directors, and for the hundreds of authors of manuals of casuistry. One also finds in the late Middle Ages that depictions by preachers of the horrid effects of original sin reach "an apex," and that the rigors of God's final judgment are presented in such a way that "it would not be possible to accuse oneself too much." Thus Delumeau describes an "acculturation culpabilisatrice,"[109] just as Elias describes, for the same centuries, an "advance of the shame frontier."

The extraordinary thing about these two complex historical processes—acculturation in shame, acculturation in guilt—is that they are almost never discussed together.[110] Yet in the anthropological literature of recent decades there are numerous studies that highlight the conflict between shame and guilt as inner restraints on what is perceived as wrongful behavior. Without minimizing the difficulty of fixing on one or more of the competing definitions of shame and guilt, it may be said that the former implies a loss of esteem among one's peers, while the latter involves a sense of having transgressed a precept whose validity is perceived to be independent of social norms. Thus the same action can be both moral and immoral, by different standards; for example, members of a migrant subculture of Greek shepherds recognize that stealing is sinful, yet they see stealing from outsiders as honorable.[111] To grasp

---

[109] Delumeau, *Sin and Fear*, 1.3.18. Delumeau is rightly taken to task for his psychologizing penchant (e.g. talk of a guilt-based "Christian neurosis") by Heiko A. Oberman, *Sixteenth Century Journal* 23 (1992): 149–50, and the problem is sometimes exacerbated by infelicitous translation. For example the translator has "cultural dissemination of the guilt complex" (115) for "acculturation culpabilisatrice" (*Le péché et la peur*, 203), and "it would have been impossible to acquire too much guilt" (203) for "on ne saurait trop se culpabiliser" (ibid., 237). On the other hand, the evidence that Delumeau presents for a gradual intensification of the religious sense of guilt—precisely for an "acculturation culpabilisatrice," and not for a "guilt complex"—is in my view overwhelming.

[110] The one exception I know of is Heinz Schilling, "Calvinism and the Making of the Modern Mind: Ecclesiastical Discipline of Public and Private Sin from the Sixteenth to the Nineteenth Century," in his *Civic Calvinism* (Kirksville, Mo.: Sixteenth Century Essays and Studies, 1991), 41–68.

[111] For example, J. G. Peristiany, ed., *Honour and Shame: The Values of Mediterranean Society* (London: Weidenfeld and Nicholson, 1965); on questions of definition, see Gerhart Piers and Milton B. Singer, *Shame and Guilt: A Psychoanalytical and a Cultural Study* (Springfield, Ill.: Thomas, 1953).

the relevance for early modern European history of the conflict between the morality of shame and the morality of guilt, one need only consider the persistence of the code of the vendetta in Renaissance Italy, and the vehement denunciations of deeds of blood by Italy's popular preachers.[112]

In Erasmus' Low Countries, the social habit of taking vengeance for injuries to one's honor had been brought well under control by the sixteenth century,[113] but the tension between *amour propre* and the Christian ethic was surely felt in other ways. The ideal of *docta pietas* makes the most sense if it is understood as an effort to build a bridge between what we might now call acculturation in shame and acculturation in guilt. In effect, Erasmus employed the classical notion of a morality based on self-esteem as a corrective to what he saw as an excessive emphasis on mortification and self-abnegation in contemporary religious culture; at the same time, he invoked the austere simplicity of the New Testament as a corrective to the worldly pride of a purely secular ethic. Unlike Luther or the mature Calvin, Erasmus wrote textbooks for humanistic schools as well as works elucidating Scripture; unlike Castiglione, he wrote commentaries on the Psalms as well as a manual of polite behavior. The fact that Erasmus sought to balance very different outlooks does not mean he always succeeded. It does mean, however, that the distinctive features of his vision of a Christian civility, and its profound coherence with the experience and aspirations of the world in which he lived, can only be brought out by comparing his works not only with those of other religious reformers, but also with those of other arbiters of manners and taste. Accordingly, this discussion will close with a brief sample comparison between one of Erasmus' principal works on education, the *De pueris statim ac liberaliter instituendis* (1529),[114] and two other works that deal with education, albeit in very different ways: Martin Luther's *Eine Predigt, daß man Kinder zur Schule halten sollte* (1530),[115] and the *Galateo* (1552) of Giovanni della Casa, papal diplomat and Archbishop of Benevento.[116]

---

[112] Anna M. Enriques, "La Vendetta nella Vita e nella Legislazione Fiorentina," *Archivo Storico Italiano*, series 7, 19 (1933): 85–146, 181–223.

[113] R. C. van Caenegem, *Geschiedenis van het Strafrecht in Vlaanderen van de Xie tot de XIVe Eeuw* (Brussels: Paleis der Akademien, 1954), 231–45.

[114] I quote from the translation by Beert C. Verstraete, CWE 26:295–346; Latin text references are according to the column/letter form used in LB 1, and given also by Margolin.

[115] Edited by O. Brenner and O. Clemen, in Martin Luther, *D. Martin Luthers Werke*, 61 vols. in 76 (Weimar: Böhlau, 1909–1983), 30/2:522–88. I quote from the translation by Charles M. Jacobs and Robert C. Schultz, "A Sermon on Keeping Children in School," in Martin Luther, *Luther's Works*, ed. Jaroslav Pelikan and Helmut T. Lehman, 55 vols. (Philadelphia: Muhlenberg Press, Fortress, 1958–1986), 46:209–58.

[116] Giovanni della Casa, *Il "Galateo,"* intro. Carlo Steiner (Milan: n. p., 1910), and *Galateo*, trans. Konrad Eisenbichler and Kenneth R. Bartlett (Toronto: Centre for Reformation and Renaissance Studies, 1986).

It may seem that these works are so different as to preclude any useful comparison among them. Luther and Erasmus are both addressing parents, and both seek to break down the reluctance of parents to provide for their children a sound but costly Latin education, yet where one is preaching a sermon, the other offers a model rhetorical declamation according to classical principles, with ideas drawn mainly from Quintilian and Plutarch.[117] Della Casa's treatise is cast in the form of advice from an elderly courtier who is not a learned man, and thus is all the more sensitive to the external forms of politeness that will make his young kinsman well liked and advance his career. Yet each author confronts in his own way the fundamental theme of nature and nurture. "If the Scriptures and learning disappear in the German lands," Luther asks, "what will remain but a disorderly and wild crowd of Tartars or Turks, indeed a pigsty and mob of wild beasts?"[118] Erasmus willingly borrows from Plutarch the principle that nature can be improved by method (*ratio*) and practice (*exercitatio*),[119] and Della Casa seems to modify this humanist formula in keeping with his own emphasis on social decency.[120] In light of their common concern for how human nature can be molded or trained for the better, a brief examination will show that each of these works builds on premises that are akin to Elias' "advancement of the shame frontier," or Delumeau's "acculturation culpabilisatrice."

As one might expect in a sermon, Luther counts on his listeners' fear of the wrath of God to make them do what they might not do willingly, in this case to keep their sons in school long enough to learn the liberal arts. The common idea that parents have a responsibility to raise up their children for the service of God and the community[121] is, for Luther, sharpened by his acute sense of the fragility of human institutions, especially those that support the preaching of the Gospel. In what seems a reformulation of a humanist commonplace, he presents the preacher (not the orator)[122] as the upholder of human community; indeed "peace, the greatest of earthly goods ... is really a

[117] On Erasmus' sources for *De pueris*, see Margolin, 63, 89–91.

[118] *Luther's Works*, 46:217; cf. 237: "If there were no worldly government, one man could not stand before another; each would necessarily devour the other, as irrational beasts devour one another."

[119] CWE 26:311: "As a general rule, human happiness depends on the prerequisites: nature, method and practice" = LB 1:497A, with Margolin's note.

[120] Eisenbichler and Bartlett, *Galateo*, 50: "It is therefore not true that against nature there is neither rein nor master. On the contrary there are two of them: one is good manners (*il costume*), the other reason."

[121] CWE 26:306: "This is a duty which you owe to God and nature . . ." = LB 1:494B.

[122] For humanist echoes of the classical *topos* on the civilizing power of oratory (cf. Vergil's Neptune in bk. 2 of the *Aeneid*, and Cicero, *De inventione*, 1, 2), see James D. Tracy, "Against the 'Barbarians': the Young Erasmus and His Humanist Contemporaries," *Sixteenth Century Journal* 11 (1980):7–8.

fruit of true preaching." Thus the withering away of schools that train learned men—potential preachers—would mean the collapse of all civilized order in chaos and confusion.[123] Accordingly, those who stand in the way of their children's education will face an angry God: "You have been earnestly commanded to raise them for God's service, or be completely rooted out—you, your children, and everything else…. Both you and they will be damned, not only here on earth but eternally in hell." It will not do to shunt the burden off on others who keep their children in school, for all who have the means of doing so must be willing for their children to be trained for service of the estates ordained by God, that is, the preaching office and the civil government. And woe to the negligent, by whose fault the land may descend into godless chaos! "No conscience can bear to be guilty of even one of the things that have been mentioned…. Your heart will then have to cry out that your sins are more than the leaves or the grass."[124] Luther was not insensitive to the income opportunities opened up by education, nor to the pleasures of learning,[125] but he had no time here for side issues; nothing less than the continued preaching of the Word depended on making parents aware of the duties for which God would hold them accountable.

The *persona* in which Della Casa chooses to speak makes fun of those educated in the liberal arts,[126] but when he comes to talk of moral principles he sounds very much like Cicero: "men are very desirous of beauty, measure, and proportion," and the speaker's young kinsman must understand that beauty and proportion are found not only in external things, but "just as much in speech and behavior."[127] Many forms of behavior are in fact unseemly and must be avoided. Thus those who "place their hands on whatever part of the body it pleases them" are indulging in "an indecent habit (*sconcio costume*)"; a well-mannered man will not soil his fingers at table, for a dirty napkin "is a disgusting thing to see"; to speak lightly of God is not only sinful but ill-mannered, for "it is unpleasant to hear"; and well-mannered women must avoid

---

[123] *Luther's Works*, 46:226 (the quote), 218, 223, 237; German phrases like "zu grunde gehen" or "gehts zu boden" (*Luthers Werke*, 30/2:525, 532, 557) convey an urgency not fully captured by the English "perish."

[124] *Luther's Works*, 46:222–23, 230.

[125] Ibid., 235, 243.

[126] Eisenbichler and Bartlett, *Galateo*, 16: "It is not fitting to be melancholy or distracted in the company of others. This may be accepted of people who have long pursued studies in the arts which, as I have heard, are called 'liberal arts,' but it should not, under any circumstances, be allowed of other people."

[127] Ibid., 51–52, using, as the translators note, a definition of beauty from Cicero's *De officiis*; cf. 48–49 for the idea of molding a young man according to good custom, just as the sculptor Polycleitos carved a statue [the Doryphoros] to fit the ideal of beauty described in his *Canon*.

not only words that are plainly indecent, but also those that "could appear to be indecent, vulgar or coarse."[128] The distinctive feature of this treatise is that it gives a social dimension to the humanist–classical ethic of self-esteem: one must avoid doing or saying things that may even seem to infringe on the self-esteem of others. While another speaks, one must not yawn, and give the impression of being bored, or drum one's fingers, as if one had a low opinion of his words.[129] Similarly, one might seem to disdain others by dressing out of keeping with one's age and status; to challenge others by boasting of one's riches or nobility; and to reproach others by professing to despise what they admire. In general, "it is proper to accept [men] readily not for what they are truly worth but rather, as with money, for their stated value."[130] The church's doctrine of sin is visible in the background, though not of immediate interest: "It is most advisable for those who aspire to be well liked to flee vices, especially the fouler ones, [but] I undertook to show you men's errors and not their sins."[131] Thus, if Luther addresses the underlying structure of reality as seen by faith, Della Casa deals with the play of surface impressions that occupy men's everyday thoughts.

Though published in 1529, *De pueris statim ac liberaliter instituendis* was written much earlier, as Jean-Claude Margolin shows, probably during Erasmus' visit to Italy (1506–1509). The treatise follows (and borrows from) similar works by Italian humanists of the Quattrocento, differing from them in its insistence that, as the title suggests (*statim* = at once), boys should be introduced to the rudiments of learning as early as three or four.[132] This emphasis points to one of the principal themes of *De pueris*, namely, that character can easily be trained at a tender age, but only with difficulty as boys grow older: "Nothing will the child learn more readily than goodness, nothing will it learn to reject more than stupidity, if only parents have worked to fill the natural void from the start." To be sure, one often hears that children are naturally prone to evil, "but these accusations against nature are unfair. The evil is largely due to ourselves," for it is we who corrupt young minds before teaching them what is right. Elsewhere Erasmus acknowledges that even in the earliest years of life "it is always easier to forget good habits than to unlearn bad ones." This truth caused "great perplexity" to the pagan philosophers, since

---

[128] Ibid., 5, 9, 17, 41.
[129] Ibid., 6, 9, 10, 11.
[130] Ibid., 12, 14, 21.
[131] Ibid., 54.
[132] Margolin, 13, 26–27, 102–3; CWE 26:297–98.

they had no knowledge of what Christian theology teaches, "that since Adam, the first man of the human race, a disposition to evil has been deeply ingrained in us." Yet even here, original sin (to give the doctrine its name, as Erasmus does not) is not seen as the prime culprit: "The greater portion of this evil stems from corrupting relationships and a misguided education, especially as they affect our early and most impressionable years."[133]

Of particular interest for this discussion is a long section (about a fifth of the treatise) that has the earmarks of a later addition.[134] In these pages Erasmus focuses not on private tutors, but on the cruelty of certain *ludimagistri* or heads of schools; indeed, he ranges far enough from the subject of early childhood to add some interesting comments about hazing practices among university students.[135] The cruelties Erasmus describes (and claims to have seen firsthand) are indeed gruesome, all the more so because the victims were visited with savage punishment in the name of religion. In the case of a master who ordered one of his charges whipped in Erasmus' presence, "the man of the cloth turned to me and commented, 'He [the boy] did not do anything to deserve this, but he simply had to be humbled'—yes, 'humbled' (*humiliandus*) was the word he used."[136] Indeed, it was this man's belief that whipping "was the only way to humble high spirits (*ad dejiciendam ingeniorum ferociam*) and check youthful waywardness." Erasmus himself remembered, in this context, a once-admired teacher who, "wishing to ascertain for himself how well I could stand up to the rod, charged me with an offense I had never even dreamed of committing and then flogged me."[137] In another case, when a boy of "hardly

---

[133] CWE 26: 312, 321 = Margolin, 497D, 502B.

[134] Margolin, 503F–509A = CWE 26: 324–34, from "There are teachers whose manners are so uncouth" to "this abuse is so widespread that no one can ever speak out sufficiently against it." The passage is marked as an insert because its subject (cruel "ludimagistri" or heads of schools) departs from the consistent focus of the rest of the treatise on private tutors; because of verbal signals that Erasmus is wandering from his theme ("Sed ad pueritiam redeo," 507 F = "Returning to my main theme," 331, and "Cum plagosis rixari desinam, si unum hoc adjecero," 509 A = "I will stop quarreling with flogging schoolmasters, but I wish to add one more point," 334); and because the lines immediately before and after the putative insert make sense if connected together ("and it is from those we like and respect that we learn most eagerly," 324 = 503 F, "It is also beneficial if the prospective teacher adopts a fatherly attitude towards his pupils," 334 = 509 A). If this one passage is excepted, Margolin's comment about the tight organization of the treatise is quite correct ("La structure de ce texte est particulièrement serrée," 13).

[135] Margolin, 507C–D (with Margolin's note on the derivation of the Latin "beanum" from the French "becjaune" or yellow-beak, from the practice of smearing a new student's mouth and chin with urine) = CWE 26: 331.

[136] Margolin, 505A–C = CWE 26: 327.

[137] Margolin, 504E–F = CWE 26: 326. Margolin, 550 nn. 561, 562, identifies the man as Romboldus, one of Erasmus' teachers at the residence run by the Brethren of the Common Life in 's Hertogenbosch. I have suggested Jan Synthen, also a member of the Brethren, one of his teachers at the town school in Deventer: Tracy, *Erasmus: The Growth of a Mind*, 27–29.

twelve" was punished brutally for an offense committed by the master's nephew, the man in charge was "one of those 'evangelicals' to whom money was the sweetest thing on earth."[138]

The veracity of at least one of these tales has been questioned,[139] but the precept that boys must be "humbled" for their own spiritual good is at least consistent with the exaggerated emphasis on humility in literature produced during this period by the Brethren of the Common Life,[140] with whom Erasmus as a boy had some acquaintance. Perhaps more to the point, there is a striking contrast between the picture Erasmus presents of a pusillanimous education under the aegis of religion and the conception of education that humanists drew from Quintilian and other classical authors. Instead of focusing on sinful pride as the obstacle to moral development, this tradition spurned corporal punishment as something worthy of slaves, and sought to build on self-esteem; boys of a noble or "generous" disposition, like horses with spirit, would respond much more readily to the inducement of praise.[141] Thus Erasmus says of the harsh discipline he is describing that "a thoroughbred horse responds better to stroking than to kicks and spurs.... You should not handle a character of high mettle (*generosum ingenium*) as you would a lion's whelp." In one place he directly confronts a biblical warrant for corporal punishment with the superior teaching of the ancient Greeks. "Someone may din into our ears such Old Testament proverbs as, 'He that spareth the rod hateth his son.'" But this "frigid ... moral wisdom" is suitable only for the Jews of Old Testament times,[142] or for training a pack-ass; for the moral instruction of the young, Erasmus recommends a philosopher quoted by Diogenes Laertius, who "tells us that there are two sharp spurs that will rouse a child's natural talents, shame and praise."[143] But it is not Erasmus' way to let pagan philosophy have the last word. The real problem with a Christianity predicated on humiliating the human spirit is that it is false Christianity. Quoting

<hr />

[138] Margolin, 506D–507C = CWE 26:329–30; both Margolin and Verstraete take the word "evangelicals" (*evangelici*) as referring to members of religious orders, and the ironic reference to greed seems indeed to imply a contrast with vows of poverty.

[139] P. J. M. Bot, *Humanisme en Onderwijs in Nederland* (Utrecht: Het Spectrum, 1955), 62–63.

[140] Jacobus de Voecht, *Narratio de Inchoatione Domus Clericorum in Zwollis*, ed. M. Schoengen (Amsterdam: Mueller, 1908).

[141] For example, Quintilian, *Oratoriae institutiones*, 1.3.14 (against corporal punishment); Pier Paolo Vergerio in Woodward, *Vittorino da Feltre and Other Humanist Educators*, 97–98: "It is a mark of soundness in a boy's nature that he is spurred by desire of praise," like a horse with mettle, "which needs neither whip nor spur."

[142] Margolin, 93, notes how the vocabulary of this passage evokes the ritualistic religion that Erasmus habitually denounces under the name of "Judaism."

[143] Margolin, 505C–D, 507F–508A = CWE 26:327, 332.

Saint Paul's injunction to fathers (Eph. 6:4) not to provoke their children to wrath, but bring them up in the admonition (*disciplina*) of the Lord, Erasmus continues: "What this 'admonition of the Lord' means, you will easily understand once you consider with what gentleness (*mansuetudo*), patience, and affection Jesus taught, supported and encouraged his disciples as he gradually led them onwards." Elsewhere he brings the two parts of his critique together: let pupils "hear some men praised for their goodness, others condemned for their evil"; such tales of honor and dishonor are "the rod of correction more worthy of Christians and followers of the gentle Jesus."[144]

In sum, while Luther seeks to heighten his listeners' sense of guilt on a particular point, and Della Casa draws out some of the practical implications of an ethos of self-esteem, Erasmus argues that this classical ethos has more in common with the precepts of Christ than does a form of religion that depends on breaking the human spirit. To my knowledge, no other humanist of the fifteenth or sixteenth century had the audacity to combine faith and reason in quite this way. From a theological perspective, one may wonder to what extent his optimism about the malleability of human character depends on a rather minimalist interpretation of the doctrine of original sin (as in the passage quoted above). From a historical perspective, however, it is difficult not to see Erasmus' characteristic emphasis on the gentleness of Christ[145] as a healthy corrective to the pusillanimous asceticism that is clearly visible in, for instance, some works produced by the Brethren of the Common Life.[146] Thus *docta pietas* was very far from being a sleight of hand. It was a viable response to the cultural and religious tensions of the sixteenth century, and we impoverish only ourselves if we are not able to reconstruct the ways in which it "made sense" to Erasmus, and to many of his contemporaries.

It has not been the purpose of this essay to suggest that those of us who pay Erasmus the courtesy of taking him seriously have the luxury of

[144] Margolin, 506B–C, 508B = CWE 26:327–28, 332.
[145] See the two-page addition to his note on "My yoke is sweet and my burden light" in Matthew 11, *Novum Testamentum* (Basel, 1519), 43–44.
[146] See the characterization of the Brethren in R. R. Post, *The Modern Devotion* (Leiden: E. J. Brill, 1969).

dismissiing postmodernist theories out of hand. Rather, I have been at pains to recognize that deconstructionist criticism, in raising doubts about the transparency of texts in general, raises all the more doubts about the interpretation of an author who revels in ambiguity as Erasmus did; and that theories which regard class conflict as the fundamental reality are inimical to any program for harmonizing or reconciling disparate values, as Erasmus sought to do both in his ideals of *bonae literae* (joining the esthetic and the moral) and *docta pietas* (joining the Christian and the classical). Thus if one wishes to argue that the "dissimulating" Erasmus nonetheless "makes sense," one must do so, consciously or unconsciously, on the basis of a theory of interpretation, and for this purpose I have suggested a way of reading the letters that Erasmus himself did not publish in light of Gadamer's hermeneutics. Similarly, if one wishes to argue that the moral and religious ideals of Erasmus represent something more than "sleight of hand," one has to show how they made sense in the historical context, and this I have attempted to do with the help of the framework of acculturation, as proposed by Elias (for acculturation in shame) and Delumeau (for acculturation in guilt). Some readers might be more comfortable with a straightforward denunciation of postmodernism and its seemingly nihilistic premises. But in an essay that in its own way honors Erasmus, it has seemed more appropriate to seek, as he sought, to maintain channels of civil communication with those with whom one may strongly disagree, and thus to do one's part in making the circle of intellectual discourse not narrower, but wider.

APPENDIX
ERASMUS ON THE PAPACY

PUBLISHED LETTERS

To Lorenzo Campeggio, 6 December 1520, Allen 4: Ep. 1167, lines 416–23:

Quid mihi necessitudinis cum Luthero? aut quid ab illo sperem praemiorum, ut ab eo stare velim aduersus doctrinam Euangelicam? aut adversus Ecclesiam Romanam, quam opinor a catholica non dissentire? aut adversus Pontificem Romanam totius Ecclesiae Principem, qui nec episcopo meo peculiari velim adversari? Non sum tam impius ut dissentiam ab Ecclesia catholica, non sum tam ingratus ut dissentiam a Leone, cuius et favorem et indulgentiam in me non vulgarem sum expertus.

To Luigi Marliano, Bishop of Tuy, 25 March 1521, Allen 4: Ep. 1195, lines 27–30:

Ego tamen nullis machinis a statu mentis dimoueri potui. Christum agnosco, Lutherum non novi; Ecclesiam Romanam agnosco, quam opinor a Catholica non dissentire. Ab hac me nec mors diuellet, nisi illa palam divellatur a Christo.

UNPUBLISHED LETTERS

To John Colet, [c. 5 March 1518], Allen 3: Ep. 786, lines 22–29:

Regnant in omnibus principum aulis personati theologi. Curia Romana plane perfricuit frontem. Quid enim impudentius his assiduis condonationibus? Et nunc bellum praetexitur in Turcas, cum re id agatur ut Hispani depellantur e Napoli. Nam Laurentius nepos Campaniam sibi vindicare conatur, filia Nauarrae Regis in uxorem ducta. Qui tumultus si procedant, tolerabilius fuerit Turcarum imperium quam horum Christianorum ferre.

To Johann Lang, 17 October [1518], Allen 3: Ep. 872, lines 14–21:

Puto illae conclusiones placuerunt omnibus, exceptis paucis de purgatorio; quod isti nolunt sibi eripi, ut *pros ta alphita* faciens. Vidi Sylvestri insulsissimam responsionem. Video *ten tou Romanou Archiereos* (ut nunc est ea sedes) *monarchian* pestem esse Christianismi; cui per omnia adulantur Praedicatores facie prorsus perfricta. Sed tamen haud scio an expediat hoc ulcus aperte tangere. Principum hoc erat negocium; sed vereor ne hi cum Pontifice colludant, in praedae partem venturi.

To Martin Bucer, 2 March 1532, Allen 9: Ep. 2615, lines 256–60:

Multa paulatim corrigi poterant, quedam erant dissimulanda. Si Pontificis regnum obstabat Euangelio, huius tyrannis erat in primis frangenda, id quod neutiquam erat difficile, nisi quidam reclamanta proverbio totum maluissent quam dimidium.

Erika Rummel

MONACHATUS NON EST PIETAS
Interpretations and Misinterpretations
of a Dictum

~

WHEN ERASMUS' *ENCHIRIDION* FIRST APPEARED in 1503, it attracted little attention. Eventually, however, the book and the controversial statement *monachatus non est pietas* were discovered and caused considerable indigna- tion, not surprisingly because its epigrammatic form gave the phrase a certain shock value.[1] However, on reading the protestations of Erasmus' critics, one finds that they vastly overinterpreted the remark. To understand the hostile reaction it generated, let us put the phrase in context and examine its constit- uent parts. What did Erasmus mean by *pietas*, what was his attitude toward monasticism, and what is the rhetorical force and meaning of the negative copula *non est*?

Let us begin with the term *pietas*.[2] Erasmus himself provides us with the following definition: "*Pietas* ... is a state of mind or disposition (*animi affec- tus*) which encompasses love of God and love of our neighbor."[3] Elsewhere he explains that by treating our neighbor charitably, we pay our debt to God: "This is how our heavenly creditor taught us to pay our debt."[4] This type of *pietas*, then, links the individual to God on the one hand and to fellow human

---

[1] The phrase appears at LB 5:65C: "Monachatus non est pietas, sed vitae genus pro suo cuique corporis ingeniique habitu, vel utile, vel utile."

[2] For the most recent analysis of Erasmian *pietas*, see John W. O'Malley's introduction to CWE 66 (Toronto, 1989).

[3] *Adversus febricitantis cuiusdam libellum responsio*, LB 10:1675B.

[4] *Enchiridion*, LB 5:63E.

beings on the other in a sort of heavenly accounting system. Being pious means paying one's dues and righting the balance of life, as it were.

Secondly, *pietas* can mean otherworldliness, in the eyes of many people, the monk's virtue par excellence. Erasmus himself did not subscribe to this view. He did not think that the regular clergy had a special or exclusive claim on *pietas* in the sense of otherworldliness. *Pietas non est ipsa professio*, he wrote: the profession of vows itself does not constitute piety.[5] On the contrary, some monasteries were, as he put it, "in the midst of worldly affairs and so entangled in them that they are no less parted from the world than are kidneys from a living body."[6] Conversely, there were lay persons who exemplified the virtue of otherworldliness. They remained in the world, but distanced themselves from secular concerns. Thus, one could "leave the world another way," as Erasmus explained, by leading a virtuous life and keeping company with good men.

Thirdly, piety can take the shape of *docta pietas*, learned piety. Erasmus neatly circumscribes its function when he writes: "Let there be the greatest zeal for learning . . . but let there be no impious curiosity."[7] *Docta pietas*, then, is the opposite of *impia curiositas*, that is, prying, quibbling, and speculating about sacred matters. The pious scholar observes the proper limits in his research, Erasmus explains in *Hyperaspistes II*: "Pious people dispute about such matters [free will and divine foreknowledge] only insofar as it is right to do so. . . . They examine with reverence what has been vouchsafed us from the sacred books."[8] *Docta pietas* was free of vanity and intellectual pride; its learning was not abstract but focused on living the philosophy of Christ. Its goal was "to be changed, moved, inspired, and transformed until you become one with what you are learning."[9] An important aspect of the Erasmian concept of *docta pietas* is its peaceful nature. It may not prepare a person for "the wrestling ground of the Sorbonne" but it will lead to "Christian tranquillity."[10] The pious scholar does not quibble about minutiae. Erasmus says: "I do not think it belongs to Christian peacefulness to stir up a tragedy concerning minor points."[11] For the same reason those who have attained *docta pietas* bear with their weaker brethren. They have no use for ceremonies, but they do not insist

---

[5] *Responsio ad Petri Cursii defensionem*, LB 10:1765B.
[6] CWE 66:173. Cf. CWE 66:22.
[7] *Methodus*, in Holborn, 151. Cf. *Ratio verae theologiae*, in Holborn, 206.
[8] LB 10:1408F, 1409B.
[9] *Enchiridion*, LB 5:77B.
[10] Allen 3: Ep. 858, lines 32–33. Cf. *Methodus*, in Holborn, 162.
[11] *Hyperaspistes II*, LB 10:1534D.

that they be abandoned, "seeing that this practice cannot be reformed without tumult,"[12] and that dissension and upheaval are foreign to *docta pietas*.

Fourthly, *pietas* is a spiritual quality; indeed, this is the underpinning of the Erasmian concept of *pietas*. He habitually contrasts it with the external observance of regulations. In fact Erasmus postulates a negative correlation between piety and ceremonialism: "As ceremonies grew . . . ," he writes, "genuine piety grew cold."[13] *Pietas* cannot be confined to mechanical action; it is a dynamic quality, the manifestation of living faith as opposed to the dead letter of the law. Erasmus laments:

> Monastic piety is everywhere cold, languid, and almost extinct because they [the common people] are growing old in the letter and never take pains to learn the spiritual sense of Scriptures. They do not hear Christ crying out in the Gospel: "The flesh is of no profit; it is the spirit that gives life," nor do they hear Paul, who adds to the words of the master: "The letter kills, it is the spirit that gives life."[14]

Although Erasmus does not reject ceremonies out of hand and indeed acknowledges the supporting role they play in a person's spiritual progress, he maintains the Pauline priority of invisible over visible things. "Visible worship is not condemned," he says, "but God is appeased only by invisible piety."[15] *Pietas*, he emphasizes, is a state of mind and has nothing to do "with diet, or dress, or any visible thing." It is neither in our words, nor our apparel, nor our compliance with ceremonies; rather it is a quality of the mind.[16]

None of Erasmus' ideas concerning *pietas* are novel or unprecedented. They are supported by the authority of Scripture and the Fathers and embodied in Scholastic definitions. Thus it was not what Erasmus said about piety that gave offense, but rather the context or the mode of expression he chose. Had he spoken of piety in a hortatory or encomiastic mode, he would not have raised any eyebrows, but Erasmus chose a polemical approach. Praise of piety in Erasmus is frequently joined with criticism of contemporary practices and is meant as a reproach to some group. *Docta pietas* is contrasted with the arid speculations of Scholastic theologians. Praise of piety in the sense of otherworldliness was coupled with reproaches of the worldliness and corruption of modern representatives of the church; praise of piety as an internal quality invariably led to the condemnation of monastic regulations. Of course

[12] LB 5:1120B.
[13] CWE 66:22.
[14] CWE 66:35.
[15] CWE 66:81.
[16] CWE 66:127; *Ratio verae theologiae*, in Holborn, 253.

this corrective approach was not an exclusively Erasmian feature. Voices demanding reform, a *restoratio* or return to the pristine customs of the early church, had become increasingly louder during the fifteenth century, but in the sixteenth century the cry for reform turned into an organized movement: the Reformation. As a result, criticisms that had not been programmatic in their original historical context were now perceived as slogans and catch-phrases of the Reformation. Erasmus, too, had the misfortune of seeing his words radicalized in this fashion. He observed that what he had written long before Luther rose to prominence was given a new significance in the light of these later developments. Thus Erasmus' comments on *pietas*, which were by and large traditional, were endowed with a controversial meaning by readers who had been sensitized to the language of the Reformers and read them as a rallying cry for the Reformation.

Let us now look at Erasmus' views on monasticism. While his concept of *pietas* appears to have remained static throughout his life, his attitude toward monasticism underwent considerable change as it was being shaped by his personal experience as well as by the communal experience of the Reformation. On a personal level, Erasmus felt that he was not suited for the life of a religious; on the level of communal experience, he could not but join the voices protesting the moral bankruptcy of the regular clergy. Erasmus' own lack of monastic vocation and his criticism of clerical abuses do not mean, however, that he rejected monasticism in principle or despised monks as a class. Rather, we find that he expresses a considerable range of views on the function and value of religious orders, from praise for the monastic ideal and admiration for exemplary representatives (such as Jean Vitrier) to sharp criticism and bitter satire of its abuses. Apart from ad hoc comments arising from specific occasions, it seems to me that Erasmus' attitude passed through three broad stages. The first stage was marked by idealism and goodwill, which was dampened by a series of disappointments and followed by, in the second place, a critical, not to say hostile phase which lasted into the 1520s. This in turn was succeeded by a third period in which Erasmus' remarks became more temperate, whether this moderation was the result of changing views or merely of a more cautious approach.

Let us look at the first phase which lasted from his entry into the monastery at Steyn to his Paris years. The melodramatic autobiographical accounts we have concerning this period leave the impression that he was coerced into entering the Augustinian order, but we must not forget that these accounts date from the second, hostile phase in his life. It may be fairer to say that

Erasmus' options at the time were limited, that his expectations of the monastic life were unrealistic, and that his sense of self was undeveloped—all of which added up to his making a choice that turned out to be less than satisfying. In the time immediately following his profession of vows, however, he certainly treated them as valid and made an earnest effort to live up to them. This first phase, which is characterized by goodwill, is represented by the tract *De contemptu mundi*, written in the late 1480s. Cast in the form of an exhortation to a young man to leave the world, the epistle is aimed at persuading the reader of the merits of the monastic life. In *De contemptu mundi* Erasmus describes what a religious community at its best had to offer. The reality, however, was not in accord with the idealistic picture he drew in that hortatory piece. The institution reflected the shortcomings of its human members, as Erasmus was to discover.

The negative experiences of the next decade first led to an emotional crisis and then made him cynical. He now entered a phase of outspoken criticism of monasticism, using a variety of literary approaches to give expression to his views: homiletic fervor in the *Enchiridion*; wit and paradox in the *Praise of Folly*; popular humor and satire in the *Colloquies*. To this phase belong his colorful descriptions of monks as "vultures" preying on the populace, as wranglers locked "in gladiatorial combat," and as a "new race of Jews," who would find that "common sailors and waggoners" would be preferred to them on the Day of Judgment.[17]

During this second phase of his life, Erasmus made a concerted effort to escape some of the consequences of his youthful decision. The dispensation he obtained from Pope Leo X in 1516 gave him the right to hold certain benefices, released him from the obligation to reside in his monastery and wear the garb of a canon regular, and absolved him from the charge of apostasy or any other ecclesiastical censures in this context: "He may have permission to reside for the term of his life outside the houses of his aforesaid order in any convenient place of good repute living reputably in other respects, to wear a symbol only of his former habit as a regular canon beneath the reputable garb of a secular priest."[18]

While Erasmus may be regarded as a "failed monk,"[19] he cannot be called an apostate, a term nevertheless applied to him by his critics; for example, Bat-

---

[17] *The Funeral*, in Craig R. Thompson, trans., *The Colloquies of Erasmus* (Chicago: University of Chicago Press, 1965), 361; *Praise of Folly*, CWE 27, 132.
[18] CWE 4: Ep. 517, lines 42–46.
[19] O'Malley, CWE 66: xix.

tista Casali, Ambrosius Catharinus, Vincentius Theoderici, and Ortensio Lando called him "runaway," "apostate," and "one who had abandoned the cowl."[20] Although Erasmus never "ran away" or officially renounced his vows, he did voice serious doubts about their validity by 1525. In a letter fragment that was perhaps never sent, he defends himself against the charge of apostasy and writes candidly: "Granted that the term apostate is correctly applied to someone who has changed his dress, it certainly does not apply to me, who had never been a monk. For it is voluntary profession (*spontanea confessio*) that makes a man a monk; not forced profession (*coacta*)." He returns to this theme throughout the letter. Describing his resistance to the urgent representations of his guardians, who wanted him to take the vows, he concludes: "I entered the monastery, not because I had changed my mind, but because I was defeated" (*non mutata sententia sed victus*). He repeats a few lines later that his entry was forced: *manifesta vis erat*. "Although I never approved in my mind of this kind of life," he continues, "I bore with it on account of the unavoidable scandal." When he left the monastery and changed his dress, it was done "with the formal approval of my superiors" (*authoritate majorum*) and confirmed by a papal dispensation (*mox impetrata a pontifice venia*). He concludes with another oblique reference to the questionable validity of his vows: "Even if I had, due to circumstances changed my dress without papal authorization, I would not be an apostate because I never agreed to this kind of life (*nunquam hoc vitae genus approbarim*)."[21]

The letter remained unpublished during Erasmus' lifetime, but his published comments on monasticism were enough to make him *persona non grata* to the regular clergy. "I have no fiercer enemy," Erasmus reported in 1527. "They have been agitating now for nine years, offended somewhat by my *Enchiridion*, but worse by my *Moria*."[22] Yet we notice a certain softening of Erasmus' attitude toward monasticism, a new conservatism in reaction to what Erasmus perceived as extremism and radicalism among the Reformers. This mood is reflected in a letter of October 15, 1527, to an unidentified monk who sought Erasmus' counsel on whether to abandon the monastic life.

---

[20] Erika Rummel, *Erasmus and His Catholic Critics*, 2 vols. (Nieuwkoop: De Graaf, 1989), 2:114, 132, 144.

[21] Allen 5: Ep. 1436, lines 20–22, 76–77, 89, 99–100, 112, 120–21. Allen published the letter under the year 1524, but it answers charges made by the pseudonymous "Taxander" in 1525. On the correct dating and context see Erika Rummel, "*Nihil actum est sine authoritate maiorum*: New evidence concerning an Erasmian letter rejecting the accusation of apostasy," *Bibliothèque d'Humanisme et Renaissance* 54 (1992): 725–31.

[22] Allen 7: Ep. 1805, lines 104–7.

Erasmus warned him against the Reformers' splendid promises of Evangelical freedom:

> Believe me, if you knew them better, you would be less dissatisfied with your life. . . . I don't see anyone improved [who has left his order]; at least among my acquaintances, I find everyone worse, so that I am very sorry that I once praised spiritual freedom in my book; although I did so in good faith and could not have anticipated that such a race of people would arise. I wished for a little curtailment of ceremonies and a great increase in true piety, but now ceremonies are abandoned in such a way that instead of spiritual freedom we have uncontrolled carnal license.

Germany, he continued, was full of hungry tramps in rags, men who had abandoned their monasteries and vows, among whom was "no sobriety, no sincerity. Wherever they are, discipline and piety are at a low ebb." Erasmus reminded his correspondent that he was leading a privileged life:

> You live in a very comfortable place, in a most healthy climate; you are greatly comforted by conversation with learned men; you do not lack good books, you do not lack ability. What can be sweeter in this life than to leisurely enjoy these meadows and have a taste, as it were, of the blessed life in heaven, especially in this day and age than which nothing can be more turbulent and calamitous. . . . I swear on my life, if I had the least strength left in my body to sustain the monastic life, I would rather live there with you than be the most honored bishop at the imperial court. You know neither your own good fortune nor the misery of our time.[23]

We find here echoes of the idealistic portrayal of monastic life in *De contemptu mundi;* there, too, Erasmus speaks of monasteries as halls of learning where a man might enjoy good books and good conversaion; he also describes the raptures experienced in a solitude with God which allows the monk a "glimpse of that eternal light."[24]

His softening attitude is also evident from the changes he introduced to his 1529 edition of the *Enchiridion.* Although he left the controversial statement *Monachatus non est pietas* intact, he added a lengthy section to the preface, in which he quoted Jerome's praise of monks and nuns as "a blossom and most precious stone among the adornments of the church"[25] and challenged the regular clergy of his day to claim Jerome's praise for themselves by living up to the example.

---

[23] Allen 7: Ep. 1887, lines 6–50. Cf. Allen 4: Ep. 1239, line 12; Allen 5: Ep. 1436, lines 127–29.

[24] LB 5: 1258C.

[25] Allen 3: Ep. 858, lines 531–32.

But the most significant document for this third, temperate phase is Erasmus' preface to his 1533 edition of the Psalm commentaries of Haymo, the ninth-century bishop of Halberstadt. There we find an enthusiastic description of the monastic ideal: "When we use the term monk," he writes, "we speak of the sum of heroic virtues." "Who would not love those men, who are truly dead to the world and have given themselves completely to God?" Their company is edifying, they are loving and charitable, they exemplify all virtues; in a word, a monastic community is "the image of the city of God." Reversing his practice of weakening any praise of monastic ideal by contrasting it with reality, he minimizes such considerations:

> Here, I know, they will immediately object that most monks are very different from this image. If we hate the good because of the bad, we cannot approve of any kind of life. So what remains to be done? Nothing but to love humanity, to interpret what is doubtful in the best possible light, to wink at lesser faults, try to remedy rather than exasperate the more severe faults, and respect the order and institution itself.[26]

These conciliatory remarks are a far cry from the implacable spirit exhibited in some of his earlier writings. How do we interpret this shift? I think it is best explained as an adjustment, an example of "serving the time" in the best sense of the phrase. We have seen that Erasmus expressed regret at the radical language he had used in earlier writings. An even more poignant expression of regret can be found in a letter of 1530: "I wish I could undo everything and start all over again!" (*Utinam liceret omnia ab integro retexere*).[27] He felt that his earlier writings had been given a twist he had not intended, that they had been right for the times, but too incendiary in the present circumstances. The tone adopted in the preface to Haymo shows that Erasmus was adapting his words to the new situation, which called for a peacemaker rather than a Socratic gadfly. And we may conclude that it is Erasmus' tone that has changed rather than his convictions. Alternatively, we could say that his views on monasticism changed not absolutely but relatively: his opinion of monks had not improved, but his opinion of the Reformers had deteriorated.

We now come to the consideration of the force of the negative equation *Monachatus non est pietas*. My interpretation of the phrase in the context in which it appears is: Being a monk is not the equivalent of, or does not amount to, or is no guarantee of, or perhaps tells us nothing about, a person's piety.

---

[26] Allen 10: Ep. 2771, lines 49–50, 87–92.
[27] Allen 8: Ep. 2315, lines 299–300.

But if Erasmus meant any or all of these things, why did he not express himself in an unequivocal manner, or rather why did he express himself in a provocative form that lent itself to misinterpretation? The explanation lies in the genre of the *Enchiridion*.

The treatise is a protreptic, that is, a piece of hortatory rhetoric, and the controversial phrase suits the genre. *Monachatus non est pietas* is a paradox, a standard rhetorical figure of thought. What makes it a paradox? It challenges the associations readers would form in their minds on reading the phrase, the equivalences they would automatically establish between *Monachatus*, *pietas*, and a third term, *religio*, which was subliminally present because it was considered a synonym of both. In Forcellini's dictionary we read under *pietas*: *Eadem fere est ac religio* ("it is practically the same as *religio*"). Erasmus himself acknowledged that the reader would make this connection since in the common view "*pietas* was the same as *religio*."[28] Similarly, he noted that readers were under the impression that "the word *religio* means the same as the word *monachismus*."[29] If the three terms were thought of as synonyms by the general reader, they could be used interchangeably. Thus, *Monachatus non est pietas* was no different than saying *religio non est religio*—a paradox.

The use of the paradox as a figure of thought was recommended in classical handbooks of rhetoric as "giving force and lending charm" to a composition.[30] According to Aristotle, the paradox was a kind of maxim, but unlike the straightforward maxim it was not self-evident and needed clarification. Quintilian explains this process of clarification as follows: "After raising alarm [with a paradoxical statement], we go on to something trivial or quite inoffensive."[31] The follow-up shows that the shocking statement is really innocuous. This is exactly the procedure followed by Erasmus in the *Enchiridion*. He shocks readers with what appears to be an alarming statement, *Monachatus non est pietas*, but immediately follows it up with the explanation that should remove any offense given: Monasticism is not piety, but a way of life which may or may not be beneficial to the person in pursuit of piety. His critics, however, passed over the second half of the sentence which contained the corrective, and generally ignored the figure of thought.

---

[28] *Apologia brevis ad viginti et quattuor libros Alberti Pii quondam Carporum comitis,* LB 9:1148F.
[29] Allen 7: Ep. 1858, lines 466–67.
[30] Quintilian, *Institutio oratoria*, 9.1.2.
[31] Ibid., 9.2.23.

Let us examine their criticism in detail. We know of three printed attacks on the passage in question. The first appeared in 1528, when the Spanish Franciscan Luis Carvajal discussed it at length in his *Apologia monasticae religionis*. Then, in 1531, the passage was attacked twice: by the Italian nobleman and scholar Alberto Pio in *Tres et viginti libri in locos lucubrationum variarum Erasmi Roterodami* and by the Louvain Dominican Eustachius Sichem in his *Apologia pro pietate*.

Pio's rather idiosyncratic interpretation of the Erasmian dictum may be dealt with in brief. Far from treating the phrase as the paradox it is, he declared that it unequivocally expressed Erasmus' opinion of monasticism. In fact, "it is expressed in such a manner that it needs no exegete … it is very clear that your goal is nothing short of annihilating monasticism … ou make out that monasticism is not piety but something histrionic (to put it thus), a sort of theatrical skill which must be eliminated … for that is the gist of your views." In Pio's opinion, the monastic life was not only equivalent to piety, but was "a special and great kind of piety, for it leads to the perfection of life."[32] Erasmus answered Pio's book at length, but referred only in passing to his exaggerated interpretation of the phrase, noting that his critic "carped at what he did not understand." "The more Pio exaggerates," he added, "and the more detailed his response, the more ridiculous he will appear in the eyes of those who have read my words."[33]

More significant than Pio's quirky interpretation is Carvajal's treatment of the Erasmian phrase, for he misinterprets it as a definition, thus transferring it from its native rhetorical setting to a logical one. He lays the groundwork in his dedicatory letter to Cardinal Quiñones, and in the prefatory letter to the reader he portrays Erasmus as an inveterate enemy of monks: "In the many and varied books published by him not one can be found that is free of that uncontrolled malice with which he raves against our institution." Carvajal accordingly warns the reader against "Erasmus' machinations against the holy orders." Having set the stage in this fashion, he immediately focuses on the controversial phrase in the *Enchiridion*. "Let us examine your definition," Carvajal writes:

> So you say: *monachatus non est pietas*. Now Aristotle teaches that a nega-
> tive definition is invalid, and Erasmus makes the undoubtedly invalid

[32] Alberto Pio, *Tres et viginiti libri in locos lucubrationum variarum Erasmi Roterodami* (Paris: Josse Bade, 1531), 98v, 100v.
[33] *Apologia brevis ad viginiti et quattuor libros Alberti Pii quondam Carporum comitis*, LB 9:1149A.

statement: *monachatus non est pietas*. Is this how they taught you dialectic? But of course Erasmus looks down on logic, physics, and metaphysics, and the other arts of which he is ignorant. Instead, he makes a great deal of rhetoric, of which he drank in a wonderful quantity.[34]

We see that Carvajal takes what is in Erasmus a rhetorical figure and subjects it to the technical rules of dialectical disputation. This process invalidates the phrase since, in logical terms, it cannot serve as a definition, for a negative equation is not unequivocal, admitting of multiple solutions, or, in terms of language, interpretations.

Carvajal then continues in the dialectic mode, offering the following syllogism: Giving alms is pious. St. Francis instructed the members of his order to give alms. Thus the members of the Franciscan order are pious.[35] He adds another, similarly problematic syllogism. Living according to the Gospel is piety. St. Francis defined the life of a Franciscan as living according to the Gospel. Thus to be a Franciscan is to be pious.[36] Conversely, if a Franciscan is found not to be pious, he is not truly a monk. This, according to Carvajal, is like saying: "If he is a man, he is a living being; if he is no living being, he is not a man. We proceed from the negation of the genus . . . to the negation of the species. . . . But Erasmus has not studied logic." Carvajal next proposes his own definition of being a monk: *Monachatus est vita evangelica*, monasticism is living according to the Gospel. He invites Erasmus to check this definition against the rules of religious orders, "and he will find that I have provided a very good definition of 'being a monk.'"[37] He adds an *argumentum ad hominem*: When Erasmus himself was a member of the Augustinian order he was content to admit that being a monk meant leading a pious life, but "now that you have cast off the cowl, being a monk no longer means being pious."[38] As we know, Erasmus had not in fact "cast off his cowl," but Carvajal was perpetuating here a common misconception about his status.

Finally, Carvajal links Erasmus with Luther. He cites the popular saying that "Erasmus laid the egg and Luther hatched the chicken" and uses the statement in the *Enchiridion* to underscore this point: "Luther says: *Monachatus est impietas*. You say: *non est pietas*. You see how the two of you are in agreement?

---

[34] Luis Carvajal, *Apologia monasticae religionis* (Salamanca, 1528), 3r, 4r, 6v.

[35] Ibid., 6v: "Fateberis [eleemosynam] esse opus plenum pietatis. Franciscus . . . professionis suae candidatos monuit ut divenditis rebus suis eas pauperibus erogarent. Ergo monachatus auspicatur initium a pietate, est ergo pietas."

[36] See 55 n. 42.

[37] Carvajal, *Apologia monasticae religionis*, 13r.

[38] Ibid., 6v.

But you are more destructive than Luther because you were first to propagate this definition to the world. Luther would perhaps never have said *est impietas* if you had not said *non est pietas* first."[39]

In his reply to Carvajal, sarcastically entitled *Responsio adversus febricitantis cuiusdam libellum* (*Response to Someone Suffering from a Fever*) — a reference to Carvajal's preface in which he says that he wrote his apologia even though he was in poor health and laboring under a fever — Erasmus immediately pointed out the problems and fallacies in Carvajal's argument. He noted that the statement in question was not a formal definition, but "whenever Carvajal hears the verb 'is', he jumps to the conclusion that it is a definition." Dialectical rules did not apply to a general rhetorical statement, but "our man is only interested in logic, physics, and metaphysics, and quite oblivious to grammar," he said, neatly turning around Carvajal's reproach that he, Erasmus, was interested only in grammar and knew nothing about logic.[40]

Erasmus argued that in a rhetorical composition there is nothing wrong with a negative followed by a corrective statement of the type "a is not b but rather c." "Monasticism is not piety but a way of life etc.," he explains, was like saying: "Sound is not the collision of bodies but the noise arising from the collision."[41] These were perfectly reasonable statements in a rhetorical context.

Erasmus might have rested his case here, but he goes on and makes what I consider a tactical mistake. After pointing out that his medium was rhetoric and not logic, he proceeds to engage Carvajal on his own turf, that is, he tries to beat him at the dialectical game. Citing Carvajal's definition of monasticism, "monasticism is living according to the Gospel, therefore monasticism is piety," he offers the following retort: "My reply is: If what he says is the truth, all Christians have professed the rule of St. Francis, and all are monks who live according to the Gospel, and especially the apostles."[42] Furthermore, he rightly observes that, by the rules of logic, his own statement, *Monachatus non est pietas*, cannot be converted into Luther's *Monachatus est impietas*: "If I said that a cup of wine contains no medicine, could someone come along and convert this into 'contains poison'—you need to be a true expert in logic to reason

[39] Ibid., 12r.
[40] *Adversus febricitantis cuiusdam libellum responsio*, LB 10:1675A, E.
[41] Ibid., LB 10:1675A.
[42] Ibid., LB 10:1675A–B: "'Regula,' inquit [Carvajal], 'Francisci haec est. Evangelium Domini nostri Jesu Christi observare. Si hoc est pietas, monachatus est pietas.' Respondeo: si verum dicit, omnes Christiani professi sunt Francisci regulam, et omnes sunt monachi, quicunque vivunt secundum regulam Evangelicam, in primis Apostoli."

in this fashion! I said 'it is not piety' but what I added is enough to exclude what Luther says."[43]

The dispute continued in 1530, with Carvajal publishing a reply, entitled *Dulcoratio amarulentiarum Erasmicae responsionis* (*A Sweet Speech against the Bitter Response of Erasmus*). In his prefatory epistle Carvajal provided the reader with a whole catalogue of Erasmian errors, but with respect to the notorious phrase *monachatus non est pietas*, he felt that he had cause for satisfaction. "I must say," he wrote, "that Erasmus is not tenacious in everything. For, whereas he said *Monachatus non est pietas*, he now recants, saying *Monachatus est professio vitae evangelicae perfectioris*, being a monk means professing a life according to the Gospel in its more perfect form." He was pleased with this recantation, as he called it, and congratulated Erasmus on his reversal: "Congratulations, Erasmus, continue to speak in this Catholic fashion. Be done with your Lucianic scoffing and follow the teachings of Christ and the tenets of the church." Feeling that he had won a victory over Erasmus, Carvajal declared jubilantly: "In this matter I plainly deserve a triumphal procession, for I have forced Erasmus to recant his ignorant and equally impious definition and to substitute in its place a truly catholic one."[44]

Commenting on Erasmus' foray into dialectic, Carvajal pointed out that Erasmus' dialectical reasoning was inept. To conclude from the statement "monks live according to the Gospel" that "all who live according to the Gospel are monks, therefore all Christians are monks" was silly.

> Oh, great dialectician! For he argues like this: Man is a living being, a horse is a living being, therefore a horse is a man. A brainy dialectician indeed! But, from what topos is this derived, Erasmus? If A is in category B and C is in category B, it does not follow that A = C.... Who will not be amazed at Erasmus, the dialectician? But he is now a decrepit old man and has forgotten the rules of conversion [of terms], which the dialecticians teach."[45]

As for Erasmus' claim that one could not convert "Monasticism is not piety" into "Monasticism is impiety" and his effort to set his views clearly apart from Luther's, Carvajal called his explanation an evasive maneuver: "Your description does not exclude the Lutheran position, indeed it attracts it as a magnet attracts iron."[46]

---

[43] Ibid., LB 10:1677D.
[44] Luis Carvajal, *Dulcoratio amarulentiarum Erasmicae responsionis* (Paris: Simon Colinaeus, 1530), 5v, 74r, 40v.
[45] Ibid., 42v–43r.
[46] Ibid., 72r–v.

He also rejected Erasmus' suggestion that he saw definitions every-where: "I don't jump to the conclusion that the verb *est* always indicates a def-inition, but when the occasion demands a definition, as in the case of your book, it is my view that one must not give an inept and impious one, as you did."[47] This is an important objection. Carvajal's point here is that matters per-taining to religion and theology must be dealt with in a "theological" (*viz.* dia-lectical) manner. A rhetorical treatment was not acceptable. This is an argument often proffered by Erasmus' critics, and more generally, it is a prom-inent theme in criticisms of humanistic writings by Scholastically trained theologians. A pertinent example is the Valladolid verdicts. In 1527 Erasmus' works were investigated by Spanish theologians at a conference in Valladolid. The question of his usage came up repeatedly. Three participants referred to Erasmus' "inappropriate language" (*impropria locutio*). Three others noted that his manner of speaking was "not in use" among theologians or "did not accord with the common usage of the scholastic doctors." Another stated cat-egorically: "In theological matters one must write and speak theologically (*theologice*)."[48] Carvajal's objection was thus an important one and reflected a fundamental disagreement or misunderstanding between humanistically and scholastically trained writers.

Erasmus did not pursue the dispute with Carvajal but instead addressed an open letter to the Franciscans, asking them to "silence such asses,"[49] and he claims that Carvajal was indeed silenced as a result. The effect, if any, was, however, short-lived because Carvajal's accusations were soon recycled by the Dominican Eustachius Sichem.

Erasmus and Sichem were enemies of long standing. Erasmus first com-plained of the Dominican in 1520 after he published two tracts against Luther, linking the Reformer with Erasmus. In his attack on the *Enchiridion* in 1531, Sichem again drew parallels between Erasmus' and Luther's teaching. It was of no use to condemn Luther, he wrote, "if he prevailed in the books of others." Erasmus, who pronounced Sichem's book "boorish and infantile," did not reply to his accusations, but expressed his disapproval in a letter to Julius Pflug, then councillor to Duke George of Saxony. He offered this comment on Sichem's pamphlet: "He assumes that all eloquent men are heretics; on the

---

[47] Ibid., 42r.
[48] Text published by V. Beltran de Heredia, *Cartulario de la Universidad de Salamanca* VI (Salamanca: Publicaciones de la Universidad, 1973). The quotations are on 73, 74, 90, 44, 55, 108, 32, respectively.
[49] Allen 8: Ep. 2275, line 58.

basis of the fifth rule in the *Enchiridion* he shows that I indiscriminately condemn all ceremonies. . . . He says furthermore that I disapprove wholesale of many admirable monks and nuns since the monastic life consists to a large extent of ceremonies. . . . Elsewhere he comes to the foolish conclusion that I by far exceed Luther's impiety; he is shameless in his lies."[50]

In his book Sichem had written:

> There is no difference between [Erasmus'] sentiments and those of Luther. Luther says: "Monasticism is impiety." Erasmus maintains: "Observance of rites turns monks into the worst kind of man." Oecolampadius and his followers say: "Monasticism is a departure from Christ." And similarly Erasmus says of monks: "You think you are the best of men, but you are the worst of men, you, a Christian, have turned into a Jew." How does this differ from saying that monasticism is Judaism, a regression from Christ to Moses, that monasticism is impiety, although perhaps Erasmus did not dare to come out with this and said instead "Monasticism is not piety."[51]

There is no strict logical progression of thought in Sichem's comparison of Erasmus, Oecolampadius, and Luther, only loosely connected, but cleverly arranged, quotations. Unlike Carvajal, Sichem offers no formal syllogisms. He avoids the incorrect conversion "monasticism is not piety" into "is impiety," claiming a psychological connection instead. The implications of the two statements were the same, he said. The only difference was that Erasmus expressed himself covertly while Luther had spoken candidly. Sichem returns to this interpretation at the end of his book, concluding: "Erasmus says that [monasticism] is not piety, indeed he is saying, like Luther, that it is impiety— that is the tacit message of the fifth rule."[52]

Of the three attacks, Carvajal's is the most significant one because it is representative of the fundamental conflict between humanists and scholastics over method and language. But both Carvajal and Sichem are also representative of the Reformation era in their readiness to discover Lutheranism lurking under every criticism of the church. Given this atmosphere, the intransigence of humanists and scholastics on the issue of language and the paranoia prevailing in the late 1520s and early 1530s, it was inevitable that the Erasmian dictum *Monachatus non est pietas*, in itself a fairly innocuous statement, should generate such hostile reaction and, in this course, become subject to misinterpretation.

---

[50] Allen 9: Ep. 2522, lines 94–100.
[51] The text of Eustachius Sichem, *Apologia pro pietate in Erasmi Roterodami Enchiridion canonem quintum* (Antwerp: Vorsterman, 1531) has been edited by J. Coppens (Brussel: Paleis der Academiën, 1975). The passage quoted is on page 68.
[52] Ibid., 90.

Hilmar M. Pabel

THE PEACEFUL PEOPLE OF CHRIST
The Irenic Ecclesiology
of Erasmus of Rotterdam

~

*E*RASMUS OF ROTTERDAM was no doubt the most famous pacifist among the Renaissance humanists. His condemnation of war, especially war among Christians, and his uneasiness with the doctrine of the just war are well known.[1] Peace was so necessary for him and for his conception of the *respublica christiana*, of a Christendom founded upon the study of languages and of good letters and above all upon the teachings of Christ handed down by Scripture, that he would prefer an unjust peace to a just war. It would be a mistake, however, to interpret Erasmus' pacifism solely or principally in terms of politics. Discussions of the lack of political realism in Erasmus' pacifism or of his reaction to the just war theory, although important, do not get to the heart of his advocacy of peace and his denunciation of war. Erasmus' pacifism was ultimately rooted in his religious worldview, in the essence of his theology, which he called the *philosophia Christi*. Peace was the way of Christ; to be a follower of Christ meant, among other things, to be a devotee of peace.

---

[1] For various interpretations of Erasmus' views on war and peace see Roland H. Bainton, "The *Querela Pacis* of Erasmus: Classical and Christian Sources," *Archiv für Reformationsgeschichte* 42 (1951): 32–47; J. A. Fernandez-Santamaria, "Erasmus on the Just War," *Journal of the History of Ideas* 34 (1973): 209–26; Ross Dealy, "The Dynamics of Erasmus' Thought on War," *Erasmus of Rotterdam Society Yearbook* 4 (1984): 53–67; Rudolf Padberg, "Erasmus contra Augustinum: Das Problem des bellum justum in der erasmischen Friedensethik," in *Colloque Erasmien de Liège*, ed. Jean-Pierre Massaut (Paris: Société d'Edition "Les Belles Lettres," 1987), 278–96; and Otto Herding, "Erasmus — Frieden und Krieg," in *Erasmus und Europa*, ed. August Buck (Wiesbaden: Otto Harrassowitz, 1988), 13–32.

That peace is fundamentally a religious and theological reality is evident in Erasmus' ecclesiology. His most famous plea for peace, the *Querela pacis*, is more than a mere polemic against warfare. More than denouncing the evils of war, it reminds Christians of their corporate religious duty to embrace and promote peace. Although Christians may speak different languages and live in different countries, they are all members of Christ's church. Unless the church, the community of Christians, dwells in peace, it has no hope for survival. Erasmus warns: "Remove peace and the whole community of Christian life is destroyed."[2] The *Querela pacis* first appeared in 1517, the year that Luther posted his Ninety-Five Theses. In 1521, when Luther was excommunicated by Pope Leo X and put under the imperial ban by Charles V, Erasmus wrote to Justus Jonas, the German humanist and partisan of Luther. He pointed out to Jonas that the word "church" lacks any meaning if it does not include the notion of concord, for "what is our religion, if not peace in the Holy Spirit?"[3]

Discussing Erasmus' ecclesiology, James Tracy rightly remarks: "Tranquillity was to be found in the church, the house of the Lord."[4] What is more, *only in the church* can peace truly prosper. Erasmus believes that "outside the confines of the church there is no peace."[5] The flock or sheepfold of Christ functions as an apt image for Erasmus' irenic concept of the church. In his commentary on Psalm 22 (23) he describes a sheep as "a harmless and a peaceful (*imbelle*) animal, armed neither with horns, nor with teeth, nor with shoes, nor with nails; nor is it fortified with poison for its own defense."[6] Ideally, Christians should be like sheep: harmless and peaceful.

Erasmus' pacifism and ecclesiology are inextricably bound up with the *scopus* or the central focus of his life and thought: the person of Jesus Christ. Not without reason do we speak of Erasmus as a Christian humanist. Christ is the goal of humanist scholarship, for Erasmus promotes the liberal arts for Christ's glory.[7] He views political authority in terms of Christ since he believes that it was of supreme importance for a prince to have "the best possible understanding of Christ."[8] Jesus embodies "the model of all piety"; for Christians he is the great exemplar, "in whom alone are all the patterns of the

[2] *Querela pacis*, CWE 27: 303.
[3] CWE 8: Ep. 1202, lines 10–11.
[4] James D. Tracy, *Erasmus: The Growth of a Mind* (Geneva: Droz, 1972), 219.
[5] *In Psalmum XXII Enarratio Triplex* (1530), ASD 5–2: 344.
[6] Ibid., ASD 5–2: 339.
[7] CWE 6: Ep. 961, lines 22–23; CWE 8: Ep. 1219, lines 53–56; "Pro docilitate," *Precationes aliquot novae* (1535), LB 5: 1202A–B.
[8] *Institutio principis christianis* (1516), CWE 27: 212.

holy life."[9] Christians are called to imitate Christ; to make him the goal of their lives; to love, marvel at, and want nothing but Christ or because of Christ.[10]

Christ, the prince of peace, is the preceptor of "concord and mutual love."[11] In his teaching "you will find nothing anywhere which does not breathe the spirit of peace, which does not savour of love."[12] To obey and follow their Lord and Master, Christians must be a people of peace. Christ stands at the center of Erasmus' irenic ecclesiology. The church takes its origin from Christ,[13] and it is one with him.[14] Erasmus most often defines the church in terms of Christ. He employs the images of the body of Christ, the bride of Christ, the flock or sheepfold of Christ, the house of Christ, the new city of Christ, and the dove of Christ.[15] Another term sums up his basic concept of the church: the people of Christ. The church is composed of men and women who put their faith in Christ their savior, obey Christ their teacher, and pattern their lives after Christ their example.

Brian Gogan has stated: "Erasmus' view of the church ... was predominantly pneumatic."[16] For the renowned Christian humanist the church is primarily a spiritual entity rooted in a communal allegiance to Christ. Erasmus' pneumatic ecclesiology appears to be entirely unrelated to the late medieval preoccupation with the visible structures of ecclesiastical power. Ever since the Great Schism (1378–1417) conciliarism had been the burning issue of debate: did a general council, above and beyond the pope, have normative, supreme authority in governing the church?[17] Erasmus demonstrates his lack of interest in such questions when he complains that, while some theologians equate the entire church with the pope, they switch their allegiance to a general council if the pope tries to resist their ambitions. Do not such dogmas prepare the way

[9] *Enchiridion* (1503), CWE 66:72, 86.

[10] Ibid., CWE 66:61.

[11] *Querela pacis*, CWE 27:299.

[12] *Dulce bellum inexpertis* (1515), in Margaret Mann Phillips, *The "Adages" of Erasmus: A Study with Translations* (Cambridge: Cambridge University Press, 1964), 328.

[13] *Christiani matrimonii institutio* (1526), LB 5:704A.

[14] *Concionalis interpretatio in Psalmum LXXXV* (1528), ASD 5–3:332.

[15] Willi Hentze, *Kirche und kirchliche Einheit bei Desiderius Erasmus von Rotterdam* (Paderborn: Verlag Bonifacius-Druckerei, 1974), 41–50; Georg Gebhardt, *Die Stellung des Erasmus von Rotterdam zur römischen Kirche* (Marburg an der Lahn: Oekumenischer Verlag Dr. R. F. Edel, 1966), 114–30; Tracy, *Erasmus: The Growth of a Mind*, 219.

[16] Brian Gogan, *The Common Corps of Christendom: Ecclesiological Themes in the Writings of Sir Thomas More* (Leiden: E. J. Brill, 1982), 326. Hentze would agree with Gogan. He writes that for Erasmus the church has a "geistig-geistliche Wirklichkeit." See Hentze, *Kirche und kirchliche Einheit*, 215.

[17] See Yves Congar, *L'Eglise de saint Augustin à l'époque moderne* (Paris: Les Editions du Cerf, 1970), 305–51.

for tyranny if so much power is placed in an impious and base individual?[18] Erasmus turns out to be neither a supporter of papal absolutism nor a conciliarist.[19]

To be sure, despite all his criticisms Erasmus never rejects the papacy, nor does he deny the visible institutions of the church. Manfred Hoffmann emphasizes that Erasmus

> did not attempt to substitute for the existing church an unstructured, undogmatic fellowship of freedom and spirit. Rather, he wished for the church's external means of grace to operate according to their spiritual purpose. This pertains particularly to the ministry of proclaiming God's word as incarnate in Christ and the Scripture.[20]

Indeed, Erasmus' massive manual on preaching, the *Ecclesiastes sive de ratione concionandi* (1535), represents the culmination of his contribution to the pastoral office of the church. He also appreciates the liturgical and sacramental life of the church, as his Mass in honor of the Virgin of Loreto (*Virginis matris apud Lauretum cultae liturgia*, 1523/1525) and his treatises on confession (*Exomologesis sive modus confitendi*, 1524) and marriage (*Christiani matrimonii institutio*, 1526) demonstrate. Nevertheless, church government, pastoral ministry, liturgy, and the sacraments all depend on a fundamental spiritual understanding of the church. At the heart of this ecclesiology is a personal and corporate commitment on the part of Christians to express their love for Christ by living according to his teaching on peace.

Today scholars recognize that "traditional Christianity was the matrix of experience, the prism in which Renaissance man would seek a focus for his feelings."[21] They have, for the most part, abandoned the old view of Erasmus as a skeptic and an intellectual threat to Christianity. Claims that "Erasmus certainly does not think in terms of the Church" or that "the Church as such does not mean anything to him"[22] can therefore no longer be upheld. Erasmus values the church highly. To be a "living member of the most holy body of the church" is an essential mark of human happiness and dignity, he says.[23] The

---

[18] *Ratio verae theologiae* (1520 ed.), in Holborn, 206.

[19] Harry J. McSorley, "Erasmus and the Primacy of the Roman Pontiff: Between Conciliarism and Papalism," *Archiv für Reformationsgeschichte* 65 (1974): 49–54.

[20] Manfred Hoffmann, "Erasmus on Church and Ministry," *Erasmus of Rotterdam Society Yearbook* 6 (1986): 30.

[21] Timothy Verdon, "Christianity, the Renaissance, and the Study of History," in *Christianity and the Renaissance: Image and Religious Imagination in the Quattrocento*, ed. Timothy Verdon and John Henderson (Syracuse: Syracuse University Press, 1990), 5.

[22] C. Augustijn, "The Ecclesiology of Erasmus," in *Scrinium Erasmianum*, 2 vols., ed. J. Coppens (Leiden: E. J. Brill, 1969), 2: 135.

church is constantly in Erasmus' mind and at the tip of his pen. After the Reformation had destroyed the unity of Western Christendom, Erasmus prays for the peace of the church,[24] and suggests ways of restoring that peace.[25] His last written work treats the theme of the purity of the Christian church.[26]

My examination of Erasmus' ecclesiology adopts a more historical approach than the studies of John Guarnaschelli, Georg Gebhardt, and Willi Hentze, who have produced systematic presentations of Erasmus' thinking on the church.[27] Although I begin by organizing Erasmus' ecclesiology according to an ordered series of perspectives, I do so within an historical framework. The principal point of reference is the Protestant Reformation, which presented the greatest challenge to a Christendom founded on peace. The year 1519 will serve as the main historical conjuncture, for in that year Erasmus began to take notice of Luther.[28] The first part of this essay, "Foundations," lays the groundwork for Erasmus' irenic ecclesiology. The church is Christ's peaceful people, called to shun the divisive forces of vice and to embrace virtue in order to imitate Christ and to promote greater Christian harmony. This groundwork was fully in place before Luther had broken with Rome. The second part, "Developments," analyzes the development of Erasmus' irenic ecclesiology in reaction to the Reformation.

FOUNDATIONS

Any discussion of Erasmus' religious thought must begin with his first major work, the *Enchiridion militis christiani* (1503). This holds true for his thinking about the church, and thus one cannot agree with the assessment that the "Church is not dealt with in the *Enchiridion* for a good reason; its value is not great."[29] The ecclesiological image that Erasmus employs most frequently in his famous manual of Christian piety and that conveys most forcefully the importance of concord for the church is the body of Christ. The body of

---

[23] *Concio de puero Jesu* (1511/1514), CWE 29:69.

[24] *Precatio ad Dominum Jesum pro pace ecclesiae* (1532), LB 5:1215E–1218D.

[25] *De sarcienda ecclesiae concordia* (1533), in Raymond Himelick, trans., *Erasmus and the Seamless Coat of Jesus* (Lafayette, Indiana: Purdue University Press, 1971), 29–97.

[26] *De puritate tabernaculi sive ecclesiae christianae* (1536), ASD 5–2:277–316.

[27] John S. Guarnaschelli, "Erasmus' Concept of the Church, 1499–1524: An Essay Concerning the Ecclesiological Conflict of the Reformation" (Ph.D. diss., Yale University, 1966). For complete references to Gebhardt and Hentze see 61 n. 15, above.

[28] Erasmus first addressed himself to the developing conflict surrounding Luther in a letter of April 14, 1519, to Luther's patron, Elector Frederick of Saxony. See CWE 6: Ep. 939.

[29] Augustijn, "The Ecclesiology of Erasmus," 140.

Christ occupies such an important place in Erasmus' theology that "it must be taken as one of the fundamental strands in the fabric of his thought."[30]

The choice of the body of Christ as an image of the church forms part of Erasmus' "Pauline preoccupation"[31] within the *Enchiridion*. He quotes extensively from Saint Paul's treatment of the church as the body of Christ, reproducing the texts of Rom. 12:4–6, 1 Cor. 12:12–27, and Eph. 4:15–16. Together these passages emphasize that the church, Christ's body, consists of many members of various ranks of dignity and of function who are nevertheless united because of their common head, Christ.[32] In adducing these Pauline passages, Erasmus demonstrates his resolute belief in the unity of the church, in the church as a unified, harmonious organism under Christ, her principle of unity.

Erasmus quotes the Pauline passages on the body of Christ in a chapter entitled "Beliefs worthy of a Christian." He does this in order to convince his readers that as Christians, as members of Christ's body, they must treat each other with mutual care and love. Ernst-Wilhelm Kohls not surprisingly calls Erasmus' concept of the church in the *Enchiridion* a "community of love."[33] This is an apt description, provided we understand Erasmus' view of the church as a community of love *under Christ*, remembering the Christocentric character of his thought. That the church is a community of love is already evident several pages before Erasmus' discussion of the beliefs that Christians ought to have. In the famous fifth rule of the *Enchiridion,* Erasmus makes clear that the subordination of the visible to the invisible, of the flesh to the spirit, is the cardinal principle of Christian piety, and at the same time he censures a senseless and undue attachment to the external manifestations of religious life. In this fifth rule he expounds the true nature of charity. The greatest of the theological virtues is completely devoid of all ceremonialism. Charity does not consist of "frequent church attendance or genuflecting in front of the images of saints or burning candles or repeating a specified number of little prayers." Erasmus explains the Pauline concept of charity: "to edify our neighbour, to consider everyone as members of the same body, to regard everyone as one in Christ, to rejoice in the Lord at your brother's prosperity as if it were your own and to heal his misfortunes as if they were your own."[34]

[30] John W. O'Malley, "Erasmus and Luther, Continuity and Discontinuity as Key to their Conflict," *Sixteenth Century Journal* 5, no. 2 (1974):55.

[31] James K. McConica, *English Humanists and Reformation Politics under Henry VIII and Edward VI* (Oxford: Clarendon Press, 1965), 20.

[32] CWE 66:95–96.

[33] Ernst-Wilhelm Kohls, *Die Theologie des Erasmus*, 2 vols. (Basel: Friedrich Reinhardt Verlag, 1966), 1:161.

In "Beliefs worthy of a Christian" Erasmus advises his reader to take thought for the needs of his neighbor and urges: "Make this one simple reflection: 'He [the neighbor] is my brother in the Lord, a member of the same body, redeemed by the same blood, a partner in the same faith, called to the same grace and happiness of the future life.'" The mutual love of the members of Christ's body is rooted in all that they have in common. Erasmus here points out some of the basic components of their love and unity by invoking their commonality in the redemption of Christ their head, in their Christian faith, and in the heavenly inheritance to which they are all called. Considerations such as the ties of citizenship, family, and friendship do not really matter. What binds Christians together in love is that they are all brothers in Christ and "members one of the other" in the body of which Christ is the head.[35] Through Christ, moreover, the church is united with God the Father, and so Erasmus concludes: "All these are one: God, Christ, the body and the members."[36] The church then, as the *Enchiridion* makes clear, is a peaceful unity of Christians who love one another under the headship of Christ.

Those who have not learned this lesson, who in effect have not accepted Paul's doctrine of the body of Christ, earn a sharp rebuke from Erasmus. He fulminates:

> Your fellow member bares his teeth from hunger, and you belch up partridge flesh. Your naked brother trembles with cold, and so much of your wardrobe is eaten away by moths and rotting with decay. You gamble away a thousand ducats of gold in a single night, while some poor girl, driven by poverty, prostitutes her virginity, and a soul perishes for which Christ gave his life.

One cannot belong to the church, the body of Christ, and be insensitive to the needs of the fellow members of the body. This lack of sensitivity and love demonstrates that one has nothing in common with the members of the body and therefore that one has nothing to do with Christ the head.[37]

In 1518, fifteen years after the first edition of the *Enchiridion*, Erasmus published the first edition of the *Ratio verae theologiae*, which in 1519 served as one of the prefaces to his second edition of the New Testament. Erasmus' ecclesiology emerges in the *Ratio* when he writes of Christ and his people. Christ the heavenly teacher founded a new people who have nothing to do

---

[34] CWE 66:79.
[35] CWE 66:94.
[36] CWE 66:95.
[37] CWE 66:96

with spite, envy, or lust, but who in the flesh lead a life similar to that of the angels. They do not know divorce, for they can bear evils or correct them. As they neither distrust nor deceive anyone, they have no use for oaths. They lay up their treasure in heaven so that they have no desire for money. The morals of Christ's people are innocent; they possess the purity and simplicity of children. Anger, cursing, and vengeance are all foreign to the Christian people. The highest form of peace and concord, the peace of the members of the one body, holds sway among them. For them mutual charity makes everything the common property of all.[38]

Although Erasmus conceives of the church as a people of pacific virtue, he does not forget that this people is also the people of Christ. The community of people who shun the vices of division cannot be conceived of apart from Christ, for it is a new people called into being by him. Christians avoid vainglory, referring "all to the glory of Christ alone," and are innocent of ambition, subordinating themselves to everyone "on account of Christ." Christ's people are "so wise after the fashion of their teacher the heavenly Spirit, they so live according to the example of Christ that they are the salt of the earth and the light of the world, like a city situated in a high place [cf. Matt. 5:13–14], visible to everyone from all directions."[39] Christians are a spiritual people, for they imitate Christ, are taught by the Holy Spirit, and depend entirely on heaven. They cast aside the helps of this world and possess a wealth, wisdom, nobility, power, and happiness with which this world is unfamiliar.[40]

Besides virtue in general, unity, love, and harmony are important characteristics of the church for Erasmus. These last three attributes are variations on the great theme of peace, which Erasmus values highly out of loyalty to and love for Christ. That the church must be a people of peace is clear from Erasmus' two famous pleas for peace among Christians. The first is an essay of 1515 on the adage *Dulce bellum inexpertis*, the second his *Querela pacis* of 1517. In both works Erasmus expresses his shock at the warlike temperament of many of his fellow Christians. In waging war against each other they prove to be more depraved than the bellicose heathen of antiquity.[41] Not only do they disobey Christ their Lord, who taught nothing but peace and mutual love, but they even force him to witness to their disregard for his teaching by butchering each other under the banners of his cross.[42]

---

[38] Holborn, 193–94.
[39] Holborn, 194.
[40] Holborn, 193.
[41] *Bellum*, in Phillips, *"Adages" of Erasmus*, 335.

In the *Querela pacis* Erasmus employs the scriptural images of the church as Christ's sheep (John 10:11, 14), as the branches of Christ the vine stock (John 15:50), and as chicks gathered under the wings of Christ the hen (Matt. 23:37).[43] He also refers to the church in *Bellum* as Christ's vine branches and invokes the Pauline metaphor of the body of Christ.[44] It is absurd that sheep should fight with sheep, branch with branch, chick with chick, and member with fellow member of the same body, for like is supposed to live in harmony with like. Erasmus most emphatically portrays the church as Christ's peaceful people by insisting upon the commonality of all Christians. In his manifestos on peace Erasmus elaborates upon this commonality and stresses it with greater urgency than he did in the *Enchiridion*. In the *Querela pacis* he writes that the decision to call the Christian people a church implies a common purpose. They "all share the same house, serve a common prince, fight for the same cause, have been initiated by the same sacraments, enjoy the same benefits, live on the same pay, and seek a joint reward."[45] Erasmus exclaims in *Bellum*:

> What an absurd thing it is, that there should be almost continuous warfare between those who are of the household of one Church, who are members of the same body and glory in the same head, that is Christ; who have one Father in heaven, who are quickened by the same Spirit, initiated into the same mysteries; redeemed by the same blood, regenerated by the same baptism, nourished by the same sacraments, fighting under the same commander, eating the same bread, sharing the same cup; having a common enemy in the Devil, and finally called together to the same inheritance![46]

That Christians should be "fighting under the same commander" does not sound out of place in an essay by a Christian pacifist. Christians are constantly engaged in a spiritual battle against the devil and sin. In the *Enchiridion* Erasmus equips his Christian soldiers with their most reliable weapons: prayer and a knowledge of Scripture.[47] In *Bellum* he holds that "it is not fitting for Christians to fight, except in that noblest of all battles against the most hideous enemies of the Church—against love of money, against anger, against ambition, against the fear of death."[48] The Christian people must fight a moral

---

[42] Phillips, *"Adages" of Erasmus*, 321–22; *Querela pacis*, CWE 27:309.
[43] CWE 27:302–3.
[44] Phillips, *"Adages" of Erasmus*, 329.
[45] CWE 27:303–4.
[46] Phillips, *"Adages" of Erasmus*, 327.
[47] CWE 66:30–32.

and spiritual battle against vice under their commander, Christ Jesus. Given their commonality in Christ, however, they may not disobey him by conducting *military* campaigns against each other. The church's life is a life of peace in imitation of the prince of peace. Those who love war are outside the church and have nothing to do with Christ. Erasmus asks in the *Querela pacis*:

> What is there in common between the church and an armed camp? One signifies bringing together, the other tearing apart. If you take pride in being a member of the church, what have you to do with wars? If you are outside the church, what have you to do with Christ?[49]

In *Bellum* and in the *Querela pacis* Erasmus mentions an important element of the commonality of the Christian people. They all share the same sacraments. This is not a new idea. In his *Panegyric for Archduke Philip of Austria* (1504) Erasmus impresses on Philip the necessity of princes to preserve peace. Christians would not go to war with each other if their leaders remembered that "the Christian church is one family ... and that we are members of the same body, ruled by the same head in Christ Jesus ... and that we receive sacraments which are common to all."[50] In 1514 Erasmus wrote Antoon van Bergen, abbot of Saint Bertin in Saint-Omer. His letter, a prelude to his condemnation of war in *Bellum*, lists being "nurtured upon the same sacraments" as one of the common characteristics of Christians, "who are members of one body."[51]

Hentze aptly refers to the "Sakramentengemeinschaft," a communion in the sacraments, as a chief feature of Erasmus' ecclesiology.[52] The sacraments confer grace, and furthermore they gather the many into one.[53] True, they are vehicles of salvation; yet they also function as signs of the unity of the church, of the members of Christ's body.[54] As Erasmus writes in the *Querela pacis*, the "holy sacraments" are "the special symbol of the closest union between Christians."[55]

Baptism and the Eucharist are the most sacred symbols of Christian unity. In his *Paraphrase on Romans* (1517) Erasmus follows Paul's teaching at the beginning of Romans 6 that in baptism Christians die together with

---

[48] Phillips, *"Adages" of Erasmus*, 336.
[49] CWE 27:303.
[50] CWE 27:56.
[51] CWE 2: Ep. 288, lines 39–41.
[52] Hentze, *Kirche und kirchliche Einheit*, 51–57.
[53] Otto Schottenloher, "Erasmus und die Respublica Christiana," *Historische Zeitschrift* 210 (1970):313.
[54] Hentze, *Kirche und kirchliche Einheit*, 100.
[55] CWE 27:304.

Christ to sin. Erasmus also links baptism to his favorite Pauline image of the church, the body of Christ, an image that shows the unity of the members with each other and with Christ. Yet in referring to Christians as being "grafted to the body of Christ through baptism"[56] he goes beyond the original text, for Paul does not use the image of the body of Christ in Rom. 6:5, the particular passage in question. The text reads: "For if we have been planted together in the likeness of his death, we shall be also in the likeness of his resurrection" (AV). In his edition of the New Testament, Erasmus departs from the Vulgate by translating the key word, σύμφυτοι, as "insitii facti sumus"— "we have been grafted on."[57] The Vulgate reads: "complantati facti sumus"— "we have been planted together." In a note of 1516 in his *Annotations on the New Testament* he argues that Paul is "alluding to the grafting on of a plant, which corresponds to the communion of the body of Christ."[58] In the context of Rom. 6:5 the idea of grafting on suggests to Erasmus the incorporation of believers into the body of Christ, into the unity of the church. Baptism brings about this incorporation, allowing Christians to share in the communion of the body of Christ.

Erasmus makes the case for baptism as a sacrament of unity much more explicitly in the *Querela pacis*. He wonders whether the sacraments have any effect on Christians, who are so used to fighting each other on the battlefield. He reminds his readers: "Baptism is common to all; by this we are reborn in Christ, cut off from the world, inserted among the members of Christ. What can be so much a united whole as the members of the same body?" Baptism initiates Christians into the church, whose essence is unity, and promotes this unity by doing away with all distinctions among Christians, since "through baptism there is neither slave nor free man, neither barbarian nor Greek, neither man nor woman, but all are the same in Christ who brings all into harmony."[59]

Whereas baptism signifies the entry into the unity and harmony of the body of Christ, the Eucharist preserves the church's unity. For Erasmus, the Eucharist is, as Otto Schottenloher remarks, the "central sacrament of the church."[60] It is the great sacrament of concord. This is evident in Erasmus' thought as early as the publication of the *Enchiridion* in 1503. To illustrate the

---

[56] CWE 42:37.
[57] LB 6:594A.
[58] Anne Reeve and M. A. Screech, eds., *Novum Testamentum: Erasmus' Annotations on the New Testament: Acts—Romans—I and II Corinthians* (Leiden: E. J. Brill, 1990), 376.
[59] CWE 27:304.
[60] Schottenloher, "Erasmus und die Respublica Christiana," 312.

primacy of the invisible and of the spiritual over the visible and material he states that Christ despised "the eating of his own flesh and the drinking of his own blood if they were not eaten and drunk spiritually as well."[61] Erasmus explains how one worthily celebrates the sacrifice of the Mass every day. If one celebrates Mass without trying to overcome one's selfishness and lack of concern for the misfortune of one's neighbors, one remains "in the 'flesh' of the sacrament." Partaking of the Eucharistic sacrifice means that "you are one spirit with the spirit of Christ, one body with the body of Christ, a living member of the church; if you love nothing but in Christ; if you consider all your goods to be the common property of all men; if you are afflicted by the misfortunes of others as if they were your own."[62] The Eucharist animates the church, grounding its members in concord and inspiring them to treat each other with mutual love.

Erasmus vents his frustration in the *Querela pacis* at Christians who refuse to acknowledge the Eucharist for what it is. He asks: "What did the communion of holy bread and loving-cup ratify but a kind of new concord which should never be broken?" Yet he laments that "the heavenly bread and mystical chalice do not unite Christians in the friendship which Christ himself held sacred, and which they renew daily and represent in sacrifice." Erasmus is unwilling to allow those who prefer war to peace to receive the sacrament: "Does any man dare to approach that sacred table, the symbol of friendship, the communion sacrament of peace, if he intends to make war on Christians, and prepares to destroy those whom Christ died to save and to drink the blood of men for whom Christ shed his own blood?"[63] The "communion sacrament of peace" is intended solely for Christ's people who, out of loyalty to Christ and to his teaching, must be a people of peace. It is impossible to be a true member of the church without loving other Christians and without living in peace with them.

Erasmus sets down his most elaborate description of the church in 1518. In the *Ratio verae theologiae* and in the preface to the third edition of the *Enchiridion*, addressed to the Benedictine abbot of Hugshofen, Paul Volz, he portrays the church, "the entire people of Christ,"[64] as a social order consisting of three concentric circles with Christ as the common midpoint. This is, as Georges Chantraine points out, a "new image for Erasmus," probably

[61] CWE 66:70.
[62] CWE 66:71.
[63] CWE 27:302, 304.
[64] Holborn, 202.

suggested to him by John Colet and inspired by the celestial hierarchies of Pseudo-Dionysius.[65] Closest to the midpoint is the first circle which contains the clergy: those "who are nearest Christ—priests, bishops, cardinals, popes, and those whose business it is to follow the Lamb wherever He may lead them."[66] In light of their exalted position of closeness to Christ, the members of the first circle must live a life worthy of their position, shunning "love of pleasure, longing for money, ambition and lust for life." Their proper function is to preach the Gospel and to "speak with pure prayers to God and to intercede for the salvation of their flock."[67] The clergy must pass on Christ's purity to the members of the second circle, the secular princes. These serve Christ with their weapons when they fight enemies in just wars, and with their laws when they punish criminals.[68] Furthest away from Christ in the third circle are the common people who, despite their lack of cultivation, nevertheless belong to the body of Christ.[69]

Chantraine is correct in claiming that the Erasmian image of the church is not as "exclusively vertical" as the Dionysian image of the hierarchies. He argues: "For Erasmus, Christ is the center of attraction of the Christian people and the center for the diffusion of charity." Christ is not only the unique source of love for "the priests and princes but also for the entire Christian people," who do not occupy a place in the three hierarchies of Pseudo-Dionysius.[70] The church is built up around Christ, who is its sole reason for existing. He is the goal of the actions of his people, the target at whom they must aim. Erasmus consequently warns: "Do not move the central mark from its place."[71] Christ is equally the focal point for all Christians, but his central position does not prevent Erasmus' image of the church from being a hierarchical one. True, the three concentric circles do not easily allow for a vertical hierarchy, but they do indicate a spatial hierarchy set up or measured in terms of the distance from the center that is Christ. The clergy stand closest to Christ; therefore they hold the first place in the Erasmian hierarchy of circles. Even if, as Erasmus holds, "every man according to the measure that is given him must strive upwards to Christ,"[72] it is still the role of the clergy to draw those who

[65] Georges Chantraine, *"Mystère" et "Philosophie du Christ" selon Erasme* (Gembloux: Editions J. Duculot, 1971), 123.

[66] Letter to Volz, CWE 66:14.

[67] Holborn, 202.

[68] Holborn.; letter to Volz, CWE 66:14.

[69] *Ratio*, Holborn, 202; letter to Volz, CWE 66:15.

[70] Chantraine, *"Mystère" et "Philosophie du Christ,"* 124.

[71] Letter to Volz, CWE 66:14.

[72] Letter to Volz, CWE 66:15.

belong to the second and third circles to Christ. The princes and magistrates, farther away from Christ than priests and bishops, have the important power of governing the temporal order, but the common people lack any mark of distinction. Those whom Erasmus places in—one could almost say, relegates to—the third circle are weak and need to be treated "with paternal indulgence."[73]

Although the popes, bishops, and priests hold the most prominent place in the ecclesiastical hierarchy, this does not mean that the clergy by itself constitutes the church. Nothing could be farther from the mind of Erasmus. His image of the three concentric circles refers, as he says in the *Ratio*, to the "entire people of Christ." He warns in an essay on the adage *Sileni Alcibiadis* (1515) that the word "Church" should not merely denote "the priests, bishops and supreme pontiffs," for "they are in truth nothing but the Church's servants." Correcting the identification of the church with the clergy, Erasmus maintains: "No, it is Christian people who are the Church."[74]

The contrast between these two definitions of the church—as the clergy or, alternatively, as all Christians—appears very clearly in the *Julius exclusus* (1517/1518), an attack upon the warrior pope, Julius II (d. 1513), which Erasmus never claims to have written, but which most scholars nonetheless attribute to him. Julius unsuccessfully attempts to storm the gates of heaven to attain his eternal reward. Saint Peter appears to test the spiritual worthiness of the deceased warrior. He reproves Julius for having engaged in warfare. Julius replies that wars enlarge the church. Peter rejoins: "But if the church is the Christian people, bound together by the spirit of Christ, you seem to have ruined the church by provoking hideous wars throughout the world, so that you could be evil and pestilent with impunity." Then follows Julius' haughty retort: "What we call the church is the holy temples, the priests, particularly the Roman curia, and above all myself, the head of the church."[75] According to Peter, Julius' church is a "false body of Christ" attached to a "false head of Christ."[76] The gates of heaven remain firmly shut to the pontiff who restricts the church to the clergy.

Erasmus subjects the clergy of his day to vehement criticism. Prelates who lead lives of avarice and licentiousness, who immerse themselves in political affairs, and who are a party to warfare are anathema to him. Yet Erasmus

[73] Ibid.
[74] CWE 34:271.
[75] CWE 27:191.
[76] CWE 27:194.

criticizes only the failings of individuals, not of their offices. Indeed, he holds the various degrees of holy orders in high esteem. "There is something heavenly about a priest," he remarks in *Sileni Alcibiadis*, "something more than human; nothing is worthy of his exalted position except what is heavenly.... This is the man chosen out of the heavenly body, which is the Church, by that heavenly Spirit for appointment to the highest place."[77] Erasmus calls a bishop "a vicar of Christ and guardian of His heavenly spouse."[78]

The dignity and "exalted position" of priests and bishops lie not in the exercise of power but in their service to the Christian people. They must be pastors, devoting themselves to their flocks in their ministry of preaching and teaching. "The Christian world," Erasmus continues in *Sileni Alcibiadis*, looks to a priest "for its food of sacred learning, it looks for the counsel that leads to salvation, for fatherly consolation, for a pattern by which to live."[79] The clergy, moreover, have to be warriors for virtue. Erasmus wants "to see priests most highly respected ... for their high standard of sacred learning and their outstanding virtues." He wants them to be "revered ... for their integrity and strict way of life."[80] In the *Praise of Folly* Erasmus interprets the cross carried before the bishop as a symbol of victory over all human passions, and the cardinal's white surplice as a sign of "supreme purity in life."[81] Popes, he says in *Sileni Alcibiadis*, should "be warlike—but against those true enemies of the Church: simony, pride, lust, ambition, anger, impiety."[82] Finally, all members of the clergy are to be propagandists for peace. Erasmus issues this command for churchmen in the *Querela pacis*: "In private and in public they must preach, proclaim, and inculcate one thing: peace."[83]

The clergy rightly occupy the first of the three concentric circles that represent the church. Although they are its servants, the clergy at the same time form the church's spiritual leadership. They have the duty and the authority to preach and to administer the sacraments. They must also witness with their conduct to the principal characteristics of the people of Christ: virtue and especially peace.

[77] CWE 34:276.
[78] CWE 34:274.
[79] CWE 34:277.
[80] CWE 34:275.
[81] CWE 27:138.
[82] CWE 34:275.
[83] CWE 27:313.

DEVELOPMENTS

The second edition of the *Ratio* appeared in 1519, the year in which Erasmus first confronted the simmering Reformation conflict by advising Luther to moderate the tone of his writings.[84] He was quick to point out that he did not belong to Luther's camp and often professed his loyalty to the Roman pontiff and the Roman church. In September 1520 he assured Pope Leo that he was "not mad enough to make some bold move against the supreme vicar of Christ."[85] To another correspondent he affirmed: "Assailed as I have been from so many quarters which I could name and wooed with honeyed words from others, it has never been possible to detach me from my veneration for the church of Rome."[86] In a letter of December 6, 1520 to Cardinal Lorenzo Campeggi he expressed his belief that the Roman church does not "dissent" from the Catholic church and declared: "I am not impious enough to dissent from the Catholic church, I am not ungrateful enough to dissent from Leo."[87] In 1522 he told Pedro Ruiz de la Mota, the Bishop of Palencia: "neither death nor life can tear me away from the society of the Catholic church."[88] To Ulrich von Hutten and the rest of Luther's followers Erasmus declared in 1523 his belief that the Roman church, which is no less a church for its "multitude of evils," is orthodox.[89] The "society of the Catholic church" from which Erasmus in 1530 urged the Strasbourg Reformers not to be removed represents in effect the Roman church, which Martin Bucer and company had forsaken.[90]

Erasmus' irenicism was the principal reason for his allegiance to the Roman church. In an apology of 1525 against the criticisms of his New Testament made by Pierre Cousturier (Petrus Sutor), a Carthusian monk who had received his doctorate in theology from the University of Paris in 1510, the humanist theologian remarked that he prefered not to leave the community of the Roman church because he loved concord and hated strife.[91] Erasmus assured Pope Clement VII (1523–1534): "I have always submitted myself and

---

[84] CWE 6: Ep. 980, lines 45–58.
[85] CWE 8: Ep. 1143, lines 55–56.
[86] CWE 9: Ep. 1337A, lines 31–33.
[87] CWE 8: Ep. 1167, lines 472–74.
[88] CWE 9: Ep. 1273, lines 30–31.
[89] *Spongia adversus aspergines Hutteni*, ASD 9–1:173.
[90] *Epistola ad fratres inferioris Germaniae*, ASD 9–1:329.
[91] *Apologia adversus Petrum Sutorem*, LB 9:790B–C. For the controversy between Cousturier and Erasmus see Erika Rummel, *Erasmus and His Catholic Critics*, 2 vols. (Nieuwkoop: De Graaf, 1989), 2:63–71.

everything of mine to the judgment of the Roman church, and should offer no resistance even if she were to judge me unjustly; for I will suffer anything rather than be a cause of subversion."[92]

Sometimes Erasmus combines his love of peace with his loyalty to the Roman church. In 1521, he promised the Faculty of Theology at the University of Louvain: "as far as in me lies, I will not abandon the peace of the Catholic church, the truth of the Gospel and the dignity of the Roman pontiff, while this is possible."[93] To the bellicose Hutten and his crowd Erasmus insists that if the evils of the Roman curia can be reformed only with warlike tumults that throw everything into confusion, it would be better to let the sleeping evil be.[94] Erasmus even goes so far as to tell the Strasbourg Reformers: "If Paul were alive today, he would not disapprove, I think, of the church's state of affairs, but he would raise his voice against human vices." These vices had to be eradicated but, of course, without tumult.[95]

Erasmus' irenic conception of the church would not permit him to join Luther or Bucer or anyone else who repudiated the church of Rome. Separation from the Roman and Catholic church and the formation of new churches meant dissension and discord within Christendom. Yet this is irreconcilable with what the people of Christ should be: a people of concord. Erasmus' irenic ecclesiology bound him to the Roman church. If he had joined the Reformation, he would have been unfaithful to what he perceived the nature of the church to be. Erasmus' concern for peace in the church seems to take precedence over the need for virtue; or rather with the onset of the Reformation concord becomes the supreme virtue in the church. A corrupt curia is not too high a price to pay for the preservation of ecclesiastical concord. Even the authority of wicked popes must remain inviolate and be tolerated in order to prevent upheavals. This sentiment is made clear in Erasmus' *Epistola de interdictu esu carnium*, a short treatise of 1522 that criticizes the church's laws on fasting.[96]

Three writings of the 1520s show Erasmus' irenic ecclesiology in action. In 1520 Erasmus coauthored with Johann Faber, a Dominican from Augsburg, a short and anonymously published *Consilium*.[97] It aims at composing the

---

[92] CWE 10: Ep. 1418, lines 48–51.
[93] CWE 8: Ep. 1217, lines 161–63.
[94] *Spongia*, ASD 9–1:174.
[95] *Contra pseudoevangelicos* (1530), ASD 9–1:308.
[96] ASD 9–1:38.
[97] The full title of the tract is *Consilium cuiusdam ex animo cupientis esse consultum et romani pontificis dignitati et christianae religionis tranquillitati.*

Lutheran affair for the benefit of the tranquillity of the church. The authors object to the widespread slandering of Luther. Wildly branding him as a heretic would accomplish nothing. The proper way to deal with him is to refer his case to three impartial arbitrators of great distinction: Charles V, the newly crowned German emperor; Henry VIII, the king of England; and Louis II, the king of Hungary. If this solution would not do, let a general council of the church pronounce judgment upon Luther's teachings. Perhaps if Luther was proven to be in error, he would come to his senses.[98] For the sake of the peace of the church Erasmus sought to remove Luther's case from the arena of theological mudslinging to a more civil and controlled environment in which an orderly settlement could be reached.

The pacification of a Christendom divided by doctrine also serves as the main theme of two publications of 1524. In the colloquy *Inquisitio de fide* Erasmus tries to teach his readers that Lutherans and Catholics are in full agreement on the essential doctrines of Christianity. The whole controversy between them is unnecessary. Having quizzed Barbatius, his Lutheran interlocutor, on the articles of the Apostles' Creed, the Catholic Aulus concludes: "When I was at Rome, I did not find all so sound in the faith."[99] The church that both Barbatius and Aulus profess is "the body of Christ, that is to say, a certain congregation of all men throughout the whole world who agree in the faith of the Gospel, who worship one God the Father, who put their confidence in his Son, who are guided by the same Spirit of him; from whose fellowship he is cut off that commits a deadly sin." The church "is nothing else but the profession of one God, one Gospel, one faith, one hope; the participation of the same Spirit and the same sacraments."[100]

As in the *Enchiridion*, *Bellum*, and *Querela pacis*, so too in the *Inquisitio*, this unity expresses itself through the commonality of Christians. They worship the same triune God, and share the same Gospel, the same faith, the same hope, the same sacraments. (The idea of the participation in the same sacraments, however, poses a problem that Erasmus overlooks, since the Lutherans acknowledged only two sacraments, five fewer than the Catholics had.) Erasmus' long-standing insistence upon the unity of the people of Christ

[98] Wallace K. Ferguson, ed., *Erasmi Opuscula: A Supplement to the Opera Omnia* (The Hague: Martinus Nijhoff, 1933), 352–61, esp. 359–60.

[99] Craig R. Thompson, ed., *Inquisitio de fide: A Colloquy by Desiderius Erasmus Roterodamus* (New Haven: Yale University Press, 1950), 73.

[100] Thompson, *Inquisitio de fide*, 69.

emerges again quite appropriately in the attempt of the *Inquisitio* to unify Lutherans and Catholics and thus to restore the unity and peace of the church.

The *Inquisitio* was certainly not "a subtle strafing before the bombardment."[101] The *De libero arbitrio* (1524) was no bombardment, for it represented Erasmus' final great attempt to reconcile Lutherans and Catholics. Here he responds to Luther's denial that human beings possess freedom of choice in matters pertaining to salvation. Unlike Luther, Erasmus believes that one cannot determine with certainty from Scripture whether human beings have free will. After examining scriptural passages that seem to uphold free will and those that seem to deny it, he opts for the traditional view in favor of free will as the more probable one. Erasmus realizes that Luther's assertions stem from the desire to emphasize that salvation depends entirely on God's mercy. The Christian humanist sought to "appease" the Reformer with a "more accommodating view."[102] The beginning and accomplishment of salvation is solely due to God's grace; in the intermediary stage, "progress," free choice is operative but only in cooperation with grace.[103] Yet the contribution of free choice is "exceedingly trivial," and what is more, "this very thing which it can do is a work of the grace of God who first created free choice and then freed it and healed it."[104]

Luther refused to be appeased. He retorted in 1525 with his *De servo arbitrio*, upholding the bondage of the will. Luther disapproved of Erasmus' efforts at moderation and peace. Already in 1521, the Reformer complained that the humanist, in all his writings, was interested in peace, but not in the cross.[105] In the *De servo arbitrio* Luther informed Erasmus:

> Let me tell you, therefore—and I beg you to let this sink deep into your mind—that what I am after in this dispute is to me something serious, necessary, and indeed eternal, something of such a kind and such importance that it ought to be asserted and defended to the death, even if the whole world had not only to be thrown into strife and confusion, but actually to return to total chaos and be reduced to nothingness. (128)

[101] Steven Ozment, *The Age of Reform: 1250–1550* (New Haven: Yale University Press, 1980), 294.

[102] E. Gordon Rupp and Philip S. Watson, trans. and eds., *Luther and Erasmus: Free Will and Salvation* (London: SCM Press, 1969), 90.

[103] Ibid., 89–90.

[104] Ibid., 90.

[105] *D. Martin Luthers Werke: Briefwechsel*, 15 vols. (Weimar: Herrmann Böhlaus Nachfolger, 1930–1978), 2:387.

Erasmus should refrain from complaining about the loss of peace and from trying to remedy the religious conflict, for "this tumult has arisen and is directed from above, and it will not cease till it makes all the adversaries of the Word like the mud on the streets." (130) If the preaching of the Word provoked tumults, then so be it. Yet to "wish to stop these tumults ... is nothing else but to wish to suppress and prohibit the Word of God." (129)[106] With the *De libero arbitrio* Erasmus' attempt to accommodate Luther had failed. Luther did not share Erasmus' pacific sensibilities.

What underlies the difference between Erasmus' attempt at conciliation and "Luther's combative speech"[107] is not an antinomy between humanism's preference for peace and the Reformation's relentless quest for truth. As Marjorie O'Rourke Boyle points out: "Erasmus sought the truth as certainly did Luther." (155) The difference between Erasmus and Luther is not a matter of peace versus truth but, in part, one of rhetoric. Erasmus prefers the more moderate art of persuasion against Luther's uncompromising assertiveness. For Erasmus, truth is discovered through deliberation and is disseminated through persuasion. Persuasion is the art of politics, and Boyle compares Erasmus to a statesman, whereas Luther is a judge who prosecutes Erasmus' erroneous position as "Christ's legal advocate." (58)[108] In Luther's opinion the bondage of the will is an open-and-shut case, and it needs to be asserted with boldness and defiance.

Conflicting rhetorical strategies do not, however, provide the only explanation for the opposition between Erasmus and Luther. They also had two distinct approaches to theology. Chantraine has discussed these at length and has remarked that Erasmus' theology is more "catholic" since its dynamic is one of "both ... and," whereas Luther understands theology in terms of "either ... or."[109] Thus Erasmus can reconcile both the need for God's grace and the cooperation of the human will in salvation. For Luther, on the other hand, grace and free will are mutually exclusive.

The *Consilium, Inquisitio de fide*, and *De libero arbitrio*, three applications of Erasmus' irenic ecclesiology in practice, are all free of the spirit (or demon, as Erasmus might say) of contention over controverted dogma. This is true

---

[106] Page numbers are from Rupp and Watson, *Luther and Erasmus*.

[107] Marjorie O'Rourke Boyle, *Rhetoric and Reform: Erasmus' Civil Dispute with Luther* (Cambridge: Harvard University Press, 1983), 101.

[108] Page numbers are from Boyle, *Rhetoric and Reform*.

[109] Georges Chantraine, *Erasme et Luther: Libre et serf arbitre* (Paris: Editions Lethielleux, 1981), 145, 449. For a similar view see Manfred Hoffmann, "Erasmus on Free Will: An Issue Revisited," *Erasmus of Rotterdam Society Yearbook* 10 (1990): 119–20. See also O'Malley, "Erasmus and Luther," 47–65, esp. 65.

even of the *De libero arbitrio* since the humanist only reluctantly enters the "tangled labyrinth" of free choice, wishing, moreover, to engage in a "temperate discussion" that would pursue "the matter without recrimination because this is more fitting for Christian men."[110] Erasmus intensely disapproved of dogmatism, of the multiplication of articles of faith, of the bitter disputes which this multiplication engenders. In the preface to his 1523 edition of the works of the Church Father, Saint Hilary of Poitiers, he professes: "The sum and substance of our religion is peace and concord. This can hardly be the case unless we define as few matters as possible and leave each individual's judgment free on many questions."[111] Four years earlier, referring to the Lutheran affair in a letter to Jan Slechta, a Bohemian nobleman, Erasmus maintains that many people would be reconciled to the Roman church if everything were not indiscriminately defined as an article of faith. Such articles should remain few in number.[112]

Erasmus' dislike of dogmatism did not, however, mean that he cared little for the church's teachings, that he was adogmatic or undogmatic, as Joseph Lortz held.[113] Erasmus rejected the Reformation along with its dogmas. He remained loyal to the teachings of the church of Rome out of faithfulness to what he called the consensus of the church, a sign of the truth of the church's teaching. This notion of consensus played an important role in his thinking about the church in the context of the Reformation.[114]

The idea that the consensus of all people confirms the truth of a proposition goes back to Aristotle. The Stoic and Epicurean philosophers adhered to the principle of the *consensus omnium*, and Cicero introduced it to the Roman world. The Roman emperors, beginning with Augustus, employed the *consensus omnium*, the consensus of the gods, and/or the consensus of the armies to legitimize their rule.[115] The consensus of believers was an important concept in the early Christian church. It sanctioned the election of bishops and the decisions of synods and, as Klaus Oehler states, made possible the unity of the pre-Constantinian church, which lacked a visible centralized organization.[116]

[110] Rupp and Watson, *Luther and Erasmus*, 35, 36.

[111] CWE 9: Ep. 1334, lines 232–34.

[112] CWE 7: Ep. 1059, lines 235–41.

[113] Joseph Lortz, *Die Reformation in Deutschland*, 2 vols., 4th ed. (Freiburg im Breisgau: Herder, 1962), 1:132.

[114] For a thorough treatment of Erasmus' concept of the consensus of the church see James K. McConica, "Erasmus and the Grammar of Consent," in *Scrinium Erasmianum*, 2:77–99.

[115] Klaus Oehler, "Der Consensus omnium als Kriterium der Wahrheit in der antiken Philosophie und der Patristik," *Antike und Abendland* 10 (1961):105–16.

Erasmus employs the concept of consensus before and outside the context of his confrontation with the Reformation. The "consensus of pious people over so many centuries" subscribes to the truth and the certainty of Scripture, he writes in the *Enchiridion*.[117] In *Paraphrases on the New Testament*, consensus often denotes the concord among the members of the church and their unity in Christ. By a unity of hearts and minds (*consensus animorum*) Christians form one bread and one body.[118] Philip, the poor, humble, Jewish man, is quite different from the rich, powerful, Ethiopian eunuch whom he baptizes. The difference in person is not relevant, however. All that matters is the same faith and a "consensus in Jesus Christ."[119]

On two occasions, in 1526 and 1527, Erasmus defines the church in terms of the consensus. In letters to the German humanist Willibald Pirckheimer, having confirmed his rejection of the Eucharistic teaching of Oecolampadius, Erasmus calls the church "the consensus of the Christian people throughout the whole world" and "the consensus of the entire Christian people."[120] These definitions of the church reflect two key elements of Erasmus' ecclesiology: the centrality of Christ, and peace. The church is the people of Christ that abides in consensus, a species of concord, as Gogan explains, that is relevant "to matters of thought and principles of human behaviour."[121] It embodies the people of Christ in harmonious agreement on matters of doctrine.

Sometimes Erasmus speaks of the consensus of all Christians. At other times the consensus of the church appears as the consensus of so many popes, bishops, theologians, church fathers, saints, martyrs, councils, and universities.[122] Gogan consequently believes that Erasmus "fell into an intellectually aristocratic approach to the church" since he "tended to restrict the bearers of consensus to the enlightened few," excluding the great unwashed of "the mass of believers."[123] Such an assertion is open to debate, however. On some occasions Erasmus mentions the consensus of the Christian people or of the Christian world in conjunction with that of the "enlightened few."[124] Furthermore,

---

[116] Ibid., 117, 122.

[117] Holborn, 57: "totiam saeculis piorum hominum consensus." CWE 66:55 translates: "the unanimous concurrence of generations of saintly men."

[118] *Paraphrase on 1 Corinthians* [10:17] (1519), LB 7:893B.

[119] *Paraphrase on Acts* [8:38] (1524), LB 7:702B–C. See also Schottenloher, "Erasmus und die Respublica Christiana," 321–22.

[120] Allen 6: Ep. 1729, line 27; Allen 7: Ep. 1893, lines 59–60.

[121] Gogan, *The Common Corps of Christendom*, 366.

[122] See, for example, *De libero arbitrio*, Rupp and Watson, *Luther and Erasmus*, 43; *Hyperaspistes I* (1526), LB 10:1315D–E, 1400C–D; *Ad fratres inferioris Germaniae*, ASD 9–1:338, 362.

[123] Gogan, *The Common Corps of Christendom*, 368, 369.

[124] *Exomologesis* (1524), LB 5:145A–B; *Hyperaspistes I*, LB 10:1292E–F, 1315D–E; *Ad fratres inferioris Germaniae*, ASD 9–1:338.

he tends to heap up a consensus of prelates, doctors, and the like in his polemics against the Reformers, obviously trying to overwhelm them with the authority of the enlightened ecclesiastical elite. Whether Erasmus' concept of consensus and thus of the church is populist or aristocratic is irrelevant. What does matter is the harmonious agreement on matters of faith within the church.

For Erasmus, moreover, the consensus does not only embrace a multitude of people. Essential to the consensus is also the entire history of the church. The church is the consensus of the Christian people down through the ages, the "consensus of so many centuries and nations."[125] To Luther Erasmus points out that the entire Christian people has always held sacred the memory of the ancient doctors of the faith and that the opinions of so many bishops and popes have been received and established "by such a long succession of centuries."[126] He reminds the Strasbourg Reformers that the princes of the church have taught the same things with a great consensus for so many hundreds of years.[127] The church as consensus is thus a reality that transcends the present moment and reaches back into its past. The Christian people through the tradition or consensus of the church acquire unity and concord in matters of faith.

Yet Georg Gebhardt incorrectly claims that the "consensus for Erasmus is nothing less than a result of a vote in the modern democratic sense."[128] Erasmus knows that the majority is not always right. Did not at one time the majority of bishops, persuaded by Arius' teachings, condemn the orthodox Athanasius?[129] To Luther he concedes: "Not that, as in human assemblies, I would measure my opinion by the number of votes or the status of the speakers. I know how frequently it happens that the greater part overcomes the better: I know that those are not always the best things that are approved by the majority."[130] The cornerstone of the consensus of the church is not the opinion of the majority over the centuries. This would make the consensus its own justification, the church its own legitimization. The church, the Christian people, does not exist of itself. Christ is the guarantor of the consensus; he is the origin and the head of the church. Erasmus believes in the Real Presence in the Eucharist, disputed by Oecolampadius and the Sacramentarians, because he

[125] *Explanatio symboli* (1533), ASD 5–1: 276.
[126] *Hyperaspistes I*, LB 10: 1315D.
[127] *Contra pseudoevangelicos*, ASD 9–1: 230.
[128] Gebhardt, *Die Stellung des Erasmus von Rotterdam zur römischen Kirche*, 58.
[129] *Ad fratres inferioris Germaniae*, ASD 9–1: 386.
[130] *De libero arbitrio*, Rupp and Watson, *Luther and Erasmus*, 43.

cannot accept that Christ, who is truth and charity, would allow his beloved bride, the church, to persist in such an abominable error as to worship a crust of bread in his stead.[131] Although the consensus attests to the verity of the church's dogma, it has its underpinning and meaningfulness in Christ.

The consensus of the church throughout the ages that is founded upon Christ possesses immense authority for Erasmus. With this consensus he upholds the practice of auricular confession,[132] the free choice of the will against Luther,[133] and the Real Presence of Christ in the Eucharist. In fact, Erasmus probably would have accepted Oecolampadius' doctrine if the consensus of the church had not contradicted it.[134] So authoritative is the consensus of the church that it strengthens his belief in the church's teachings. He cannot abandon the consensus. In a letter of 1525, Erasmus informs Conrad Pellican, one of the reform leaders of Basel: "Hitherto, along with all other Christians, I have always worshipped in the Eucharist the Christ who suffered for me, and I see no reason now to change my views. No human argument could make me abandon what is the universal teaching of Christendom." Towards the end of the letter he reiterates: "You have no place for the authority of prelates or councils, and so, as you are always saying, your mind is in a constant state of flux; my mind, on the other hand, has been kept firm thus far by the universal agreement of the Catholic church."[135]

On the authority of the consensus Erasmus indicts the Reformation. He blames Luther for discarding the doctors of the church from apostolic times to the present, the decisions of ancient councils, and the consensus of the Christian people.[136] What the Church Fathers have taught and religiously preserved for so many centuries in times past—whether it concern fasting, singing in church, the sacrifice of the Mass, the Eucharist, the invocation of saints, statues in church, free will, or monasticism—the Strasbourg Reformers and others dare to call "idolatry, blasphemy, an insult to Christ, and assaults upon Scripture." The Reformers cannot convince Erasmus that they are not proposing new dogmas but only restoring old ones. "As if," he retorts, "what the church has preserved and taught with a great consensus of the world for fourteen hundred years to this day is not old." The doctrines of Luther and of the Strasbourgers on the Eucharist: are they not new?[137] To the tumult-provoking

---

[131] Allen 8: Ep. 2136, lines 221–26.
[132] *Exomologesis*, LB 5: 145A–B.
[133] *De libero arbitrio*, Rupp and Watson, *Luther and Erasmus*, 43.
[134] CWE 11: Ep. 1636, lines 3–6.
[135] CWE 11: Ep. 1637, lines 69–73, 125–28.
[136] Allen 7: Ep. 1853, lines 6–9.

new dogmas of the Reformation he opposes the teachings handed down by the church for the last fifteen hundred years.[138]

Where do they stand who have defied the Christian consensus and broken with Rome and thus with the Catholic church? Does Erasmus think that Protestants have cut themselves off from the body of Christ? Erasmus never expressly casts the Protestants out of the church. Yet the implications of his critique of the Reformation, when seen in the light of his thinking on the church, seem in some respects to point to the exclusion of the Protestants from the people of Christ.

Erasmus finds it difficult to reconcile the behavior of the "evangelicals" with the spirit of Christ. Of Luther's supporters he writes: "They all have on their lips five words: Gospel, God's word, faith, Christ, and spirit—and yet I see many among them of a sort that leaves me in no doubt they are moved by the spirit of Satan."[139] He hears the evangelicals clamor for the Gospel, but he would like to see their moral conduct agree with the Gospel.[140] He repeatedly claims that the adherents of the Reformation have not become more virtuous through their Gospel; he does not know of any evangelicals who have not become worse.[141] Those who come out of the evangelical churches seem to be filled with an evil spirit. They go about with countenances of wrath and ferocity. Their leaders are greater tyrants than the Catholic bishops. Whereas the love of wealth and the lust for power crept into the popes and other prelates late in time, the reform leaders want to rule and grow rich right away.[142] "The power of the Gospel," Erasmus lectures Pellican, "does not destroy the moral law, but fulfils it."[143]

He does not, however, point his finger only at the Protestants. The calamity of the Reformation is God's punishment for the evils of all of Christendom. In particular, the bishops' neglect of their flocks explains why "God has let into our midst the wolves of heresy." God is "offended by the idleness, debauchery, pride, and lust of the priests." Yet, as Erasmus reminds the Reformers, the church from its very inception has always included evil people. Is it surprising that one still encounters reprehensible things in the church,

---

[137] *Ad fratres inferioris Germaniae*, ASD 9–1: 362, 414.

[138] Ibid., 9–1: 364.

[139] CWE 10: Ep. 1483, lines 8–10.

[140] Allen 7: Ep. 1973, lines 16–17.

[141] See, for example, Allen 7: Ep. 1887, lines 6–11; Allen 7: Ep. 1901, lines 26–34; *Contra pseudoevangelicos*, ASD 9–1: 298; Karl Heinz Oelrich, *Der späte Erasmus und die Reformation* (Münster: Aschendorffische Verlagsbuchhandlung, 1961), 95–96.

[142] *Contra pseudoevangelicos*, ASD 9–1: 292, 300.

[143] CWE 11: Ep. 1637, lines 1–2.

and is there any justification for throwing the whole church into confusion on account of some of its faults?[144] Erasmus' answer, of course, is "no." The faults of the clergy do not justify revolution against the church. Erasmus does not wish to excuse the sins of the church's leadership. He will not, however, countenance upheaval and tumult as appropriate responses to clerical corruption.

The worst sin of the Reformers is their violation of the peace of the church. Erasmus perceives in the Reformation a desire to overturn everything in order to bring about radical change.[145] Nothing handed down from the past pleases its leaders. Their attempts to change the world suddenly "have ruined the concord of the entire church."[146] It is Luther who has thrown the apple of discord into the world,[147] and also into the church, one might add, for he is the "author of this ecclesiastical tempest."[148] What is more, peace does not abide in the camp of the Reformers. The strife and discord among the leaders of the Reformation repel Erasmus from joining them and their churches. He reminds Philip Melanchthon of the differences in doctrine between him and Zwingli, and to Bucer he expresses his astonishment at the confessional infighting among Zwingli, Luther, and Osiander.[149] Erasmus, who will not depart from the peaceful abode of "the public judgment and consensus of the church," criticizes Pellican: "You go to war among yourselves."[150] The repudiators of Rome could not constitute a church among themselves because they lacked a necessary ecclesial ingredient: peace. Nor could they, to take Erasmus' ecclesiological thought to its logical conclusion, be part of the consensus of the Catholic church, for the new Protestant dogmas conflicted with the consensus.

Were the Reformers heretics, therefore? Erasmus refrained from branding his contemporaries as such. Screaming "heresy!" and "to the fire!" amounted to tumultuous behavior, something he could not condone.[151] Nevertheless, perhaps his reference to "the wolves of heresy" quoted above, and his sarcastic comment to the Strasbourgers, acknowledging their preference to refer to themselves as evangelical rather than heretical churches,[152] indicated that he did think the evangelicals were heretics.

---

[144] *Contra pseudoevangelicos*, ASD 9–1: 302–4.
[145] Oelrich, *Der späte Erasmus und die Reformation*, 53.
[146] Allen 7: Ep. 1901, line 97; Ep. 1976, line 23.
[147] CWE 8: Ep. 1228, line 30.
[148] Allen 9: Ep. 2465, lines 275–76.
[149] CWE 10: Ep. 1496, lines 83–89; Allen 7: Ep. 1901, lines 35–38.
[150] Allen 6: Ep. 1644, lines 15–17.
[151] See, for example, CWE 6: Ep. 939, lines 53–68; CWE 7: Ep. 1033, lines 80–103; *De sarcienda*, Himelick, *Erasmus and the Seamless Coat of Jesus*, 84.
[152] *Ad fratres inferioris Germaniae*, ASD 9–1: 331.

Whatever the case may be, Erasmus has harsh words for heresy and schism. His disparagement of these two ills fits into the context of his ecclesiological thought. Defending his writings from the censures of the theologians of the University of Paris in 1532, he categorically states that heretics, even if not publicly condemned, are outside the church.[153] Not only are they outside the church, but also "heretics and schismatics," he writes the following year in the *De sarcienda ecclesiae concordia*, "have always tried to split apart the Church."[154] Heretics do not believe the voice of the church; schismatics seek a new church.[155] Together they sow the seeds of discord in the church. In his catechism, the *Explanatio symboli* (1533), Erasmus makes a repudiation of these two evils a necessary condition for belief in the church:

> Whoever professes the holy church execrates and abjures every schismatic conspiracy against the tranquillity of the ecclesiastical hierarchy, and similarly all conventicles of heretics, with whatever label they use to advertise themselves. Conventicles there are without number, but there is only one dove.[156]

The one dove, an allusion to the Song of Solomon (6:8), is an apt image for Erasmus' irenic conception of the church.

The most harmful species of discord are also the worst possible vices. "There is no vice worse than heresy or schism," he tells the Strasbourg Reformers. The debauchery, lust, ambition, avarice, and the other sins of one priest cannot even equal the evil of heresy.[157] In a similar vein, "anyone who abandons the fellowship of the Church and moves into heresy or schism is worse than one who leads an indecent life in sound beliefs."[158]

For Erasmus, ecclesiastical concord ranks above all other virtues, and any vice is more tolerable than that of discord in the church. He would prefer the consensus of the church in matters of doctrine to a conventicle of pious heretics. Luther believed that the good works of a man without faith were in fact mortal sins. Erasmus held that the piety and virtue of heretics and schismatics is nothing but sin and vice. The Catholic church may contain many wicked people; nevertheless, it possesses the remission of sins. Heretics, on the other hand, Erasmus goes on to tell the Strasbourgers, live wickedly even if they live well.[159] It would seem then that outside the church there is neither

---

[153] *Declarationes adversus censuras theologorum parisiensium*, LB 9: 946E.
[154] *De sarcienda*, Himelick, *Erasmus and the Seamless Coat of Jesus*, 37.
[155] *Ad fratres inferioris Germaniae*, ASD 9–1: 408.
[156] ASD 5–1: 274.
[157] *Ad fratres inferioris Germaniae*, ASD 9–1: 422.
[158] *De sarcienda*, Himelick, *Erasmus and the Seamless Coat of Jesus*, 82.

peace nor virtue and piety. Virtue and piety are subordinated to peace, however, because they cannot exist in the church without peace. The principal evil
of heretics and schismatics lies in their rending the seamless coat of Christ.

Erasmus was, of course, not content with analyzing the sources of ecclesiastical discord: moral vice, the spirit of tumult, the departure from the consensus, the evils of heresy and schism. Much more did he value the
reestablishment of the unity of the church. This is why he published in 1533 the
De sarcienda ecclesiae concordia, a commentary on Psalm 83 (84).

Erasmus explains why he chose to expound this psalm: "We have chosen
the eighty-third psalm for comment because in it the Holy Spirit, arguing
with the utmost plainness and cogency, urges upon us that blessed and lovely
peace of the Church, a subject useful and beneficial at any time, but in this age
of proliferating sects more essential than any other."[160] This introduction
manifests what seems to be a new emphasis in the ecclesiological thought of
Erasmus towards the end of his life: the role of the Holy Spirit in the church.
God the Father governs the church through the Holy Spirit.[161] The third
person of the Trinity quickens the bride of Christ. The flock of Christ "is led
by the Spirit of Christ."[162] Under the same Spirit's influence the Catholic
church hands down inviolable truth.[163] He would not have allowed the
church to err for the past thirteen hundred years.[164] Most importantly, the
Holy Spirit is the Spirit of peace and unity. With the "glue of peace" he recon-
ciles those who are at odds with each other.[165] In the *Explanatio symboli*
Erasmus teaches that just as the Spirit binds together the Father with the Son,
so too he links the church to Christ "with a secret and indissoluble bond." Not
only does he unite the church to Christ; he also unifies all the members of the
church.[166] The Holy Spirit is the guardian of the church's unity and for this
reason he "urges upon us that beloved and lovely peace of the Church."

To have "true peace of mind," Erasmus writes in the *De sarcienda,* Christians must "remain in the unity of the Catholic Church."[167] Erasmus' first proposal to restore this unity is a summons to moral and spiritual renewal. He
holds: "the particular source of this turmoil is the irreligious moral habits of

---

[159] *Ad fratres inferioris Germaniae,* ASD 9–1:341.
[160] Himelick, *Erasmus and the Seamless Coat of Jesus,* 29.
[161] *Ecclesiastes,* LB 5:1073C.
[162] *In Psalmum XXII enarratio triplex,* ASD 5–2:335, 341.
[163] "Ad Spiritum Sanctum," *Precationes aliquot novae,* LB 5:1200A.
[164] *De libero arbitrio,* Rupp and Watson, *Luther and Erasmus,* 48.
[165] "Ad Spiritum Sanctum," *Precationes aliquot novae,* LB 5: 1199F.
[166] ASD 5–1:216, 271.
[167] Himelick, *Erasmus and the Seamless Coat of Jesus,* 59.

men." Virtue no longer reigns supreme among the people of Christ, and as a result discord has invaded the church. Moral and spiritual renewal involves two things. First, Christians must consider each other's good characteristics and not dwell on each other's vices. Peace cannot return to the church "if everyone closes his eye to the virtues of the other fellow and has such an eye for his blemishes as are those mirrors which present an alleged image much enlarged and distorted." Yes, many monks, priests, and bishops, are utterly devoid of religion, chastity, and learning, preferring tyranny to piety. It would be wrong, however, to forget that many clerics nonetheless are pious and virtuous. The second part of moral and spiritual reform is embodied in the principle: "Let every man personally be what he ought to be." Popes, high priests, and vicars of Christ, must care "sincerely for the Lord's flock, while princes are to be "ministers of divine justice." Monks must demonstrate excellence in character; priests should meditate on the law of the Lord. Bankers, merchants, and tradesmen must go about their business honestly.[168]

Fostering a spirit of "give-and-take" between Catholics and Protestants emerges as the second point of Erasmus' peace plan. The Christian humanist urges both sides to make concessions on a number of sources of contention. To resolve the controversy over the free choice of the will he proposes the formula of justification by faith accompanied by works of charity, which are "essential for attaining salvation."[169] Erasmus allows for the prayers and good works of the living to help the dead, the invocation of the saints, and the veneration of images and relics, provided that these practices are free of superstition. Those who cannot bear such religious devotions may freely dissent from them as long as they refrain from causing an uproar. Whether or not auricular confession was instituted by Christ and whether the Eucharist should be understood *opere operante* or *opere operato,* he leaves to the opinion of the individual until a church council should pronounce on these matters.[170] Fasting should also remain, provided that no one be coerced to fast, and that those who eat do not revile those who fast and vice versa. In making these suggestions Erasmus does not wish to "dictate to the Church what decisions she should make." He only brings forward the provisional solution of concessions until the points of dispute are resolved by the proper institutional authority of a church council, until "the healing relief of the synod will work for peace."[171]

[168] Himelick, *Erasmus and the Seamless Coat,* 83–86.
[169] Ibid., 86.
[170] Ibid., 87–92.
[171] Ibid., 95.

The third and final element of the peace plan in the *De sarcienda* is an appeal to the consensus of the church. The times are such that "we see the minds of many vacillating to such an extent that if the most insignificant little nobody offered a new doctrine, however inane, it would find disciples." (97) Erasmus advises: "You must not be tossed about by every wind of doctrine: let us hold fast with steady faith to what the Catholic Church has handed down from Holy Scriptures. Let us follow in simple obedience what it teaches and await in eager hope what it promises." (81) Although he advocates concessions, he still feels "it ought to be a deep conviction of everyone that it is neither safe nor helpful in fostering peace to brashly abandon those positions which have been established by the authority of our ancestors and confirmed by the practice and agreement of generation after generation." (86)[172]

For this reason he affirms: "It was not necessary to get rid of the Mass, accepted for so many centuries, as if it were something wicked and pernicious."[173] He also recommends staying with the consensus as a sure way of dispelling the doubts about the Real Presence of Christ in the Eucharist.[174] The consensus consequently not only figures in Erasmus' thought as a conceptualization of the church. This conceptualization also serves as a touchstone for the resolution of ecclesiastical discord and as a goal to which a divided Christendom can and must aspire.

Another way of restoring peace is through prayer. In 1530, three years before the publication of the *De sarcienda*, Erasmus had urged the Reform leaders of Strasbourg: "let us, joined in prayer, beseech the Lord that, forsaking his anger, he will look kindly upon us and with his Spirit reconcile all souls in evangelical sincerity, and that you and we reform our lives."[175] In the same year Erasmus confided to Christoph von Stadion, the bishop of Augsburg, that he prayed for the peace of the church every day.[176] In the *De sarcienda* he writes that Christians, who because of their wickedness have earned the wrath of God, must turn to him with sincere hearts. Influenced by their prayers, he "will be converted to us and will turn these disordered commotions of affairs to peace."[177] Indeed, Erasmus interrupts his exposition in the *De sarcienda* to offer a prayer. He asks God

---

[172] Page numbers are from Himelick, *Erasmus and the Seamless Coat*.
[173] Ibid., 92.
[174] Ibid., 94.
[175] *Contra pseudoevangelicos*, ASD 9–1: 302.
[176] Allen 8: Ep. 2332, lines 31–35.
[177] Himelick, *Erasmus and the Seamless Coat*, 85.

to open our eyes so that seeing how lovely, how beautiful, how peaceful, how secure, how happy are your tabernacles—and furthermore, how unlike these are the tabernacles of wickedness with their array of conjectures and their dissonance of passion—and seeing that we, as one in meaning and purpose, are engaged in that happy communion of all the saints, it can truly be said of us, "Look! how good and pleasant it is to live together as brothers" (Ps. 132 [133]: 1).[178]

The prayer expresses Erasmus' ecclesiology in the context of the Reformation. The church is a community of peace. All communities that have seceded from the ancient consensus of the church to form their own new churches are in reality "tabernacles of wickedness."

When he published the *De sarcienda* in 1533, Erasmus appended to it a prayer he had written the previous year, the *Precatio ad Dominum Jesum pro pace ecclesiae*. Even the title of the *Precatio* indicates that prayer has a role to play in restoring peace to the church. Several common themes of Erasmus' ecclesiological thought emerge in the prayer. Peace is constitutive of the nature of the church; this is why the irenic Christian humanist offers up his prayer. The sad moral and spiritual state of the people of Christ has violated this peace: "We acknowledge and confess that our wicked deeds have brought this storm upon us."[179] Erasmus therefore repeatedly begs Christ to have mercy on his bride, on his people.[180] The Holy Spirit also has a role to play in and for the church. The *Precatio* implores Christ: "Send out, we ask, your Spirit, Lord." This is the Spirit who drives out the evil from Christian hearts, the Spirit by whom Christ strengthens his bride and her pastors, the Spirit through whom Christ has brought so many nations into the one body of the church, which is joined to Christ its head through the same Spirit. The *Precatio* appeals to Jesus to turn the chaos of discord into order and asks that his Spirit spread itself out over the waters of conflicting doctrines.[181]

After considering the Holy Spirit's contribution to peace, Erasmus returns to the notion of the church, first elaborated in the *Ratio* and in the letter to Volz, as a tripartite society, but this time he mentions princes before pastors. As usual, the common people occupy third place. Erasmus prays to Christ to grant the princes the fear of him (i.e. of Christ) so that they will administer the state in such a way as to take responsibility for all their actions before the King of Kings. Erasmus asks Christ to give to the clergy the three-

[178] Ibid., 82.
[179] LB 5: 1216F.
[180] LB 5: 1215E, 1215F, 1216E, 1217A, 1218D.
[181] LB 5: 1217C–D.

fold charity which he demanded of Peter (John 21:15–17), to take care of his sheep. His prayer for the common people is that Christ will give them the good will to obey his commands and the princely governors and priestly teachers that he has set over them. If each of the three orders fulfills its role, tranquillity will return to the church.[182]

Prayer for the peace of the church is essential for two reasons. First, it is a prayer made by the church, Christ's people. Their supplication acts as a sign to Christ of their contrition, conversion, and desire to live the true life of the church, a life in accordance with virtue and peace. Second, and most importantly, prayer for the peace of the church is a prayer offered to Christ, the head of the church. Christ not only hears prayers, but he also grants them. He hears the cries of his people and will, out of love for them, come to their aid. He will most assuredly restore peace to the church. Indeed, Christ is the only one who can do so, since "the storm has conquered human effort." As he calmed the winds and the waves from the boat when roused by his disciples (Matt. 8:24–26), so too will he be roused by the cries of his endangered church, of so many thousands of people who clamor: "Lord, save us, we are perishing." With one word he will silence the storm, allowing tranquillity to shine out.[183]

The restoration of the peace and unity of the church, for which Erasmus longs so dearly, is impossible without Christ. Peace, the ideal hallmark of the people of Christ, is inextricably bound up with the church's *scopus*: Jesus Christ. He is, as the *Precatio* proclaims, "the sole author and guardian of peace."[184] The *Precatio* concludes with an appeal to Christ's mercy so that with concordant hearts the chorus of the entire church might give thanks for divine mercy to the Father, and the Son, and the Holy Spirit, the triune God who is "the absolute example of concord."[185]

The ending of the prayer is significant. It justifies Hentze's claim that for Erasmus the Trinity serves as "the symbol and example of the unity of the church."[186] Erasmus does not have a great deal to say about the relationship between the Trinity and the church, but what he does say relates to his irenic concept of the church. The perfect harmony among the three divine persons in the unity of the Godhead is worthy of the church's attention and imitation. The triune God of peace, moreover, is the ultimate goal of Christ's people. In

[182] LB 5:1218A–C.
[183] LB 5:1216F.
[184] LB 5:1217A.
[185] LB 5:1218D.
[186] Hentze, *Kirche und kirchliche Einheit*, 91–92.

the epilogue to his *Paraphrase on John* (1523), published nine years before the prayer for the peace of the church, Erasmus interprets the Evangelist as postulating "two circles or spheres." One is heavenly and spiritual, the other earthly and physical. Into the first sphere John places God the Father, the Son, and the Spirit. "This sacred triad," in Erasmus' estimation, "firmly united within itself and returning into itself, is the prime example of absolute love and harmony. All who cling to the Gospel teaching with true hearts are adopted into it through faith and love."[187] In the *Ecclesiastes* Erasmus appends a fourth person to the Trinity of the Father, the Son, and the Holy Spirit: "the body of Christ, the church." In a sense Christ and his church form one person, but for didactic purposes it is better to distinguish between the two. The four persons all gravitate towards unity. The church achieves unity with the triune God through her head, Christ, God the Son: "For just as the Father, the Son, and the Holy Spirit are in nature one, so those who through faith and charity are members of Christ are taken up through him into the unity of the Trinity as far as this is possible."[188] The church, the Christian people of concord, is therefore destined for unity with the triune God, the archetype of concord and the source of the church's concord.

In the *Precatio ad Dominum Jesum pro pace ecclesiae* it is the church on earth that sings the praises of its merciful triune God. In the last year of his life Erasmus directed the thoughts of his readers to the heavenly church when, in January 1536, he published the *Enarratio psalmi XIV qui est de puritate tabernaculi sive ecclesiae christianae*. In the *Enchiridion* Erasmus had evoked the image of the church triumphant as the heavenly city of Jerusalem, "where there is no tumult of war, but everlasting peace and perfect tranquillity."[189] Similarly, Erasmus had appealed to the authority of the celestial "City of God" in *Bellum* and of the "heavenly Jerusalem" in the *Querela pacis*,[190] for the church triumphant is the abode of perfect peace and concord, and, in this respect, it serves as an exemplar for the church militant, the church on earth. In the *De puritate* Erasmus with the psalmist (Ps. 14 [15]:1) asks who will live in the Lord's tabernacle or rest on his holy mountain. God's tabernacle and his holy mountain are metaphors for the church, in which only those people will find rest who are grafted onto the body of Christ. This church is an eschatological reality, for it is one and the same with the kingdom of heaven, the mystical city of

[187] CWE 46:226.
[188] LB 5:1073F–1074A.
[189] CWE 66:38.
[190] Phillips, *"Adages" of Erasmus*, 329; CWE 27:304.

Jerusalem, whose cornerstone is Christ.[191] Who dwells in God's tabernacle? Christ certainly does. He is the pure and sinless priest who offered himself as a perfect sacrifice for the sins of humankind and who consequently presides over a new temple and a new kingdom.[192] Everyone who belongs to his royal priesthood and his holy people will find rest with Christ in the heavenly temple: men and women, the young and the old, the poor and the rich, nobles and commoners, kings and farmers, tailors and fullers, everyone who is reborn in Christ through baptism.[193]

A moral interpretation of the psalm indicates what Erasmus means by the purity of the church. This purity originates not only in the faith and baptism of Christians but also in their efforts to present themselves as living, acceptable, and pleasing sacrifices to God.[194] The pure do their best to live without sin; to do works of justice; to speak the truth; to keep from harming, disgracing, and deceiving their neighbors; and to refuse to lend money at interest and take bribes.[195] These manifestations of purity are opposed to every form of ceremonialism, to every form of worship devoid of a solid, spiritual foundation. Erasmus asserts that God is greatly displeased with "those who place their trust in the temple and its cults, while their minds and lives are stained with wickedness." Such people do not purify the temple; they pollute it.[196] Christians offer pure sacrifices by striving to overcome lust, envy, and all other vices, by living chastely with their spouses, by yearning for the life of heaven, and by offering pure prayers and thanksgiving to God. Christians who offer up spiritual sacrifices will be transferred from the earthly tabernacle to the heavenly one.[197]

The moral and spiritual requirements for finding rest in God's tabernacle cannot exist without concord. Erasmus encourages his readers to make heaven their goal by doing away with all malice, by walking in God's sight without sin, being "of one heart and mind in the truth" (*concordes in veritate atque vnanimes*). Christians pursue virtue united in their desire for and commitment to truth, for "sin is not absent when discord is present; nor does truth reside in the heart when opinions diverge; nor is sincere speech possible when doctrines conflict."[198] The truth of which Erasmus writes is Christian

---

[191] ASD 5–2: 288, 290.
[192] ASD 5–2: 292.
[193] ASD 5–2: 314.
[194] ASD 5–2: 300.
[195] ASD 5–2: 302–10.
[196] ASD 5–2: 311.
[197] ASD 5–2: 316.
[198] ASD 5–2: 314.

truth, the truth of Christian faith. Heresy undermines the concordant unity in the truth.

The psalm says that those who walk without sin (*sine macula*) and who speak the truth in their hearts will dwell in God's tabernacle and on his holy mountain. Heresy is Erasmus' first example of a *turpis macula*, of a foul blot or a base sin. He also mentions lack of faith, the hatred of one's neighbor, and the love of money and pleasure. Heresy is incompatible with the peace of the church, which cannot tolerate the blemishes of sin. The fasting, prayers, psalms, chastity, preaching, and other works of heretics and schismatics that have the "appearance of piety" are all sins because they are done outside the church. Those who seek true rest should not leave God's holy mountain, on which the church is built.[199] In explaining what it means to speak the truth in one's heart Erasmus compares heretics with atheists. Just as the fool, who says in his heart that there is no God (Ps. 13 [14]:1), tells himself a disastrous lie, so too do heretics lie to themselves when they assent to false doctrines. To speak the truth in one's heart means, first of all, to think properly about the dogmas of faith, and also to trust in God's mercy and not in one's own strength, and to acknowledge one's sinfulness and to appeal to God's mercy with a sincere heart.[200]

Erasmus' conception of the church in the *De puritate* is of one piece with his earlier writings, demonstrating a continuity in his ecclesiology that extends back to the *Enchiridion*. He expects the church to be a community of the pure. Those who persist in their wicked ways are not worthy of membership in the body of Christ on earth and cannot belong to the triumphant church in heaven. The clergy, those in the church who stand closest to Christ, must combat vice, and with their office of preaching and administering the sacraments they must serve their flocks. The priests mediate the spiritual purity of Christ the high priest to the rest of the Christian community.

Of course Erasmus is not so naive as to think that the church on earth will ever be the perfect society of the sinless. He believes that the church is

199 ASD 5–2:301–2.
200 ASD 5–2:304.

essentially made up of those who are in a state of grace, whose lives are animated by faith and charity. Yet he does not exclude the wicked, those in the state of mortal sin, from belonging to the church in an outward sense, albeit as dead members devoid of charity attached to the living body of Christ. Jean-Pierre Massaut has shown that this position, advanced against Erasmus' critics at the University of Paris, is in keeping within the Catholic mainstream from Augustine to the twentieth century.[201] In the *De puritate* Erasmus acknowledges that Christians deceive themselves if they think that they are without sin (cf. 1 John 1:8), and he concedes that even the just have their faults and pray for the forgiveness of their trespasses. The church can at one and the same time be holy and sinful because of Christ. Christians must remain in Christ; they are to put on Christ (cf. Rom. 13:14). In and of themselves they bear the blemishes of sin, but in Christ they are immaculate. Through the sacrament of penance, moreover, Christ's people can return to their "pristine innocence."[202]

Purity and innocence cannot abide in the church without peace. Where discord endures, sin remains. The church cannot be the church if it lacks peace and concord. Erasmus' favorite image of the church is the unified body of Christ, in which the fellowship that Christians have with Christ their head and with each other is rooted in the unity of love. This unity expresses itself in the great commonality of the church. Christ's peaceful people worship the same triune God, the absolute example and source of concord for the church. They share the same faith, partake of the same sacraments, and long for the same heavenly inheritance in the tranquillity of God's tabernacle.

With the emergence of the Reformation, peace, unity, and concord dominate Erasmus' thinking about the church. He remains loyal to the Roman church and will even tolerate its many failings because he loves peace and hates discord. Peace he elevates to the highest virtue; heresy and schism he despises as the worst vices. Erasmus refuses to join the Reformers not only because their mores conflict with the demands of the Gospel, but more importantly because they have divided the church. While their new dogmas convulse Christendom, the irenic Christian humanist adheres to and relies on the consensus of the church throughout the ages. Therefore the only major development in Erasmus' ecclesiological thought is one of increased emphasis.

---

[201] Jean-Pierre Massaut, "Erasme, la Sorbonne et la nature de l'Eglise," in *Colloquium Erasmianum* (Mons: Centre universitaire de l'Etat, 1968), 95–108. Massaut (109–10) notes, however, that Erasmus' position is flawed by a contradiction.

[202] *De puritate*, ASD 5–2: 302–3.

Although he continues to understand the church as a community of virtue, he nevertheless underlines the notion of the community of concord with greater urgency once Luther had thrown the apple of discord into Christendom.

The church is a people of purity and a people of peace, but above all it is the people of Christ. The church is *his* body, *his* flock, *his* bride, *his* people. In Erasmus' spiritual reinterpretation of the Christian republic, Christ becomes the central focus of Christendom. The people that gather around him must be virtuous and peaceful not for the sake of virtue or of peace but out of loyalty to Christ, "the model of all piety" and the prince of peace. They can be immaculate only insofar as they remain in Christ. He is the guarantor and underpinning of their concordant agreement on matters of faith over the centuries. When Erasmus prays for the peace of the church, he prays to Jesus. The *Precatio ad Dominum Jesum pro pace ecclesiae* and all his other religious writings uphold, in the midst of a divided Christendom, the vision of the church as a peaceful people united by their love of and devotion to Christ.

Erasmus after a painting by Holbein

Irena Backus

ERASMUS AND THE SPIRITUALITY
OF THE EARLY CHURCH

~

W̶HAT EMERGES FROM THE various recent partial accounts of Erasmus' attitude to the early church is a rather predictable and hazy picture with the following main features. First, we are told that Erasmus relied on the Church
Fathers not only as witnesses to the text but also, in his *Annotations*, as exponents of the theology of the "golden era."[1] Second, it has been said that
Erasmus did not use the Fathers "uncritically."[2] Third, historians have mar-
veled at the impressive list of Erasmus' patristic editions.[3] Why did he edit
some or all of the works of Jerome (1516), Cyprian (1520), Arnobius the
Younger (1522), Hilary of Poitiers (1523), John Chrysostom (1525, 1527, 1530),
Irenaeus (1526), Ambrose (1527), Athanasius (1527), Augustine (1528–29), Lactantius (1529), Basil of Caesarea (1532) and Origen (published posthumously)?
Various replies have been given to that question. According to Robert Peters,
Erasmus edited only those Fathers whose doctrines were of immediate use
for his controversies.[4] According to Jacques Chomarat, Erasmus (and

---

[1] See especially Erika Rummel, *Erasmus' Annotations on the New Testament* (Toronto: University of Toronto Press, 1986), 53: "Erasmus epitomized this movement toward spiritual renewal
through a return to the *vetus theologia*, when he contrasted the 'golden river' of patristic theology
with the 'shallow runnels' of scholasticism."

[2] See Rummel, *Erasmus' Annotations*; and Peter Walter, *Theologie aus dem Geist der Rhetorik:
Zur Schriftauslegung des Erasmus von Rotterdam* (Mainz: Matthias-Grünewald-Verlag, 1991), 256:
"Sie sind die nicht unkritisch rezipierten *veteres*, die Erasmus den *neoterici* vorzieht."

[3] See esp. Walter, *Theologie aus dem Geist der Rhetorik* , 150, and C. Augustijn, *Erasmus von
Rotterdam: Leben-Werk-Wirkung* (Munich: C. H. Beck, 1986), 92.

[4] Robert Peters, "Erasmus and the Fathers: Their Practical Value," *Church History* 36
(1967): 254–61.

Froben) aimed above all at filling in gaps in the market.[5] John C. Olin and
Peter Walter contend, for their part, that Erasmus' patristic editions were a
part of a reform program and should be considered in some sense equivalent
to his *New Testament*.[6] The fourth interesting feature of historians' treatment
of Erasmus and the Fathers has been studies on Erasmus and a particular
Father. Charles Béné and André Godin have thus examined, respectively, the
influence of Augustine and Origen on Erasmus' methodology, especially his
exegesis,[7] while Olin and (more recently) Jan den Boeft have examined
Erasmus' view of Jerome and Ambrose.[8] Fifth, and most recently, Peter
Walter has argued that Erasmus takes from the Church Fathers and especially
from Augustine his use of classical rhetoric to uncover the meaning of the
Bible.[9]

Without initially wishing to challenge any one of these approaches or
hypotheses, I should like to fill in some details in what emerges as a vague picture. The questions I shall be asking here are first, what light do the hitherto
unstudied prefaces to Erasmus' patristic editions throw on his view of the
early church? Second, I shall examine his view of the Fathers in the more specifically theological and equally little-studied controversy with Luther surrounding the *Explanatio symboli*, the catechism Erasmus published in 1533.

PREFACES TO THE FATHERS

On reading the prefaces as a series one is struck by two things: the sheer
quantity of technical details, which does not concern us here, and the varying
emphasis with which Erasmus makes basically the same points. It quickly

---

[5] Jacques Chomarat, *Grammaire et rhétorique chez Erasme*, 2 vols. (Paris: Société d'Edition "Les belles lettres," 1981), 1:480.

[6] John C. Olin, "Erasmus and the Church Fathers," in Olin, *Six Essays on Erasmus* (New York: Fordham University Press, 1979), 35: "In Erasmus' program to restore theology, Holy Scripture of course came first, especially the Gospels and Epistles. . . . But after this literature came the Fathers. Their authority derived from their closeness in time as well as in spirit to the divine source." Walter, *Theologie aus dem Geist der Rhetorik*, 151: "Diese Ausgaben vieler wichtiger Kirch-enväter sollten ebenso zur Wiederherstellung und Erneuerung von Kirche und Theologie bei-tragen wie die Ausgabe des Neuen Testaments."

[7] Charles Béné, *Erasme et Saint Augustin* (Geneva: Droz, 1969); André Godin, *Erasme, lecteur d'Origène* (Geneva: Droz, 1982).

[8] John C. Olin, "Erasmus and Saint Jerome: The Close Bond and Its Significance," *Erasmus of Rotterdam Society Yearbook* 7 (1987): 33–53. I refer to J. den Boeft's paper, *"Pectus vere Romanum immo Christianum"* given at the 11th Patristic Conference (Oxford, August 1991) and due to appear in the *Proceedings*.

[9] See Walter, *Theologie aus dem Geist der Rhetorik*, 256–61.

becomes clear that Erasmus' view of the spirituality of the early church and of its importance for his contemporaries never underwent any fundamental changes. I shall now examine the main prefaces in chronological order.

JEROME

In the letter to William Warham, dated April 1, 1516, Erasmus presents a picture of Jerome not substantially different from that in his *Vita Hieronymi*. It is not only Erasmus' identification with Jerome which is striking but also his very deliberate presentation of Jerome as a member of an intellectual (and therefore spiritual) elite, the values of which are inherited and promulgated by Erasmus himself, the Erasmus who attacks the judgment of the multitude which venerates relics at the expense of writings of saints from the past. The reason for this is found in the progressive decline of rulers into barbaric tyranny, which caused bishops to become more interested in civil rule than in the office of teaching handed down to them by the apostles.[10] As the duty of teaching was assumed by those who were completely unsuited for it, the ancient doctors were, for the most part, cast into oblivion. Such of their writings as did survive, survived in a corrupt form. This oblivion is particularly regrettable in the case of Jerome, the Christian Cicero, unequaled in erudition, linguistic skills, knowledge of sacred and profane letters, and a man of phenomenal industry and a perfect follower of Christ. His commentaries have become adulterated with unlearned editors' fabrications, all the more numerous as Jerome's prose is intended for the learned and "not for the ordinary mortals." Erasmus' task has thus been to present a Jerome free from barbarous accretions, with clarifications added in the form of *scholia*. The edition is intended by Erasmus as a sort of companion volume to the recently published *Novum Instrumentum*, and Erasmus assures Warham that "alongside the Gospels and the Epistles there is no reading matter more suitable for Christians."[11] If he will have done nothing else, contends Erasmus, he will have separated the true Jerome from the false.[12]

On the face of it, theology plays little or no part in Erasmus' high regard for Jerome; his importance lies in his having been the perfect gentleman scholar, source of inspiration, and the model for Erasmus himself. If we juxtapose this portrayal with the *Vita Hieronymi* appended to the 1516 edition, we see that it too underplays the theological side, while promulgating even more

[10] Allen 2: Ep. 396, lines 65–85.
[11] Allen 2: Ep. 396, lines 187–88, 325–26.
[12] Allen 2: Ep. 396, lines 358–65.

forcefully the gentleman scholar who traveled in the East largely for his own education,[13] who was betrayed by his Origenist friend Rufinus,[14] and who was a sharp critic of monks, clerics, and virgins unworthy of their name.[15] The medieval stereotype of lives of Jerome, particularly of the *Legenda aurea*, portraying him as the perfect monk, the perfect ascetic, and the perfect miracle worker, has thus been completely turned on its head. Two passages in the *Vita* really drive that point home. First, referring to virginity in general, Erasmus questions its usefulness as a moral example to us: "how many more were moved to virtue by the sinner Magdalene, Christ's sweetheart, than by the perpetual innocence of Tekla which hardly anyone out of thousands of people can hope to imitate."[16] Then, further on, he mocks the medieval tradition of the four doctors of the church:

> There had to be four doctors of the church and four senses of the Scripture so that they correspond to the four Evangelists. To Gregory they assign tropology, to Ambrose allegory, to Augustine anagogy, to Jerome, so as not to leave him with nothing, they relegate the letter and the literal sense.[17]

While it is certainly true that Erasmus identifies with Jerome, it would not do to underestimate his very deliberate wish to "send up" the Jerome of the Middle Ages and to replace him with a figure, almost equally arbitrary, of the Renaissance gentleman. This naturally does not stop Erasmus from expressing a genuine admiration for Jerome's biblical scholarship, an example to his own. Any striving to regain the spirituality of the early church as that of a golden age is in the case of Jerome heavily tinged with irony.

---

[13] Wallace K. Ferguson, ed., *Erasmi Opuscula* (The Hague: Nijhoff, 1933), 161: "partim ut inspectis locis, quorum in Divinis litteris fit mentio penitius intelligeret quod esset scriptum, ut ipse testatur in praefatione quadam. Nec pietatis nec sacrae scientiae sibi magister esse voluit diuque discendum putavit quod doceret."

[14] *Erasmi Opuscula*, 158. Erasmus' accusation refers to 385–86 when Jerome left Rome for the East the second time. At that time the friendship between Rufinus and Jerome was still intact, as Ferguson points out in his note.

[15] Ibid.: "Neque mediocrem invidiam conflaverat Hieronymo liber ad Eustochium De virginitate, quod in eo salsissime taxet clericos et monachos ac virgines suo indignas nomine." On the early Renaissance image of Jerome see Eugene F. Rice, Jr., *Saint Jerome in the Renaissance* (Baltimore: Johns Hopkins University Press, 1985), 49–83.

[16] *Erasmi Opuscula*, 174: "Quanto plures pellexit ad bonam frugem peccatrix illa Magdalene, Christi deliciae, quam Teclae perpetua innocentia, quae ex tot hominum milibus vix ulli contigit?"

[17] Ibid., 180. On the respective dignities accorded to the four doctors see Rice, *Saint Jerome in the Renaissance*, 35.

CYPRIAN

Quite unsatirical and much more politically oriented is Erasmus' portrayal of Cyprian in the preface to his edition dated July 31, 1519, the period of Erasmus' defense of Luther in letters to Frederick the Wise and Albert of Brandenburg, and of his difficulties with the Louvain theologians. In the preface, addressed to Lorenzo Pucci, he begins by contrasting the adulterations to Cyprian's writings with those suffered by the works of Jerome. Cyprian was more fortunate in that all the works falsely attributed to him are pious. As a prime example of this Erasmus cites the *Explanatio symboli* which, he notes rightly, figures under Rufinus' name in the works of Jerome. Stylistically, Cyprian is to be preferred to Jerome not on general grounds but because he writes with less artifice, "to which Jerome is rather prone." He writes like a truly Christian bishop destined for martyrdom. "His heart is full of evangelical piety and this is reflected by his style."[18] It is no accident, Erasmus cannot resist pointing out, that a doctor of the church of this stature should be the product of a pagan school of rhetoric, and not a school of dialectics or a peripatetic academy! Although Cyprian was hailed as the most orthodox Church Father by the "Gelasian Decree," continues Erasmus, some of his views are no longer accepted by the church, the chief of them being his doctrine of rebaptism of schismatics. Yet this was the doctrine adopted by most North African bishops in Cyprian's time. Even Hilary would not accept into his church those who had been baptized by Arians, as Jerome reports.[19]

In the 1519 edition Erasmus unintentionally confuses Hilary of Poitiers with Hilary the deacon of Rome. Moreover, he seems to have a very curious conception of what constitutes Cyprian's time, which seems to extend up until the fifth century. But, what is more important, he strongly relativizes Cyprian's position and thus the very concept of orthodoxy. Cyprian followed what he thought was right but did not deem it necessary to *excommunicate* anyone who felt differently. In 1520, with the threat of excommunication hanging over Luther, Cyprian's stance was rich in meaning, as indeed was the statement on baptism, so much so that one could forgive the anachronism. Those who disagreed with Cyprian, continues Erasmus, and claimed that heretical baptism was valid were simply more anti-Donatist than he and did not wish to open the door to the erroneous belief that a Sacrament administered by a wicked priest is inefficacious. The belief in the efficacy of the Sacraments, regardless of

---

[18] Allen 4: Ep. 1000, lines 99, 101–2.
[19] Allen 4: Ep. 1000, lines 118–30.

the priest's merit, was current in the early church as is shown by Augustine's teaching on the matter, concludes Erasmus.[20]

Although nearly a hundred years of early church history are telescoped, Erasmus' point is made. Dogma in the early church was fluid; it was not a book of rules with orthodox and heterodox beliefs clearly laid down. Both Cyprian and his opponents acted for the best. It is interesting to note that, in the 1530 edition of Cyprian's works, Erasmus modified this passage to state that Cyprian, although he held his teaching from earlier sources, and was thus no heresiarch, was clearly in error "so that his successors improved upon the early doctrine as they modified it."[21] Gone was the openness of the early church; gone also the confusion between Hilary of Poitiers and Hilary the deacon of Rome. It is plain, however, that in 1519 on the issue of heretical baptism both Cyprian and his opponents are held up as an example of the non-doctrinaire position that characterized the early church and that should, it is implied, be imitated by both Pope Leo X and Luther.

ARNOBIUS THE YOUNGER

After Jerome the gentleman scholar and Cyprian the apostle of tolerance comes Arnobius the Younger, an African monk of the fifth century and author of an allegorizing *Commentary on the Psalms,* which Erasmus attributes wrongly to Arnobius the Elder (d. 330), Christian apologist and rhetorician, and teacher of Lactantius. Arnobius the Elder's *Life* was familiar to Erasmus from his Jerome studies. His edition of the *Commentary on the Psalms* appeared with a preface to the new Pope Adrian VI dated August 1, 1522, at a time when Erasmus was not unjustly accused of heterodoxy by both Catholic theologians (notably those of Louvain) and the Reformers.[22]

The main characteristic of the preface is a sense of conflict, both literary and theological. Erasmus cannot reconcile the poor Latin of the *Commentary* with what he knows of the rhetorical antecedents of its presumed author. However, contrary to his normal practice, Erasmus does not question the attribution. It is not clear whether this timidity is due to the pioneering nature of his task (nothing of either Arnobius had hitherto appeared in print) or to a desire not to appear hypercritical given his delicate position. Be that as it may,

---

[20] Allen 4: Ep. 1000, lines 134–43.
[21] Allen 4: Ep. 1000, note to line 129.
[22] See Irena Backus, "Deux cas d'évolution théologique dans les 'Paraphrases' d'Erasme," in *Actes du Colloque international Erasme,* ed. Jacques Chomarat, André Godin, and Jean-Claude Margolin (Geneva: Droz, 1990), 141–51.

Erasmus finds himself justifying Arnobius' style with some unease. The *Commentary* is poorly written, he claims, not because its author was an uneducated barbarian but because, unlike his *Opus adversus Gentes,* he intended it for the common people.[23] Augustine's sermons, he continues, show that Latin, if sufficiently simplified, could be understood in all the Roman provinces. Still feeling some doubt, Erasmus then addresses himself to the question of why the great rhetorician Arnobius should suddenly wish to write a *Commentary on the Psalms* for the common people. The chief motive would have been Christian charity, he declares.[24] No text was more popular at the time than the *Psalms of David,* and Arnobius wanted his *Commentary* to be understood by all the simple people who knew and sang the *Psalms.* His public would have been offended by a *Commentary* in learned, elegant Latin, especially as Arnobius' preface suggests that he was a newly converted Christian.[25] Were he writing in Erasmus' own time, he would be writing in the vernacular! There follows a list of solecisms and the correct observation that Jerome did not include the *Commentary* in his list of Arnobius the Elder's works. A possible reason for this omission is that the work was so well known that Jerome did not think it worth mentioning.[26] The heresies mentioned show that it cannot have been written later than the time of Arnobius the Elder. Erasmus then introduces a doubtful note: "And yet Arnobius talks about free will here and there; surely he would have mentioned Pelagius, had the latter been of an earlier date than he."[27] As the style of the *Commentary* obviously cannot be commended, Erasmus praises its conciseness. No book is more obscure than the *Psalms* and the fact that Arnobius comments on it so briefly and so clearly shows that he really understood it.

Erasmus is equally torn about the theological content of the work. Unlike Origen, Tertullian, and other *veteres,* Arnobius is so moderate in his theology that it contains nothing remotely heretical. The supposed teacher of Lactantius emphasizes the primacy and uniqueness of the Roman church and of Peter,[28] even though the latter denied Christ. More interestingly, Arnobius is both for and against monastic vows as "he does mention vows but only those by which, professing Christ in baptism, we reject Satan and the world; not that I think he would have been contemptuous of other vows, but he

---

[23] Allen 5: Ep. 1304, lines 59–66.
[24] Allen 5: Ep. 1304, lines 97–99.
[25] Allen 5: Ep. 1304, lines 113–22.
[26] Allen 5: Ep. 1304, lines 212–13.
[27] Allen 5: Ep. 1304, lines 229–31.
[28] Allen 5: Ep. 1304, lines 291–94.

obviously only considered baptismal vows of prime importance, as indeed they are."[29] It is through Arnobius' *Commentary*, says Erasmus, that the new pope can take David and therefore Christ as his model, the chief merit of the work being its author's christological and allegorical interpretation of the *Psalms*. Erasmus thus presents Arnobius as the most reformist and the most orthodox of theologians. He writes in his equivalent of the vernacular for the common people, striving for intelligibility, yet allegorizing. His work is radical, but it contains nothing heretical. He stresses both the uniqueness of Peter and his denial of Christ; he is both for and against monastic vows. The preface, if read discerningly, would have made clear to the new pope all the nuances of Erasmus' own theological position.

Thus Jerome, the rhetorician gentleman scholar, and Cyprian, the eloquent apostle of tolerance, are joined in 1522 by Arnobius (the Younger), the most reformist of all orthodox theologians, whose very rhetorical merit lies in the poor quality of his Latin.

HILARY OF POITIERS

A much more forceful view of the early church and its significance for the spirituality of his own time emerges from Erasmus' preface to the works of Hilary written only some six months later than the Arnobius preface. What Erasmus finds particularly commendable about the bishop of Poitiers is his reluctance to speculate excessively about the Trinity, which he knew to be ineffable.[30] Although he was the first Latin Father to speak out against the Arians and although (like Cyprian and Augustine) he was inclined to grandiloquence and obscurity, Hilary never indulged in "vain" disputations, vain being synonymous for Erasmus with "philosophical." In the church of Hilary's time faith expressed itself in a way of life and not in doctrine which was hardly written down. It was only as heresies surfaced that more and more was prescribed and that Christ's teaching began to be couched in a philosophical framework so as forcibly to make Christians understand what could not and should not be understood anyway.[31]

Erasmus asks how orthodox Hilary himself was. Hilary never calls the Holy Spirit God; this dogma was not yet formulated. He was zealous in combating the Arians and called them devils or antichrists, yet it is surely possible that at least some of the Arians were pious. On the other hand, Hilary himself

---

[29] Allen 5: Ep. 1304, lines 294–98.
[30] Allen 5: Ep. 1334, lines 138–40.
[31] Allen 5: Ep. 1334, lines 360–80.

taught that Christ had a divine body not susceptible to feeling pain. Erasmus therefore asks whether we should consider Hilary a heretic. Again confusing Hilary of Poitiers with Hilary the deacon of Rome (the error was rectified in 1530), Erasmus points out that Jerome himself criticized Hilary in very opprobrious terms. This is an example set by the early church which should not be followed by theologians of Erasmus' time. It is the glory of Christ, not the glory of the pope, which is important.[32]

Having acknowledged that the early church, although less rigid in her doctrinal formulations, was by no means perfect, Erasmus argues that the Holy Scriptures cannot be read without the aid of patristic exegesis. The purpose of theology is not to innovate, and, he adds, making a barely concealed allusion to Luther's followers: "for I see that some spurn ancient authors and prefer new books now springing up everywhere, so much so that they think that Origen and Jerome should, like the sexagenarians in the proverb, be cast off the bridge." The *veteres* must be revered, says Erasmus, but they must be read with discernment. Scholastic theologians should not be completely forgotten but should be read "discerningly and sympathetically."[33]

In contrast to Jerome, Cyprian, and Arnobius, the personal qualities of Hilary of Poitiers do not interest Erasmus. He uses the preface to commend the early church without a loss of sense of proportion. Hilary and the other Fathers were not perfect: their chief merit consisted in their basic devotion to Christ coupled with a lack of clearly formulated doctrine on the very theological issues that were to become controversial in Erasmus' time. Unlike his edition of Cyprian, Erasmus' edition of Hilary is not linked to any particular event such as Luther's excommunication; his assessment of the nondoctrinaire nature of the early church is thus correspondingly far less apologetic.

IRENAEUS

It is the very problem of orthodoxy and heresy that dominates the preface (addressed to the bishop of Trent, Bernard of Cles) to Irenaeus' *Adversus haereses*, dated August 27, 1526. The chief merit of Irenaeus (considered by Erasmus to be a Latin writer) was that he was a great peacemaker, as his name suggests. His own church, continues Erasmus, could well do with a few Irenaeuses "who bring peace to the world in accord with the spirit of the Gospel."[34] His information about the bishop of Lyons is drawn almost entirely

[32] Allen 5: Ep. 1334, lines 490–92, 504–7, 570–92.
[33] Allen 5: Ep. 1334, lines 923–27; quotation: lines 926–27.
[34] Allen 6: Ep. 1738, lines 14–15.

from Eusebius-Rufinus' *Ecclesiastical History*, the reliability of which is not questioned. It is true that Irenaeus *combats* heresies, which were for the most part due to their authors' excessive interest in philosophy. However, he combats these heresies by Scripture and by Scripture only, with gentleness and humility, thus following the example of the Lord himself.[35] Erasmus' detailed list of the heresies mentioned and refuted in *Adversus haereses*[36] suggests a certain fascination with heterodox thought or rather a wish to prove to his readers how great a part it played in the early church from early on. The modern reader cannot help but be struck by the sheer genius of Erasmus' insight. For him, there is no fundamental distinction between the ancient sects and the "zeal of the Jews, the pride of the Pharisees, excessive authority of priests, royal armed forces and legislation, the sophistries of our ancestors, the learning of the philosophers." All are snares set by Satan to confound the simple piety of the true Christians. However, concludes Erasmus, apparently contradicting what he had said earlier, all those evils will be turned by the Lord to a good end; ancient heresies, although they had their origin in philosophy, were refuted by philosophers: Tertullian, Origen, Chrysostom. There is good hope that a few more Irenaeuses will arise "who will resolve conflicts and restore peace to the world."[37]

The heresies that preoccupied Irenaeus were no better and no worse than the excessive despotism of priests or warmongering practices of various rulers. Irenaeus sets a particularly good example not because he fought heretics but because he fought them gently and with arguments drawn from the Scripture aiming to bring about concord, not to foment strife. He can thus, Erasmus implies, be counted as a true philosopher, that is, an advocate of the "philosophy of Christ."

AMBROSE OF MILAN

Erasmus' prefaces to the works of Ambrose (August 13, 1527), Augustine (May 1529), and Chrysostom (March 24, 1527, and June 29, 1527) all touch explicitly on the question of what constitutes a model bishop. Although Erasmus' prefaces to Hilary and Irenaeus have already made implicit that a good bishop cannot engage in vigorous and aggressive combat against opinions he considers heterodox, neither of the two bishops has been explicitly held up as models. That Ambrose should be comes as no surprise given not

[35] Allen 6: Ep. 1738, lines 116–17, 210–18.
[36] Allen 6: Ep. 1738, lines 120–95.
[37] Allen 6: Ep. 1738, lines 224–26, 262–63.

only the reputation of the bishop of Milan but also the person of Archbishop Jan Laski of Gniezno to whom the edition was dedicated. True, Jerome is the better linguist, Hilary is more eloquent, Augustine reasons better. However, according to Erasmus, no one avoids suspect doctrine better and no one combines authority with gentleness more effectively than does Ambrose.[38] Some instances of Ambrose's striving for concord are then cited, and, as in the case of Irenaeus, Erasmus expresses the wish that someone not unlike Ambrose might come along who, with similar authority, will restore peace in this wretched, tumultuous world.[39] He embodied all the virtues of a bishop: divincly given, respected by the people and by the civil rulers, so that the all-powerful Theodosius submitted to him, even though Ambrose used no weapons other than those a bishop should have, namely his tongue, his prayers, and a holy life. In contrast with other early churchmen—Cyprian, Origen, Jerome, Tertullian—no one ever spoke unkindly of Ambrose, not even heretics. Only Jerome expressed some reservations, but then Jerome too was only human.[40] Erasmus is eager to admit that Ambrose was unoriginal in his biblical commentaries, taking much from the Greeks, particularly from Origen. But he only took what was sound, dissimulating anything contentious or heterodox, "neither professing errors, nor traducing his author's intentions."[41] Thus, although he did not contribute in any major way to the corpus of Christian literature and although he was no great rhetorician, Ambrose was a great bishop with regard to his influence on the faithful and on civil rulers.

John Chrysostom

John Chrysostom, if the prefaces to the *Lucubrationes* (addressed to King John III of Portugal) and the *Commentary on Galatians* (addressed to the Cardinal of Lorraine on June 29, 1527) are anything to go by, was another exemplary bishop, although his virtues were quite different from those of Ambrose. In the preface to John III Erasmus stresses that Chrysostom's strength lay in his concern with pastoral care and in his preaching. Although he was as learned in the liberal arts as Augustine, he never showed off his knowledge but put all human learning to the service of theology "like someone moderating the effect of strong wine by diluting it with water."[42] His whole discourse was

---

[38] Allen 7: Ep. 1855, lines 20–30.
[39] Allen 7: Ep. 1855, lines 95–97.
[40] Allen 7: Ep. 1855, lines 235–40.
[41] Allen 7: Ep. 1855, lines 241–45; quotation: lines 244–45.
[42] Allen 6: Ep. 1800, lines 132–33.

adapted to make it comprehensible to the common people who at that time demanded to be taught the Christian doctrine. There is no passage in the Scriptures so obscure that it did not become easy when expounded by him. In a word, unlike Jerome, Ambrose, and Tertullian, Chrysostom is the perfect Christian orator.[43] If such orators and preachers existed nowadays, believes Erasmus, faith would not be on the decline. Emperor Arcadius did not think that the splendid city of Constantinople was splendid without an outstanding preacher of the Gospel and so made Chrysostom its patriarch. If Arcadius' and John III's example were followed by more princes, we would be closer to Christian peace with Christ reigning in us![44]

The reader cannot help but note that whereas Ambrose's particular strength as bishop lay in his making a civil ruler, Theodosius, submit to him, Chrysostom's special gift, that of preaching, served to increase the splendors that surrounded another civil ruler, Arcadius. The sketch of Chrysostom, the model bishop, is elaborated in the preface to his *Commentary on Galatians*. He was very similar to Paul, says Erasmus, in that he not only felt concern for the material needs of his faithful but also wanted to teach them the right doctrine "like a nurse feeding her child."[45] Chrysostom as bishop embodied (in accord with Paul's recommendations) three people: the father in priestly authority, the mother in his zeal to protect his faithful, and the nurse in feeding them the doctrine of salvation.[46] Furthermore, he is to be commended for his conciliatory exegesis of Gal. 2:11 (the strife between Peter and Paul), the very biblical passage which led to a controversy between Augustine (Epp. 75, 82) and Jerome (Epp. 112, 116) in which Augustine said some very uncharitable things about Peter "the head of the apostles and the herald of faith."[47] This veiled reference to the Sorbonne's condemnation of Erasmus' anti-Augustinian interpretation of Luke 22:36 and John 18:10 has at least a triple purpose. First, Erasmus points out to the cardinal of Lorraine that, in hiding behind Augustine, the Sorbonne theologians are questioning Peter's primacy (which they no doubt are). Second, he tries to show him that there is a better exegetical method (employed by Chrysostom) which dispenses with needless strife. Finally, Erasmus adds another touch to his portrait of Chrysostom as a model bishop: he could and did give a noncontroversial interpretation of a passage

---

[43] Allen 6: Ep. 1800, lines 190–204.
[44] Allen 6: Ep. 1800, lines 205, 230–38.
[45] Allen 7: Ep. 1841, lines 39–40.
[46] Allen 7: Ep. 1841, lines 46–48.
[47] Allen 7: Ep. 1841, lines 59–68; quotation: line 68.

that was the object of controversy between such important theologians as Augustine and Jerome. The perfect orator, obedient to civil powers (who were in their turn well inclined towards him), authoritative, caring and conciliatory in his exegesis: these qualities shown by Chrysostom as model bishop are very different from Ambrose's capacities for spiritual leadership.

AUGUSTINE

Augustine, as might be expected, represents yet another set of virtues, as is shown by the preface (to Alfonso Fonseca, archbishop of Toledo) to the 1529 edition. Starting off, as he often does, with some comparisons, Erasmus praises Athanasius for his teaching gifts, Basil of Caesarea for his subtlety and eloquence, Chrysostom for his rhetoric, Cyprian for his "spirit worthy of a martyr," Hilary for his capacity to talk about abstract issues, Ambrose for his modesty, Jerome for his biblical learning, and Gregory the Great for his saint-liness. However, no doctor of the church had so many gifts of the Holy Spirit bestowed upon him as Augustine; he had all the virtues of a bishop required by Peter and Paul.[48] The faults attributed to Augustine by Erasmus in the other prefaces—his excessive love for engaging in argument, his tendency to show off his knowledge of the liberal arts, his philosophizing, his lack of knowledge of Greek—play no part here. Augustine embodied the sobriety and vigilance that Paul required from a bishop: he never spoke to women unless other clerics were present, he was moderate in his pronouncements, and (like Irenaeus) he argued against heretics with arguments drawn from Scripture.[49] He was charitable, hospitable, and gentle. He did not submit the monastic communities that he founded to harsh rules. In short, "he loved perfect piety so long as it was spontaneous and not forced."[50] His writings instruct and inspire to a better life.

What of his tendencies to logic chopping? Erasmus evades the issue by stating that dialectic and rhetoric are well nigh inseparable and that it was rhetoric that Augustine was especially well versed in. He knew Platonic philosophy "which includes several elements compatible with Christian precepts," but was barely acquainted with the more pernicious Aristotelian philosophy. It was, however, this smattering of Aristotelian philosophy that conferred upon him, quite unjustly, the reputation of a dialectician. His heretical opponents, annoyed that Augustine had outdebated them, claimed to

---

[48] Allen 8: Ep. 2157, lines 10–20, 23–29; quotation: lines 14–15.
[49] Allen 8: Ep. 2157, lines 70–99.
[50] Allen 8: Ep. 2157, lines 226–27.

have been overcome by dialectical artifice whereas in fact they had simply been squashed by the weight of truth.[51] Towards the end of the preface Erasmus implies that Fonseca's educational activities in Spain mirror Augustine's methodology of "a little philosophy but not too much." "For there is a happy mean," says Erasmus, "between those who hitherto have taught humanities in schools in a sophistical and perverse manner and those who wish to abolish humanities altogether as well as schools."[52]

The respective episcopal virtues of Ambrose, Chrysostom, and Augustine vary according to circumstances and patrons. However, there is no doubt in Erasmus' mind that each of the three was a good bishop: Ambrose because of his qualities of spiritual leadership; Chrysostom because of his preaching and pastoral capacities; Augustine because of his charity, his moderate use of philosophical argument, and his sobriety. Moreover, both Chrysostom and Augustine remained close to some aspects of the Pauline ideal. It is plain that for Erasmus none of the three was perfect, nor is there any suggestion on his part that the three should be somehow put together to form the composite, perfect bishop.

THE GREEK AND LATIN FATHERS

It is interesting to see that Erasmus does not invariably and at all costs make the Church Father whose work(s) he happens to be introducing fit the virtues of the patron to whom the preface is addressed. This is particularly so in his preface to the recently deceased Pirckheimer's Latin translation of Gregory of Nazianzus' *Orationes* published in 1531. The preface dated May 15, 1531, is addressed to Duke George of Saxony, and it is plain from the outset that Erasmus does not consider Gregory a model bishop (nor indeed is there any particular reason why he should). Most of the preface is in fact devoted to praises of Pirckheimer, whose Latin translation is so good that no one any longer need read the Greek.[53] That is no bad thing as Gregory's Greek style is full of subtleties and puns which make him difficult to understand. Moreover, although his piety is equaled by his eloquence, he frequently philosophizes about theological matters which can barely be encompassed in human words. In short, Erasmus finds Gregory of Nazianzus too obscure. He compares him

---

[51] Allen 8: Ep. 2157, lines 297–320, quotation: lines 301–2.
[52] Allen 8: Ep. 2157, lines 604–7.
[53] Allen 9: Ep. 2493, lines 62–65.

unfavorably to Basil of Caesarea, his brother, equally erudite but clearer and more amusing, and to Chrysostom, more diffuse but very simple to understand because he never handles abstract issues. Erasmus then seeks out, rather fancifully, their stylistic counterparts in the Latin church: Chrysostom can be considered Augustine's "opposite number," Gregory of Nazianzus is comparable to Ambrose who "would have given his translators a great deal of trouble had he written in Greek," while Basil *stylistically* constitutes a mixture of Jerome and Lactantius.[54] He offers no word about Gregory of Nazianzus as a model churchman. In fact, although pious, Gregory represents to Erasmus a schoolman *avant la lettre*.

What of Basil of Caesarea? The *En amice lector* of 1532 and Erasmus' Latin translation of *De Spiritu sancto* of the same year contain prefaces to Sadoleto and Dantiscus respectively. In the preface to Sadoleto, Basil's pastoral gifts and his contribution to the formulation of the doctrine of the Trinity are virtually ignored. Although Erasmus praises Basil's anti-Arian zeal, he does not even mention that the Cappadocian was a bishop. What interests Erasmus above all is Basil's Greek style, particularly as compared to the other Greek Fathers. Athanasius is didactic, Nazianzus complex, Chrysostom verbose, Gregory of Nyssa piously simple. Basil's style, stresses Erasmus, leaves nothing to be desired. Moreover, like Chrysostom, he has an excellent knowledge of philosophy and the liberal arts "but does no more with them than put them at the service of piety." His expositions of the Scriptures are remarkably "nonviolent" and careful. His oratory is a mirror of his life, adds Erasmus curtly without giving any details.[55] The preface to the *De Spiritu sancto* does not substantially qualify this picture of Basil.[56]

THE EARLY CHURCH IN THE PREFACES

What do his most important prefaces show us about the spirituality of the early church and its significance to Erasmus? It is worth noting that with the exception of Chrysostom, the Greek doctors are not considered as highly as the Latin ones. Chrysostom, already "legitimized" in the Middle Ages, is the only one to be accorded the status of a "model bishop," and that is due

---

[54] Allen 9: Ep. 2493, lines 76–81, 82–85, 92–97; quotations: lines 92–93, 94–95.

[55] Allen 9: Ep. 2493, Ep. 2611, lines 50–54, 65, 68–72, 76–78, 92; quotations: lines 71–72, 78.

[56] Allen 10: Ep. 2643. On both the Greek edition and translation see Irena Backus, *Lectures humanistes de Basile de Césarée: Traductions latines (1439–1618)* (Paris: Institut d'Etudes Augustiniennes, 1990), 110–14.

largely to his gifts as a preacher. Gregory of Nazianzus is treated with the greatest circumspection; Athanasius is praised for his didactic gifts and for his *tranquillitas!*[57] Only Basil attracts Erasmus' attention because of his brilliance and his stand against the Arians but, interestingly, not primarily because of any spiritual authority he might have had. The nature of Origen's importance for Erasmus has been too well investigated to require any further elaboration.[58] Irenaeus constitutes a case apart.

If we now turn to the Latin doctors we see that the three who were in some sense "canonized" by the medieval tradition—Jerome, Augustine, and Ambrose—are also the ones that Erasmus finds the most important, although, notably in the case of Jerome, he also makes sure that he overturns the medieval image. Ambrose had the greatest spiritual authority because of Theodosius' submission to him, with Augustine, it would seem, coming a close second. Cyprian, Hilary, and Arnobius are praised for different reasons, even though the reader might ask just how seriously the preface to Arnobius the Younger's *Psalms Commentary* should be taken.

Apart from the varying degree to which its doctors serve as moral exemplars to his contemporaries, what else did Erasmus find of spiritual importance in the early church? Its stylistic and oratorical qualities were naturally important, although not all the Fathers are automatically great rhetoricians. Notably, Ambrose and Gregory of Nazianzus fare less well. It is interesting that Erasmus clearly distinguishes Ambrose's spiritual authority from his relatively meager stylistic gifts. The one in Erasmus' eyes does not automatically entail the other so that, conversely, Basil's great eloquence does not make him a great spiritual authority. Arnobius, on the other hand, is praised for his attempts to reach a larger public, albeit in barbaric Latin.

But for Erasmus probably one of the most important features of the spirituality of the early church is the fluidity of its dogma. Although his emphasis on this takes on a rather apologetic aspect in the preface to Cyprian, Erasmus' basic point is historically sound: the issue of schismatic and heretical baptism was not a clear-cut matter in Cyprian's time. His views on the fluidity of dogma find their fullest expression in the preface to Hilary, where he states in so many words that it is not the written-down doctrine that constitutes the essence of Christianity; it is conduct and way of life. This conception of Christianity enables Erasmus to relativize heresy while being careful never to condone it openly. Arianism is reprehensible to him, but that does not mean that

---

[57] Allen 6: Ep. 1790, lines 92–94.
[58] See Godin, *Erasme, lecteur d'Origène.*

at least some Arians could not behave in a Christian manner. On the other hand, Erasmus also stresses that heresy is grounded in excessive interest in philosophy and should be refuted by arguments drawn from Scripture and from nowhere else, as I have shown in Erasmus' evaluation of Irenaeus and Augustine. The doctors of the early church were not perfect, they were not all great rhetoricians, they do not incarnate for Erasmus a "golden age." However, he insists on the fact that they have much to teach us, notably in matters of the fluidity of doctrine, that the Bible cannot be interpreted without their writings, and that they have been neglected or misrepresented for too long.

CONTROVERSY WITH LUTHER OVER THE EXPLANATIO SYMBOLI

The radical nature of these views was spotted by Luther, as is shown by the controversy of 1534, the full importance of which seems to have escaped historians' attention so far. In 1534, after a reading of Erasmus' works, Luther had his famous exchange of correspondence with Nicholas Amsdorf which was published in the same year.[59] Although not nearly as theologically elaborate as the *De servo arbitrio* of 1525, the attack was surprisingly virulent and centered partly on Erasmus' understanding of the patristic tradition and its status. Luther criticized this with reference to two of Erasmus' writings, the *Explanatio symboli* of 1533 and the preface to the works of Hilary of 1523.[60] The *Explanatio symboli* is interesting in several respects. First, although in 1519 Erasmus had questioned (rightly) the attribution of the frequently cited *Expositio symboli* to Cyprian and had noted that it appears among Jerome's works under the name of Rufinus,[61] in the *Explanatio* he adopted the traditional attribution. Second, there was the problem of the authenticity of the Apostles' Creed. Following Valla, Erasmus rejected the medieval legend according to which the Creed was the work of the apostles themselves.[62] In 1519 in the *Ratio* he had

---

[59] See *D. Martin Luthers Werke: Briefwechsel*, 15 vols. (Weimar: Herrmann Böhlaus Nachfolger, 1930–1978), hereafter cited as WA Br., 7: Ep. 2086 (Nicholas Amsdorf to Luther, January 28, 1534) and Ep. 2093 (Luther to Nicholas Amsdorf, March 11, 1534). The two were published together in the same year under the title *Epistolae Domini Nicolai Amsdorfii et D. Martini Lutheri de Erasmo Roterodamo . . .* (Wittenberg: Johannes Luft, 1534). Amsdorf's letter is short and constitutes more a condemnation of Georg Witzel than of Erasmus, although he does say it is time that Erasmus was refuted "ut tandem suis coloribus, qui sunt inscitia et malitia depingeretur" (WA Br. 7: Ep. 2086, lines 15–16). For the full background to the controversy see ASD 9–1: 429–34.
[60] ASD 5–1: 177–320; Allen 5: Ep. 1334.
[61] Allen 4: Ep. 1000, lines 34–37.
[62] ASD 5–1: 196–99.

actually asserted that it was produced during the Council of Nicaea.[63] However, he always insisted that it was a Creed which summarized the earliest teaching, maintaining that the church in its beginnings did not need any extensive documents and that more and more of its doctrine was written down as heresies came into being. This is why *Catecheses* three and four of the *Explanatio*[64] contain a listing of a large number of ancient heresies—an unprecedented departure in the catechetical literature of the Middle Ages—and more importantly, this is why Erasmus in the *Explanatio* (as elsewhere in his work) insists on the fluidity of the dogma of the early church. He points out notably that the *Filioque* was a late addition to the Creed made in one text only by the Latin church.[65] In the very early church Christians were not required to believe that the Holy Spirit proceeded from both the Father and the Son. Moreover, Erasmus makes his catechumen ask in so many words why the writings of the Fathers are accepted by the church given that nearly all of them contain some heterodox statement.[66]

Erasmus' answer, as might be expected, relativizes orthodoxy and heresy. The Fathers do not possess the authority of Scripture: they were good and pious but above all they were men. An error does not make a man into a heretic; it does not follow that all Greeks were heretics just because they believed in a single procession of the Holy Spirit. What is heretical is to "impudently combat self-evident truth transmitted by public authority."[67]

What angered Luther in 1534 were not any doubts Erasmus might have had about the authenticity of the Creed or about the attribution of the *Expositio* to Cyprian. He saw very well the issues raised by Erasmus' attitude to patristic tradition. The rudiments of Christian faith, says Luther, should be presented simply and clearly, not in such a way that they raise doubts. Erasmus does not give his catechumens any solid foundations, and "he insists so much on the heresies and schisms which troubled the church from its very beginnings that he practically asserts that nothing has ever been certain in the

---

[63] Holborn, 211.

[64] ASD 5–1:247–51, 257, 260–62, 264–66.

[65] ASD 5–1:269: "Quanquam videtur a Latinis adiectum Filioque, quemadmodum et in symbolo Athanasii, quod haec particula nec habeatur in Graeco symbolo, quod aeditione secunda Novo Testamento praefixeramus, nec in ullo Symbolo, quod refertur in volumine canonum. Nondum enim tum opinor receptum erat, praesertim apud orientis ecclesias Spiritum sanctum ab utroque procedere, nec hoc exigebatur a christianis. Satis erat a Patre procedentem et in Filio manentem profiteri, sicut exprimitur in vita Andreae apostoli."

[66] ASD 5–1:277: "Audio vix ullum esse scriptorem veterem, in quo non deprehendantur aliqua a catholicae fidei regula dissonantia. Quur eorum libros recepit ecclesia?"

[67] ASD 5–1:278: "Sed haereticum est adversus evidentem et cum autoritate publica proditam veritatem rebellare procaciter."

Christian religion."[68] Then, apropos of Erasmus' preface to the works of Hilary, Luther points out that the accusations of Arianism leveled against Erasmus are not unfounded, seeing as he says there, "we dare to call the Holy Spirit God, the Fathers did not."[69] First, this is false, says Luther; second, it is playing about with words and creating difficulties where none exist.[70]

In his *Purgatio adversus Lutherum*,[71] also published in 1534, Erasmus defends himself. He has seen from the very nature of the attack that his adversary holds the standard sixteenth-century view of the Fathers and their authority: timeless spokesmen of fully formulated orthodox doctrine to be read not in their context but in the context of Luther's own time.[72] Erasmus therefore chooses his arguments accordingly: he begins by saying that all the great doctors of the church, notably Augustine, Thomas Aquinas, and Jean Gerson, include a list of heresies in their catechisms. Moreover, Athanasius, Basil, Chrysostom, Cyril, John of Damascus, not to mention Cyprian, Ambrose, Jerome, and Augustine, all include catalogues of heresies in their works. The most holy men have judged this useful so that young people could find out how firmly Christ's faith has resisted such numerous and diverse threats through the ages. Moreover, his *Explanatio symboli* was not intended for complete beginners; had it been so, he could not have written it in Latin.[73] Without really answering Luther's accusations of relativizing orthodoxy and heresy, Erasmus cannot resist pointing out the incoherence of Luther's position. If Luther admits nothing other than the authority of Scripture, how did he come up with so many new doctrines which the church ignored for so long, given that Scripture has always been the same? Is Luther going to deny that the Fathers occasionally read Scripture differently from us, that they accepted as orthodox teachings that we consider heretical, or doubted certain things that we no longer doubt? For a very long time the church did not *dare* to say that the Holy Spirit proceeded from the Father and the Son; we have no such inhibitions.[74] Hilary did not *dare* call the Holy Spirit God, not because he was a heretic "but because he scrupulously waited upon the ruling of the church, when it came to choosing the most appropriate vocabulary for

---

[68] WA Br. 7: Ep. 2093, lines 80–111; quotation: lines 91–94.

[69] WA Br. 7: Ep. 2903, lines 225–26: "Nos audemus Spiritum sanctum appellare Deum, quod veteres ausi non sunt."

[70] WA Br. 7: Ep. 2903, lines 244–60.

[71] ASD 9–1: 429–83.

[72] On this view of patristic authority in the sixteenth century see Backus, *Lectures humanistes de Basile de Césarée*, 203–7.

[73] ASD 9–1: 447.

[74] ASD 9–1: 459–60.

discoursing about the Holy Spirit."[75] In other words, certain doctrines do not figure in the Scripture; they are fixed by the church and are dependent on history just as the church is. The question legitimately posed by Luther of who therefore is to be considered a heretic, and when, does not really receive an answer.

Erasmus' view of the fluidity of patristic doctrines remained unaltered throughout his career and was far more radical than Luther's view of patristic tradition and authority. Fathers as model rhetoricians also play an important part in Erasmus' view of the early church: he cannot help but acknowledge that they expressed themselves better than the schoolmen.

Why did Erasmus edit or help to edit so many Fathers? Several reasons suggest themselves. Some were indeed of use in his own controversies, imbued as he was with patristic thought. He probably also intended to fill in gaps in the market by helping Froben publish the Fathers of whom no good editions existed. Erasmus indisputably wanted to institute some kind of reform program so as to reconvert the church to its early doctrine and language. The Fathers were to provide a valuable ethical model, although it was a model of how not to act as well as of how to act. However, the main reason why Erasmus helped publish patristic writings was to show the relative and fluid nature of the teaching they contained. Although radical in its conception of history, this view of tradition did not make Erasmus into a "radical reformer." The doctrine of the church of his time, he constantly implies, is as history-dependent as that of the early church, but this does not mean that it has to be overturned in every detail.

<hr />

[75] ASD 9–1: 462.

Germain Marc'hadour

ERASMUS AS PRIEST
Holy Orders in His Vision and Practice

~

ORDINATION IS THE HIGH POINT in the life of any Catholic priest; as a landmark in Erasmus' earthly career, it ranks next only to his birth and to his death. Despite the uncertainty about the year of his birth (generally believed to have been in 1469), he received more attention in 1969 than did Napoleon (born in 1769). Peace for once could not complain that her Apostle was slighted. He received attention again in that *annus mirabilis*, "Columbus year," because he was ordained a presbyter in the cathedral of Utrecht on April 25, 1492. That event was banal enough in that it increased the number of priests in an already priest-ridden Christendom. It has gained significance, however, because Erasmus was a different priest, less clerical, indeed somewhat anticlerical, perhaps even a congenital bachelor before he also became a committed celibate. One of his major tasks would be to complete that emergence of an enlightened laity which had begun so vigorously in his own native land with the *devotio moderna*. The *Enchiridion militis christiani* (1503), through which he exercised the priestly function of teaching, of "evangelizing," was a code offered to every baptized Christian, and demonstrated in the life of his best friend Thomas More. Updating this manual fifteen years after its first publication, Erasmus, in a new preface, placed the priests in the circle closest to the divine High Priest, yet added: "There are twice-married men whom Christ deigns to admit into the inmost circle of his friends."[1]

[1] Allen 3: Ep. 858, lines 333–34; and Holborn, 12.

More, who is here alluded to, will be granted pride of place in this paper. When Erasmus crossed the Channel in 1499, on a holiday from the University of Paris, More, his "most sweet Thomas," a law student at Lincoln's Inn, London, was himself examining a possible vocation to the priesthood.[2] By the time (1505) the two friends translated Lucian in fraternal emulation, More was a married man and Erasmus his house guest.[3] It was again under More's roof that Erasmus dashed off his *Moria*, in ironic contrast to the *Enchiridion*.[4]

Second to More among Erasmus' English friends was John Colet, whom he offered in 1521 as a model to the young clergy of Europe as he had, in 1519, presented More as a model to Christendom's lay intelligentsia.[5] Colet's embodiment of the priestly ideal is the more precious because Erasmus never wrote systematically about holy orders, unlike Saint John Fisher, whose *Defence of the Sacred Priesthood* (1525) went through many editions on the continent.[6] A true pastor who visited his flock and fed it regularly though preaching, Fisher was Erasmus' perfect exemplar for the episcopal office. To his insistent request we owe Erasmus' last book, *Ecclesiastes*, a manual of pulpit oratory, written by a priest for his brother priests.

ERASMUS' ORDINATION

How old was Erasmus on April 25, 1492? Twenty-two years and five months, if one dates his birth October 27, 1469. That this was below the

[2] Allen 1: Ep. 114 (of October 28, 1499) is the only extant letter from Erasmus in which More's Christian name is used. The dedication of *Moriae Encomium* to More endowed his surname with ironic and mystical overtones.

[3] The preface of May 1, 1506, to a translation of Lucian quotes Richard Whitford as saying that More and Erasmus were as like as twins (CWE 2: Ep. 191, line 39). Although age is not mentioned, this use of twins (*gemelli*), with half a dozen other indications, inclined me toward 1469 as Erasmus' birth year, and 1477 (rather than 1478) as More's, which reduces the age gap between them to seven years and a little over three months, considering that the respective birthdays are October 27 and February 6 or 7. John B. Gleason, "The Birth Dates of John Colet and Erasmus of Rotterdam: Fresh Documentary Evidence," *Renaissance Quarterly* 32 (1979): 73–76, makes a strong point in favor of 1466, a date Harry Vredeveld also asserts with confidence in CWE 85: 398 n. 9. See also Vredeveld, "The Ages of Erasmus and the Year of His Birth," *Renaissance Quarterly* 46 (1993): 754–809.

[4] Clarence H. Miller's critical edition of *Moriae Encomium id est Stultitiae Laus* (ASD 4–3) has revealed the care with which Erasmus revised this work.

[5] If Erasmus chose to portray Saint Jerome, More, Vitrier, and Colet, it was because they embodied his ideals: the four Lives are at once encomia and pleas for imitation.

[6] *Sacri sacerdotii defensio contra Lutherum* was dedicated on June 1, 1525, to Cuthbert Tunstal, who had examined it in manuscript. A few weeks earlier (March 14), Erasmus had dedicated to Pirckheimer an edition of Chrysostom's *De sacerdotio*, on the dignity of the priesthood (Allen 6: Ep. 1558).

canonical age should not be invoked as an argument for preferring 1466 or 1467 as his birth year. A dispensation issued by the Holy See allowed Fisher to receive the priesthood at twenty-two, on December 17, 1491.[7] As for Luther, he did not enter his Erfurt monastery until July 17, 1505 (after obtaining his M.A.), and yet he was ordained on March 3, 1507, at twenty-three.[8]

Colet was a diocesan priest; Jehan Vitrier, who shares with him Erasmus' diptych of 1521, was a Franciscan friar, while Luther was an Augustinian hermit. Erasmus belonged to a different category as a canon regular. Richard DeMolen has repeatedly stressed that he was not a monk, but the terms "monastic" and "monasticism" do duty for all these forms of the religious life as well as for Benedictines, Carthusians, and Cistercians, embracing all men and women who bind themselves to live in community under vows of celibacy, poverty, and obedience. Erasmus and Luther had taken this triple vow at their religious profession; the priesthood in itself added no new obligation.

Fisher, Erasmus, and Luther are specimens of the best category of ordinands: they were already inserted into a structure—a university college or a religious house—where they were expected to continue living in their new capacity. Their immediate superiors, who presented them to the bishop for ordination, were guarantors of their worthiness in learning and virtue. By instituting seminaries, the Council of Trent extended this conventual mold to all candidates for holy orders: a myriad modern priests have fit into this pattern of ending their formation between the ages of twenty-three and twenty-five. In the secular clergy of Erasmus' day, ordination ages varied considerably, as they do again in the post-Vatican II church. Colet, who did not need Mass stipends for a living, was ordained on March 25, 1498, in his thirties. Thomas Linacre was a physician before he received the presbyterate, and his main motive for seeking major orders may have been access to fatter ecclesiastical prebends. Other correspondents of Erasmus were ordained on the threshold of adult life. Jan Laski, born in 1499, was ordained in 1521. Johann Maier von Eck (Eckius), born on November 13, 1486, was only one month into his

---

[7] The papal bull is actually the only document which establishes 1469 as Fisher's birth year; older biographies used to make it 1459. Fisher, already a Master of Arts, needed holy orders before he could fulfil one major obligation attached to his fellowship—offering Mass for the intentions of the endowers.

[8] Born on Martinmas Eve (November 10) 1483, Luther became a priest at twenty-three years, three months, and three weeks. On the whole question, see R. J. Schoeck, *Erasmus of Europe: The Making of a Humanist* (Edinburgh: Edinburgh University Press, 1990), 107–9.

twenty-third year when ordained on December 13, 1508; like Fisher he received a dispensation from Rome.

Since Erasmus' community at Steyn belonged, like his birthplace, to the vast diocese of Utrecht, the cathedral of that city was the normal place for his ordination. In 1492, the bishop was David of Burgundy, an illegitimate son of Philip of Burgundy, and thus a half brother of Duke Charles the Bold, whose wife Margaret of York, sister to Edward IV and Richard III, patronized William Caxton in the 1470s. After the defeat and death of Duke Charles (1477), Bishop David was expelled by the population of Utrecht; he returned only after his nephew Maximilian had subdued the city by force of arms. His successor, the last prince-bishop of Utrecht, surrendered his secular power to the emperor after the Sack of Rome (1527).

Erasmus has nothing to say against the prelate from whom he received the priesthood. He praises him for examining the candidates for holy orders. That David's bastardy was no impediment to promotion in the church may shock us as grossly unfair in the light of Erasmus' being barred, as son of a priest, from access to the secular clergy. Another aristocrat, Clement VII, was unhampered in his ecclesiastical career by being born out of wedlock. His legitimacy was effected by a papal bull, and Erasmus would secure a similar dispensation later in life, after achieving a kind of nobility through the fame of his learning.

THE BLESSED SACRAMENT AND SACRIFICE

The order of presbyter was conferred by the laying on of hands, with the specific rite of the presentation of the chalice and the formula "Accipe potestatem offerendi sacramentum"—"receive the power to offer the sacrament"—or words to that effect.[9] The emphasis, then as now, lay on the ministry of the Eucharist: the achieving of Christ's presence on the altar was the ground for Saint Francis of Assisi and Saint Thomas More to claim reverence

---

[9] The Council of Florence (1439) obliged the Armenians, who had till then ordained through the laying on of hands, to include in their ritual the presentation (or "porrection") of the instruments or implements. For the presbyterate, this meant the chalice and paten. John Fisher reached the conclusion that the *impositio manuum*, being the only rite mentioned in Scripture, must be the operative gesture. More shared that view: "And that the grace by God appointed unto Holy Orders is given with that putting upon of the hands is twice declared by Saint Paul in his epistles to Timothee" (CW 8:198). See his many references to ordination under 1 Tim. 4:14 and 2 Tim. 1:6 in Germain Marc'hadour *The Bible in the Works of St. Thomas More*, pt. 3 (Nieuwkoop: B. de Graaf, 1970), 130, 133.

toward even the worst members of the clergy.[10] True, the Apostles had defined their priorities as prayer and the service of the Word (Acts 6:4), but in Saint Paul's phrase, "the dispensers of the mysteries of God" (1 Cor. 4:1), the "mystery" par excellence which the priests were called to "dispense" as loyal stewards of the Lord was that which the liturgy of the Mass continues to proclaim as "the mystery of faith." That is why Erasmus' attitude to the Eucharist is the most important element in our examination of his priesthood. I reopen the dossier, however summarily, because at least one great Erasmian scholar is still unconvinced that Erasmus was fully orthodox on this point.[11]

My first witness is Jean Richard's *Sentimens d'Erasme de Rotterdam, conformes à ceux de l'Eglise catholique, sur tous les points controversés*, a book published anonymously in 1688, and in Calvinist Amsterdam, beyond the reach of Catholic censorship. The author's thesis is that Erasmus' views "conformed" to Catholic doctrine "on all the controversial points." The most hotly controversial issue, even within the Protestant camp, was the Sacrament of the altar. On no point did Erasmus create more alarm among his Catholic friends, and more hope among the Swiss "Sacramentarians," who denied the real presence. Michael Screech is among the many critics who have laid to rest the notion that Erasmus was won over to a symbolic interpretation by the learning of Oecolampadius.[12] Richard Rex finds "striking resemblances between Erasmus' attitude to the Eucharist," and that of Fisher in the fullest statement of the Catholic faith.[13] Erasmus' statement of 1530—"I never doubted the reality of the Lord's body"—comes after dozens of protests against allegations or even mere suspicions of his having departed from the *consensus ecclesiae*. For him as for More, this unanimous consensus of the church was the most visible seat of inerrancy in matters of faith and conduct.[14]

---

[10] Young More received the Franciscan heritage through the Observant movement. Translating Giovanni Pico della Mirandola's "properties of the perfect lover," he alludes to this identification with Christ when he calls the priests of Christ "the quick reliques, the ministers of his Church." See *English Works of Sir Thomas More* (London: Cawood et al., 1557), 30. In *A Dialogue concerning Heresies* (1529), chap. 12 of bk. 3 is entitled "The author toucheth one special prerogative that we have by a priest, be he never so bad, in that his naughtiness cannot take from us the profit of his Mass" (CW 6:299).

[11] Jacques Chomarat, *Grammaire et rhétorique chez Erasme*, 2 vols. (Paris: Société d'Editions "Les Belles Lettres," 1981), 2:1099–1101.

[12] M. A. Screech, *Ecstasy and the Praise of Folly* (London: Duckworth, 1980), 117–19.

[13] Richard Rex, *The Theology of John Fisher* (Cambridge: Cambridge University Press), 145.

[14] The statement "I never doubted the reality of the Lord's body," is from the preface to Erasmus' edition of Alger's treatise defending the real presence against Berengarius: *De veritate corporis et sanguinis Dominici in Eucharistia* (Freiburg: Emmeus, 1530). See Allen 8: Ep. 2284, line 176.

Some of Erasmus' Latin words or phrases are misconstrued by those ignorant of liturgical and patristic usage and formulation: of the fact, for instance, that *conficere corpus Domini* has always meant "to make the Body of the Lord present through consecration."[15] Screech describes Erasmus' doctrine of the Mass as "Origenistic."[16] He analyzes the meaning of *repraesentare* in Erasmus' theology of the Eucharist, and points out that *transubstantiatio*, a scholastic term Erasmus disliked, was not fully "canonized" until the Council of Trent, in 1551, described it as a "fitting" term.[17] The vocabulary in this mysterious field lends itself to misinterpretation. Even More might sound "non-Catholic" when he defines the thing (*res*) of the Sacrament as "the unity and society of all good holy folk in the mystical body of Christ."[18] Such is the thing of the Eucharist, its specific purpose, the main fruit of the real presence, which of course More firmly believes in and staunchly defends.

The Sacrament of penance is the second exclusive province of the ordained minister. It is often linked in practice to the Eucharist. One goes to confession in order to be clean for communion. These two Sacraments constituted the staple of a parish priest's routine. For what is today called "the Sacrament of reconciliation," Erasmus used the Greek term *exomologesis*. His many pronouncements about auricular confession include his record of Colet as a witness to its virtue. The dean of Saint Paul's deprecated only the anguished scrupulosity which prompted endless recourse to sacramental absolution, a pastoral concern he shared with Jehan Vitrier and with a host of spiritual classics.[19]

---

[15] Chomarat is taken to task by A. Godin in *Moreana* 65–66 (June 1980):146, for rendering this phrase "consommer le corps du Seigneur" in *La Correspondance d'Erasme*, 12 vols., ed. Aloïs Gerlo and Paul Foriers (Brussels: Brussels University Press, 1967–1982), 8:151.

[16] Screech, *Ecstasy and the Praise of Folly*, 119. Origen, as the pioneer of allegorical exegesis, is not prone to stress the literal sense and, but for the immemorial faith of the church, Erasmus might have espoused the symbolic view of the Eucharist.

[17] *The Catechism of the Catholic Church* (Rome: Libreria Editrice Vaticana, and Washington: United States Catholic Conference, 1994) quotes the Council of Trent in § 1377 as follows: "by the consecration of the bread and wine there takes place a change of the whole substance of the bread into the substance of the body of Christ our Lord and of the whole substance of the wine into the substance of his blood. This change the holy Catholic Church has fittingly and properly called transubstantiation."

[18] CW 13:142. Christ's presence in the source of that virtue of efficacy. See CW 13:230.

[19] Colet is equally vehement when, from personal and pastoral experience, he approves of auricular confession and when he condemns *anxiam ac subinde repetitam* (Godin, lines 470–72; Allen 4: Ep. 1211, line 489). The same words for "anxious and continually repeated confessions" are quoted for Vitrier, who abominates them but who, unlike Colet, is halfhearted even about sounder penitents (Godin, line 128; Allen 4: Ep. 1211, lines 132–35).

Erasmus' practice should be assessed in its pre-Tridentine context. He probably did not often stand at the altar, preferring to attend Mass among the faithful. In England, a horde of priests celebrated each and every day. Many had been ordained just for that sake—to serve a chantry on behalf of a guild or even a manor house. Erasmus reports approvingly that Colet and Warham chose to skip Mass on certain days.[20] We have no reason to imagine that, when Erasmus sojourned in Fisher's palace, the bishop found anything to tax in his conduct as a priest. Ignatius Loyola, ordained on June 24, 1537, did not say Mass on his own until Christmas 1538, and he died in Rome without receiving either Holy Communion or Extreme Unction. The eleventh-century hermit Saint Romuald, when near to death, asked his two companions to leave him alone for the night. Before they returned on the next morning he had gone to God without the last Sacraments. On Sundays Erasmus would not miss Mass; even when sick, he courageously left his room to join the congregation in church. When, in 1529, Erasmus chose to celebrate Easter alone in his bedroom rather than join Oecolampadius, it was because, in the public service, the Paschal Lamb was feasted "without the Lamb" itself being present.[21] Beatus Rhenanus informs us that he used to give alms to the poor he encountered on the way home from the Eucharistic service.[22]

To this dossier let me add a recusant work published by "William Reynolde Priest" in 1593: *A Treatise Containing the True Catholic and Apostolic Faith of the Holy Sacrifice and Sacrament Ordained by Christ at His Last Supper*. Here, fifty-seven years after Erasmus' death, a Catholic polemicist uses Erasmus' testimony "the rather for that the Protestants sometimes much extol him as a great profound divine, deeply seen in the Fathers." In a sentence which Reynolde somewhat paraphrases, Erasmus says "he had rather be drawn in pieces than to become of Berengarius' opinion and think of the Sacrament as the Zwinglians do." Reynolde proceeds to quote Erasmus in the first person: "I could never be induced to believe otherwise than that the true body of Christ was in the Sacrament, for that the writings of the Gospel and Apostles express so plainly the body which is given, and the blood which is shed." Besides this "so manifest warrant from Christ and Saint Paul," it is, Erasmus continues,

---

[20] Godin, lines 472–79 = Allen 4: Ep. 1211, lines 492–98; *Ecclesiastes*, ASD 5–4:140.

[21] Léon-E. Halkin, "La piété d'Erasme," *Revue d'histoire ecclésiastique* 79 (1984), 671–718, may tip the scales a little in favor of Erasmus' orthopraxis. See also Halkin, "Erasme contre la liturgie?" in *Miscellanea Moreana: Essays for Germain Marc'hadour*, ed. Clare M. Murphy, Henri Gibaud, and Mario A. Di Cesare (Binghamton: Medieval and Renaissance Texts and Studies, 1989), 421–25; and *Erasme parmi nous* (Paris: Fayard, 1987), 327–40.

[22] Allen 1: Ep. IV, line 542.

"proved that the ancient writers, unto whom not without cause the Church yieldeth so great credit, believed with one consent that in the eucharist is the true substance of Christ's body and blood," and he adds "the constant authority of councils and so great consent of Christian people." The recusant divine ends with a prayer that his compatriots, "both English and Scottish, who have followed Berengarius in his impudent error (for so Erasmus termeth it) may also follow him in his repentance and execration of the same impudent error, whereunto Erasmus persuadeth them."[23]

Reynolde's joy at being able to enroll Erasmus as an ally contrasts with John Jortin's annoyance at having to concede that Erasmus was loyal to the Catholic doctrine of the Eucharist, except for the "monster of transubstantiation." A convinced Huguenot, Jortin dismisses the faith *consensus*, so weighty for Erasmus, as the "conspiracy of a few dark, stupid, ignorant, wicked, scandalous, factious ages of Christianity."[24] There is anger in that caricatural accumulation of contemptuous epithets; yet Jortin does not shrink from the bitter evidence. He quotes Erasmus' description of Oecolampadius' book to Pirckheimer as written "with such skill . . . and such persuasive eloquence that, if God should not interpose, even the Elect may be seduced."[25] Erasmus continues in Jortin's English: "The opinion of Oecolampadius would not displease me, if the consent of the Church did not hinder me from adopting it. . . . I cannot depart from the general consent of the Church, and I never did depart from it."[26] Amid rebukes of Erasmus for recurring to consensus, Jortin honestly proceeds to show how unshakable that bad "maxim" made a man who on most other issues was so undogmatic. One more quotation may provide the pleasure of hearing Erasmus' voice through the Augustan prose of Jortin's rendering: "Not that the words of Jesus Christ are not sufficient for me; but none should be surprised, if I follow the interpretations of the Church, upon whose authority my faith and belief of the Canonical Scriptures is founded."[27]

The other issues linked with the Eucharist are less essential, and were not raised much in Erasmus' life or writings. He warns Pirckheimer against going all the way with Luther in denying the sacrificial character of the Mass.

---

[23] William Reynolde, *A Treatise Containing the True Catholic and Apostolic Faith of the Holy Sacrifice and Sacrament Ordained by Christ at His Last Supper* (Antwerp: J. Trognesius, 1593; Menston: Scolar Press, 1970), 34.

[24] John Jortin, *The Life of Erasmus*, 2 vols. (London: J. Whitsun and B. White, 1758–1760), 2:409. I call Jortin a Huguenot because his Calvinism is that of his French ancestors.

[25] Ibid., 379.

[26] Ibid., 408.

[27] Ibid., 429.

The use of *sacrificare* and *sacrificus* to designate the Mass and its celebrant implies his acceptance of the view, so strongly defended by Fisher, that each Mass is a real sacrifice in that it reenacts sacramentally (which of course means symbolically) the unique sacrifice of Calvary. Differences of ontology or psychology continue to divide theologians when it comes to defining the "how" of this mystery. The faith itself, though it "seeks to understand" (*fides quaerens intellectum*), is never in question. Thus the Pauline phrase "in the person of Christ" (2 Cor. 2:10 and 4:6) is always being discussed and tentatively retranslated. The emphases of the *magisterium* have shifted perceptibly in our own times. Fisher and More themselves use expressions which are considered inadequate by some Catholic commentators of today.[28] We may leave Erasmus the theologian in the hands of his peers and, harboring no doubt about his Eucharistic orthodoxy, examine his pastoral concern for the ministers of God's altar.

PARADIGM OF THE CATHOLIC PRIEST

Saint Jerome was a self-conscious presbyter, as appears in his correspondence with an *episcopus* like Saint Augustine. Yet the priesthood is not stressed in Erasmus' *Vita Hieronymi*, whereas it is almost the only theme of the letter he addressed, on June 13, 1521, to Jodocus Jonas, a young German priest and supporter of Luther. That open epistle is a portrait of two priests, the Franciscan Observant Jehan Vitrier and the diocesan prelate John Colet, whom he has known personally and reveres as models. I will draw more on the "life of Colet" because Erasmus' acquaintance with the Dean of Saint Paul's lasted much longer—a full two decades—and he took almost two years between his earliest search for biographical documents (October 1519) and the signing of the letter. That he admires both men despite their differences shows that his ideal of the good priest is not a rigid one. Erasmus' own views come most to the fore where the two men agree in disagreeing with their respective superiors or with the current practice of their milieu.

Leafing through the pages on Vitrier, we discover that friar's intense love of Saint Paul, who provided the staple and the spirit of his preaching; the

---

[28] John Jay Hughes, *The Stewards of the Lord* (London: Sheed and Ward, 1970) accuses Fisher and More of having paved the way for Cranmer's Eucharistic reform by failing to stress the oneness of the celebrant on Calvary and at the altar. Brian Byron expresses dissatisfaction with the phrase "real presence." He says it weakens the equation "This is my body." See Byron, "From Essence to Presence: A Shift in Eucharistic Expression Illustrated from the Apologetic of Saint Thomas More," in *Miscellanea Moreana*, 429–44.

joy he stressed and generated when preparing his charges to die or when conducting liturgical prayer; his intransigent fidelity to Franciscan (and evangelical) poverty.

The portrait of Colet is significantly longer. The man appears as more fully, more richly human, less purely spiritual and sacerdotal, less intensely religious, perhaps as befits his belonging to the secular clergy. Erasmus mentions the livings[29] from which the dean drew income, and expresses no qualms about there being ten of them, some received before Colet was a priest. This may surprise us in view of Erasmus' own misgivings when Archbishop Warham offered him the parish of Aldington in Kent: "I cannot be a real shepherd to that flock," he objected, "since I am ignorant of the language." Warham calmed these scruples: "Instead of preaching to one tiny rural village, you teach all the pastors through your books; since the fruit is much more plentiful, how can it look unworthy of you to draw a little money from the church?"[30] Erasmus reassures us fully by adding that the first priest to whom he entrusted the cure of his parish, being too busy, was replaced by a young man, a curate chosen for his theological learning and his moral integrity. More too saw some virtue in the existing plurality; he writes "that some man may right well have the cure of divers parishes, and good causes why he so should."[31] Every one of the eight priests More nominated to shepherd a parish was already in charge of one or more: "Each in turn appointed curates, all of whom were residents," as well as being learned and virtuous; absenteeism and neglect were avoided.[32]

It is apropos of More's electing wedlock after envisaging holy orders that Erasmus, revising his 1519 letter to Hutten for its 1521 edition, denounces the vast number of those "who rashly engage in so arduous a profession without testing themselves beforehand."[33] More had tested his vocation by living several years with the London Carthusians, sharing in their "vigils, fasts and prayers."[34]

---

[29] Colet, he says, lived off these *sacerdotia* or preferments, and disposed of his private fortune for charitable purposes (Godin, lines 323–25).

[30] *Ecclesiastes*, ASD 5–4:142.

[31] CW 8:596.

[32] Seymour B. House, "Sir Thomas More as Church Patron," *Journal of Ecclesiastical History* 40 (1989):217.

[33] *Thomas More: A Portrait in Words by His Friend Erasmus*, trans. John C. Olin (New York: Fordham University Press, 1977), 7.

[34] Allen 4: Ep. 999, lines 161–62. Those means (from 1 Cor. 6:5–6) were used by Colet to tame his passions: ". . . vigiliis, ieiuniis ac precibus" (Godin, line 377).

The sheer number of priests and professed religious was almost enough to explain why they could not be an exemplary corporation. On this count, humanists and Reformers speak with one voice, nor is Erasmus the loudest in the chorus. Sacrificing quantity to achieve quality is advocated by William de Melton in an *Exhortation to those who apply for promotion to Holy Orders*,[35] printed by Wynkyn de Worde (London) between December 1507 and the end of 1515. Erasmus knew of this booklet, perhaps through Fisher, who was the author's colleague and friend, or through Colet who, as official examiner, had approved its publication.[36] "The *Sermo* is directed to be read in all grammar schools (*in omni ludo litterario*), particularly during the fortnight or month preceding the usual time of ordinations"; its purpose is to rid the church "of the swarms of dull and ignorant clerics (*a multitudine rudium et stolidorum clericorum*)."[37] This document is the more significant because Melton, though he was writing as chancellor of the diocese of York, was a Cambridge don like Erasmus himself. Erasmus may have been instrumental in bringing it to the attention of Jakob Wimpfeling, the Alsatian priest who procured its printing at Strasbourg.[38]

John Colet's address of 1512 to the English hierarchy has been quoted by hundreds of historians: "First, let those laws be recited which admonish you, Fathers, . . . not . . . to admit them to holy orders rashly." More too, no doubt with the approval of his own bishop, Cuthbert Tunstal (by whose commission he is confuting heretics), urges the prelates to obey canon law by ceasing to produce the "rabble" of priests who scandalize the church.[39] Before the first tremors of the Lutheran earthquake, *Utopia* had satirized the inflation and consequent devaluation of clergy by endowing the reasonable community of Nowhere with priests who are "very holy, and therefore very few."[40] The demand for many Masses—Henry VII left money for ten thousand to be said

---

[35] *Sermo exhortatorius . . . hijs qui ad sacros ordines petunt promoueri* (STC 17806).

[36] John B. Gleason quotes the colophon by Colet, phrased in a way which suggests that the dean was *censor deputatus* appointed by his ordinary, Bishop Fitzjames of London. This discovery reinforces his conviction that Erasmus overdramatized the feud between Colet and his ordinary. See Gleason, "The Earliest Evidence for Ecclesiastical Censorship of Printed Books in England," *The Library*, 6th ser., 4 (June 1982):137.

[37] Rex, *The Theology of John Fisher*, 210 n. 79.

[38] *Sermo ad iuuenes, qui sacris ordinibus iniciari, et examini se submittere petunt* (1514; reprint, Strasbourg, 1519). See *J. Wimpfelingi Opera Selecta*, ed. F. J. Worstbrock (Munich: W. Fink, 1965), 74. On January 24, 1529, responding to the news of Wimpfeling's death, Erasmus wrote at some length about that pastor-educator as a model priest, canonizing him especially for his "sancta libertas," Allen 8: Ep. 2000.

[39] *A Dialogue concerning Heresies*, CW 6:300, 301.

[40] *Utopia* stresses paucity as a deliberate goal: CW 4:226, 228, 230.

within a month of his death—justified, as it were, the flood of ordinations, and a late scholastic such as Gabriel Biel (d. 1495) adjusted the theology of the Eucharistic sacrifice to these facts. The medieval development of chantries was linked with popular compassion for the souls in purgatory. Earlier religious patriarchs had been of another cast. Saint Benedict was never a priest, nor was Saint Francis of Assisi, who wanted a single Mass each day in his friaries. Saint Gilbert of Sempringham (d. 1189), the founder of the only English order, agreed with them in viewing the Eucharist as a community celebration, so he allowed no priest to say Mass on his own during the novitiate.[41]

The issue of clerical celibacy, made burning by the crisis in quality, is often addressed by Erasmus. More never questioned that rule. While considering his vocation, he decided he was not called to the priesthood since "he could not shake off his desire for a wife."[42] Against Tyndale in 1532, while acknowledging with the church "that wedlock and priesthood be not repugnant but compatible," he believes, still with the church, that "the forbearing of the work of wedlock is more acceptable to God."[43] Nor does he reckon virginity "a seldom gift."[44] Léon Halkin, to define Erasmus' more nuanced position, uses the long annotation on Matt. 19:12, and points out that "for him, that which is not human is not Christian."[45] Erasmus warned priests against the illusion that marriage was an easier yoke; he confirmed some in their purpose of celibacy; he spoke sarcastically of Hedio, Capito, Luther, and Oecolampadius on the occasion of their weddings. He advocated allowing learned priests to continue their service to the church in wedlock, instead of concubinage, when they cannot lead chaste lives.[46]

Sexual impurity was the most visible of the clergy's vices, but Erasmus did not consider it the most heinous. Avarice and ambition are worse and

---

[41] Saint Gilbert, pastor of Sempringham, at first gathered seven women under a Cistercian-inspired rule. The spiritual guides were canons regular of Saint Augustine, who eventually constituted the male branch of the double monasteries. There were thirteen communities when the founder died in 1189 and twenty-five houses when Henry VIII dissolved the order in 1538. Francesco da Paola, the Calabrian hermit who in 1483 attended Louis XI's last anguish-ridden months, was not a priest. He nevertheless founded the order of Minims. He died on April 2, 1507, and was canonized as early as May 1519.

[42] Allen 4: Ep. 999, line 166.

[43] CW 8:307.

[44] CW 6:308: "Though chastity be a great gift . . . , many men have it."

[45] "Erasme et le célibat sacerdotal," *Revue d'histoire et de philosophie religieuses* 57 (1977):501.

[46] In *De conscribendis epistolis* Erasmus suggests a balanced solution for the "huge crowd of priests." The concubines, turned into wives, will live with a better conscience; bring up their offspring, now seen as legitimate, without infamy and with greater care. That will also stop the scandalous traffic of some bishops' officials, who draw an income from fines inflicted on irregular priests. See ASD 1–2: 418.

work more havoc. Colet, whose wisdom he seems to endorse, was "less harsh on priests and monks who sin only in the field of Venus, because he found them to be much less evil than such others as were proud, envious, detractors, frauds, ignorant, wholly addicted to money and ambition. Their avowed weakness made the sexual offenders humbler. Avarice and pride are more execrable in a priest than having a hundred concubines."[47] The last sentence may illustrate Colet's love of paradox, yet it conveys a commonplace. Saint Catherine of Siena (d. 1380) is often quoted as saying much the same. Saint Francis de Sales (d. 1622) points out that an avaricious minister is like Judas, for he sells our Lord; no crime is greater in an ecclesiastic or a religious.[48] The traitor is also More's reference when lashing out at the parish priests who appropriate the tithe money entrusted to them for the poor.[49]

Some impressions need to be qualified. The colloquy *Peregrinatio religionis ergo* can sound very flippant indeed, yet its very existence attests that Erasmus, always so busy with his books, did make time for the two pilgrimages he satirizes. He enriched the chapel of Our Lady at Walsingham with a prayer in Greek iambs which is still available in translation. Pilgrims of today, both Catholics and Anglicans, repeat his words to ask for the "remission of all their sins and for piety of heart."[50]

Pietas is the key virtue of humanism, with its Virgilian as well as Christian overtones. No virtue is mentioned more often in the *Enchiridion*.[51] *Impietas* is the inhuman, unnatural crime par excellence. When Lefèvre d'Etaples taxed him with impiety for making Jesus too human in his interpretation of Heb. 2:6–7, Erasmus protested with indignant vigor: "I will easily suffer charges of ignorance and error, but a charge of impiety I cannot suffer."[52] Erasmus' full acceptance of the Incarnation with all its corollaries makes him actually a more "Catholic" Christian than his fellow priests Lefèvre and Colet, who are reluctant to admit of any frailty in Jesus. Never, he feels sure, will the whole corps of Christendom share the persuasion of his Parisian critic.[53]

---

[47] This is a slight compression of the long Latin paragraph. See Godin, lines 441–52.

[48] From the bishop's third Lenten sermon of 1622.

[49] CW 13:80. More, the loyal parishioner, sees Judas as the figure also of "the parishen [sic] that stealeth his tithe from his curate," yet the priest is "the worse thief of them both."

[50] For the poem see CWE 85:120–23.

[51] *Pietas* is rendered in almost fifty different ways by the earliest English translator, sometimes through a whole line enucleating the dominant sense in the given context. See *Erasmus' Enchiridion Militis Christiani: An English Version*, ed. Anne M. O'Donnell (Oxford: Oxford University Press, 1981). The pregnancy of the word led to the semantic bifurcation of pity/piety, paralleled in French with *pitié* and *piété*.

[52] Quoted by Guy Bedouelle in *Le Quincuplex Psalterium de Lefèvre d'Etaples* (Geneva: Droz, 1979), 130 n. 3.

[53] Ibid.

"Erasmus' best are his religious poems," writes J. Kelley Sowards, endorsing the view expressed by Clarence Miller.[54] If Erasmus' response to events is apt to sound strangely secular, the same impression is given by the letters of his saintly friend, Thomas More. Faced with the domestic tribulations of Peter Gillis, More laments "the iniquitous vicissitude of mortal things,"[55] and Ammonio's sudden death inspires him with another this-worldly commonplace about fate.[56] In a similar vein Erasmus ascribes his first encounter with Colet to the god—"I can't tell which"—who had driven him to Oxford where Colet was publicly lecturing on Paul.[57] Recoiling from this unidentified deity, J. H. Lupton substitutes "some kind providence,"[58] but Erasmus was no doubt alluding to the adage from Homer about some "god always bringing like to like,"[59] and this, after all, makes belief in Providence, if less specifically Christian, the more deeply human and universal. Colet, he adds, loved topics which "prepared the soul for the immortality of the life to come."[60] Luther might shudder at this evocation of a Platonic future, so ethereal in comparison to the Resurrection. But remember the spirit of Europe in 1520. The soul's immortality had just been made an article of faith by the Fifth Lateran Council; marginal glosses to *Utopia* accuse the Christans of not believing it as firmly as do the pagans of Nowhere; and More, in his own epitaph, is grateful to be rid of worldly business, so he can "ponder the immortality of the life to come."[61] True, More goes on to express his desire to be with Christ, and Erasmus fully shared that expectation: after canonizing Colet and Vitrier, he prays their "happy souls" to intercede for him, and he looks forward to enjoying their company forever.[62]

---

[54] J. Kelley Sowards, review of *Erasmus of Rotterdam Society Yearbook* 1 (1981), in *Moreana*, 75–76 (1982): 64; Clarence H. Miller, "The Epigrams of Erasmus and More: A Literary Diptych," *Erasmus of Rotterdam Society Yearbook* 1 (1981): 24

[55] Allen 3: Ep. 601, line 10.

[56] Allen 3: Ep. 623, line 22. See my attempt to explain the secular tone of the early correspondence between Erasmus and More in "Thomas More's Spirituality," *St Thomas More: Action and Contemplation*, ed. R. S. Sylvester (New Haven: Yale University Press, 1972), 147–50.

[57] Godin, line 271.

[58] John C. Olin, ed., *Christian Humanism and the Reformation*, 3d ed. (New York: Fordham University Press, 1987), 167.

[59] CWE 31:167, adages 21 and 22. Erasmus quotes "the old proverb" (of God leading like to like) to Archbishop John Lasky in dedicating to him Saint Ambrose's *Opera* (Allen 7: Ep. 1855, line 60).

[60] Godin, lines 396–97.

[61] *English Works of Sir Thomas More*, 1421; and Allen 10: Ep. 2831, lines 108–9. The Utopian gloss is in CW 4:62.

[62] Godin, lines 607–8.

Erasmus parted company with medieval devotion by repeatedly expressing his dislike for the *Salve Regina*, a dislike shared by all Protestant Reformers. The riot of hyperboles, in a hymn born of the Crusades and the knightly
cult of the Virgin Mary, may have reminded him embarrassingly of the effu-
sive epithets which mark his own adolescent letters. He also seems to have
heard the *Salve* bawled during sea tempests by drunken sailors who ought
rather to have stood to their tacking. Nonetheless, we can safely imagine him
singing it with heart and voice at night prayer with the More household.[63]
Nor did he frown on the devotion of his English friends toward the rings hallowed by the touch of their king, Henry VIII. We find him passing a golden
one to his Antwerp banker—for wear, not for the metal.[64] This detail can be
added to the impressive array of evidence mustered by Halkin to illustrate the
traditional features, almost the ordinariness, of Erasmus' piety.[65]

The liturgical reform born of Vatican II has heeded Erasmus' plea for an
alleviation of the daily burden of vocal prayers which constitutes the divine
office. One is perhaps more surprised than edified to see busy prelates such as
Warham, Aleander, even Wolsey, faithful to its recitation. In a letter to Jacob
Batt of May 2, 1499, Erasmus, still a canon of Steyn, deplores the loss of a
hood which contained his breviary, but this item comes at the end of a list
which includes some underwear and ten pieces of gold.[66] He advocates not
praying less, but devoting more time to mental prayer, an emphasis emulated
by the mystics of the Catholic Reformation. He clearly agrees with Colet that
the binding recitation of so many prayers is a hardly bearable yoke for secular
priests with crowded schedules, and he welcomes the freedom of spirit Vitrier
manifests toward the office when traveling.[67] He encourages the faithful to

---

[63] Against Luther More defends "the common anthem of Our Lady and the most devout
Salve Regina" (CW 6:359). Erasmus' annoyance at its misuse is expressed in the colloquies "Ship-
wreck" (1523) and "A Fish Diet" (1526). See Craig R. Thompson, trans., *The Colloquies of Erasmus*
(Chicago: University of Chicago Press, 1965), 141, 142, 355. Yet Erasmus' poem on the *Salve Regina*
is an amazingly faithful rendering of it. See CWE 85:338–39.

[64] Having received an assortment of *sacrati annuli* at Padua, Thomas Lupset sent Erasmus
two golden ones (Allen 6: Ep. 1595, lines 112–15), one of which became Erasmus' Christmas gift for
Schets' wife: "Mitto uxori anulum aureum ab ipso Angliae Rege consecratum" (Allen 6: Ep. 1654,
line 32).

[65] Léon-E. Halkin, "Erasme pèlerin," *Scrinium Erasmianum*, 2 vols., ed. J. Coppens (Leiden:
Brill, 1969), 2:251: "Erasme, cependant, n'est pas de ces croyants aristocratiques qui, pour pra-
tiquer une religion éclairée, s'écartent de la voie commune. Il se veut et se sent dans l'Eglise; il
ambitionne d'être un chrétien parmi les autres, sinon comme les autres."

[66] Allen 1: Ep. 95, line 6.

[67] In annotating *iugum meum suave* (Matt. 11:30), Erasmus repeats the epithet *blandum*,
"mild," like the burden of his song. See *Erasmus' Annotations on the New Testament: The Gospels*, ed.
Anne Reeve (London: Duckworth, 1986), 53. Colet wonders why "quotidie tam prolixas preces
exhaurire cogerentur" (Godin, lines 489–90; for Vitrier, Godin, lines 139–42).

use their own words in addressing God and praises More for coining prayers instead of repeating routine ready-made formulas.[68] The Jesuits, who were being born as a Society during the last years of Erasmus' life—the first members took their vows at Montmartre on August 15, 1534—espoused his ideal of enlightened piety, with a lesser dose of ceremonies and practices for the sake of both learning and teaching, in humanities as well as the sacred sciences.[69]

ON HUSBANDING THE CHRISTIAN REVELATION

Erasmus' advocacy of *dissimulatio* is alarming unless one interprets the word in the light of patristic *oikonomia*. This "economy," or husbanding, of even revealed truths was received as normal pastoral practice right from the fervent and zealous beginnings of the church. In espousing and recommending it, Erasmus is a conscious and deliberate heir to that apostolic tradition. His urging *accommodatio* corresponds to the modern educational commonplace: "You need to know John before you teach him Latin." It calls for adjusting information, even of the most sacred kind, to the minds of the receivers.

Nowhere does Erasmus advocate this love-inspired pedagogy with more examples and more nuances than in his long epistle of May 10, 1521, to Jodocus Jonas, a young German priest whom he was warning against the intemperance of Luther and Hutten. This pedagogy is embodied in the parallel lives of Colet and Vitrier, described in a letter of June 13, 1521, in which Erasmus stresses the meritorious reticence in two priests who by temperament were outspoken, and by prophetic charisma fearless in proclaiming the truth. The Toronto translators exaggerate the contrast between those model pastors and their admiring biographer when they write: "If Ep 1202 was intended to explain and defend Erasmus' own position in the religious controversy, a position characterized by compromise and occasionally concealment, this letter presents two men who did not compromise and whom Erasmus may well have considered to be more perfect Christians than himself."[70] True, Erasmus looks up to these shining models with affectionate humility—even their tall, handsome physiques seem to symbolize heights of Christian purity above the reach of his own frail body. If they are perfect, it is not, however, because of

---

[68] Allen 4: Ep. 999, lines 272–73: "Habet suas horas, quibus Deo litet precibus, non ex more, sed e pectore depromptis." More composed a number of prayers, one written in the margins of his Book of Hours. See CW 13: 214–31.

[69] See John W. O'Malley, *The First Jesuits* (Cambridge: Harvard University Press, 1993).

[70] CWE 8: Ep. 1211, 225. "This letter" refers to Allen: Ep. 1211.

their refusal to compromise but because their love of souls, especially of the weaker consciences, prompts them to curb their own intransigence, and to hold their tongues for fear of occasioning scandal.

Why did Vitrier put up with the petty, or even idiotic, regulations of his friary? Because "he was ready to endure everything rather than be a cause of stumbling to any mortal man, following in this as in other things the example of his favourite, Paul."[71] Paul's name sends us to 1 Cor. 8:9 and 1 Cor. 9:19–22, the tacit inference being that Luther, who is so fond of the Apostle, should learn from him, not only the liberty of the spirit, but also the pastoral concern not to hurt tender consciences, nor to expose sore eyes to the full glare of the Christian revelation. Though boldly and proudly free from all human yokes and fears, Paul makes himself the slave of his catechumens, especially those in greatest need of nursing or breast-feeding in the faith. A concrete instance of Vitrier's circumspection is given apropos of an "accommodating" counsel he once gave to Erasmus about the Lenten fast, not before "looking round for his companion, who at the time was a layman, for fear he might be shocked."[72] In the very wording of his indulgent advice, the friar took the presence of the lay brother into account. When he crossed the Channel to visit Colet, it was not he who played the trenchant Stoic, but "another member of the same order."[73]

As for Colet, the vehement enunciator of startling paradoxes, two considerations help him curb his tongue: to avoid harming his reputation, a human motive which has some scriptural sanction too, and the nobler motive — to avoid scandal. "As he thus had himself always under suspicion, he avoided everything in which he might give offence to others."[74] That concerns his behavior, but two other statements have to do with the speaking of his mind: "in his opinions he differed widely from the majority, but ... showed great wisdom in adjusting himself to others in order not to give offence."[75] Before revealing to Erasmus his dislike of Aquinas, "Colet concealed his feelings two or three times and said nothing."[76] One last lesson for the hasty and violent Reformers is that Colet's discontent, born of his exposure to ancient theologians, never led him "to contend against the legislation of the church."[77]

---

[71] CWE 8: Ep. 1211, lines 45–47.
[72] Godin, line 150.
[73] Godin, line 240.
[74] Godin, lines 392–93.
[75] Godin, lines 402–3.
[76] Godin, line 416.
[77] Godin, line 458.

Very clearly, then, Erasmus' biographical diptych does not recommend a frontal assault on ideas and practices that need correcting. "Un mystique intransigeant" is André Godin's definition of Vitrier,[78] based on an acquaintance with the primary sources. But according to Erasmus' portrait, Vitrier, like Colet, learned to discipline his congenital impulse and prophetic impatience; to wink and dissemble at some abuses when taking vocal issue was likely to bear no fruit. Both of our good priests were led into this gentler attitude by the spirit of Christ, who is meek and compassionate for the multitude. Jesus is their model when they reserve their anger for the wolves who play the shepherds in order to fleece and devour the flock.[79] If they never tamper with the truth, they temper the expression of it. I find a perfect coherence between these exemplary *Lives* and the hardly less elaborate epistle which prepared Jonas for them—the two were published in the same *Epistolae ad diversos* of August 1521. They build the policy of *accommodatio* on the rock of inspired precedent. Christ attunes himself to the feelings of the Jews; he says one thing to the multitudes, another to his disciples.[80] So does Saint Peter in his preaching. Saint Paul "twists" the inscription on the Athenians' altar "into evidence for their faith, with the alteration and omission of several words."[81] "A Christian, I admit, ought to be free of all pretense," but there are occasions "when it is right for truth to remain unspoken."[82]

This sort of advice was apt to confirm the image of its author as a slippery eel, Luther's *anguis*, but in fact Erasmus' tread is firm: our two epistles are surrounded, in the *Epistolae ad diuersos*, with at least ten others which harp on the same string. The message of moderation and modulation, of steering cautiously between rock and whirlpool, is not limited to young clergy undergoing a crisis of identity; it is also addressed to magnates such as Cardinal Campeggi, Bishop Marliano, and Lord Mountjoy. Erasmus begins to inculcate this policy at least as early as July 6, 1520, when he writes: "The truth should not always be expressed, and the way it is expressed makes a great difference."[83] Allen's footnote to this sentence includes precious references to later letters which show silence to have been a leitmotiv in Erasmus' pastoral music, while shrillness increased on the part of both Luther and his opponents. "Though it is never right to go against the truth, it can be expedient to

---

[78] This is Godin's subtitle for a twenty-three-line paragraph. See Godin, 43.
[79] The bishops are expressly mentioned: Godin, line 453.
[80] CWE 8: Ep. 1202, lines 74–76.
[81] Godin, lines 112–13.
[82] Allen 4: Ep. 1202, lines 125–27.
[83] Allen 4: Ep. 1119, lines 40–41.

conceal it; that can even be a deed of piety and mercy."[84] "Truth possesses efficacy and is invincible, but should be dispensed with evangelical prudence."[85]
He is prepared "to forfeit a significant portion of the truth rather than shatter
the concord."[86] As imperial counselor, Erasmus is tempted to endorse Plato's
view that governors need the ruse of sound deception if they are to sway the
multitude. He mentions it to Leo X via Campeggi, to Charles V via Marliano,
and even to Luther via Melanchthon.[87] But as a Christian priest he cannot
condone even "good dupery: no room in Christians for lying!"[88]

This string of epistolary warnings tallies with several annotations to the
New Testament. We already heard Erasmus' remarks on Acts 17:22–31—Paul's
strategy to win the ear of the Athenians. Here is his comment on 1 Cor. 7:39:
"The first mark of a piety worthy of the Apostles is to cater to the salvation of
all as far as one may, and to apply one's care to succor even the weak members
of the church." As for Holy Scripture, "it is the task of a pious and prudent
steward to accommodate it to the community's way of life."[89] As early as the
Enchiridion, Erasmus echoed the Apostle's special solicitude toward "the weak
brethren for whom Christ died."[90] Such a phrase assumes that Christ is no
mere *praeceptor* or *archetypus* or even *scopus*, but the redeemer. His friendship,
which Erasmus prizes for himself and to which he calls his readers, involves
the equality of all genuine friendship, the total sharing praised in the first
adage.

The mystical union between head and member, which is Erasmus' ideal,
is attuned to the mysticism of Colet and Vitrier, and is a far cry from a desic-
cated asceticism. Pastoral chores never prevented those priests from making
time for sacred studies and contemplation. Vitrier performed the two specific
tasks of the priest: "he taught the people and offered sacrifice."[91] Colet

---

[84] Allen 4: Ep. 1167, lines 164–66; Ep. 1195, lines 105–9.

[85] Allen 5: Ep. 1331, line 20.

[86] Allen 5: Ep. 1331, lines 23–24.

[87] Allen 4: Epp. 1167, 1195; and Allen 6: Ep. 1523.

[88] Allen 5: Ep. 1523, lines 85–86.

[89] *Annotations on the New Testament: Acts, Romans, I and II Corinthians*, ed. Anne Reeve and
M. A. Screech (Leiden: E. J. Brill, 1990), 467. In Allen 4: Ep. 1183, lines 83–85, Erasmus imagines
Saint Peter himself compelled to connive at things he could not approve if he were now ruling the
church.

[90] Holborn, 85. In the 1518 preface to Volz, Erasmus repeats the echo to Rom. 14:15 and 1
Cor. 8:11 by extending the notion of weak brothers to the unlearned masses—"imperitae multitu-
dini, pro qua mortuus est Christus" (Holborn, 5). Cf. the colloquy *Ichthyophagia* (1526): "Et
procul abest a charitate Christiana, qui ob potum aut cibum, quo recte quis uti potest, exasperat
fratrem, pro cuius libertate mortuus est Christus" (ASD 1–3:505).

[91] Godin, lines 173–74: ". . . docebat populum et Christo sacrificabat." The dative "Christo"
is unexpected, since Christ is the victim and the priest of the sacrifice. The phrase may reflect the
"ministrantibus Deo" of Acts 13:2, in which the verb, Erasmus says, means "offered sacrifice."

achieved the same balance at Saint Paul's School. Although teaching was the main goal, Mass was celebrated daily on the premises, and the boys stood up from their seats and knelt when the bell announced the consecration.[92]

Godin draws a parallel between the two *Lives* and Erasmus' *Convivium religiosum* of the same period. The "religious banquet" follows the pattern of meals at Colet's frugal table. A reading from the Bible triggers an exchange which is not limited to professional scholars. Neatness is the dominant concern.[93] An image of Christ transfigured adorns the wall, with the Father saying "Hear ye him" (Mark 9:6). The scandal of the weak comes up for discussion. Joy is presented as the sign of a good conscience and a faithful Christian hope, especially at the hour of death.[94]

ECONOMY IN MATTER AND MANNER

Oikonomia, as we have seen, is Erasmus' resolute program. He sees it as an expression of *pietas*. Although he will not endorse Plato's advocacy of lying as an instrument of government, he is no Stoic enemy to officious lying which causes no harm, and to a partiality which may achieve fairness even at the expense of strict justice. In his first extant letter to Erasmus, More confesses to a good deal of diplomatic concealment in dealing with his friend's hopes of benefice and patronage,[95] and yet Erasmus shared the letter with Peter Gillis, who proceeded to share it, through publication, with every literate European, including the prelates who might have been hoodwinked by More's not speaking the whole truth. Later, More would beat about the bush rather than admit Erasmus' authorship of *Julius exclusus*. His evasive formulas did not prevent the truth from emerging, and he may have welcomed that timely emergence.

The handling of truth will never become a simple moral and spiritual issue. Saint Paul's Jesus is "yea" and "amen" in 2 Cor. 1:20; his name in Rev. 3:17 is Amen. Yet, *pace* Luther the great hater of "amphibology," the same fearless Apostle is the greatest advocate of a pedagogy which adjusts the good

---

[92] Godin, note to line 338.

[93] Godin, appendix 3, 127–133. Compare the verbs "nitent," "niteat" with the "nitidum" of Colet's meals (Godin, line 298).

[94] The quality of death is emphasized as a test of genuine piety in Erasmus' colloquy *Funus* (ASD 1–3:537–51); "alacritas spiritus" marks the death of Vitrier's charges (Godin, lines 111–17). The good Utopian also dies "alacriter" (CW 4, 222).

[95] Allen 2: Ep. 388, lines 32–85.

news to the mentality and the mental capacity of its recipients. "Dispensing the truth is a matter of wise husbanding."[96] The content of revelation is not threatened by the manner of its handling. While stressing the basic harmony of early Christian classics, More adds that "once they varied in the manner of their doctrine." Here "manner" means, above all, terminology.[97]

In his *De conscribendis epistolis*, a manual for letter-writing, Erasmus gives a specimen of "oblique request."[98] He uses the nautical metaphor by which More, in *Utopia*, defends the biased indirect approach[99]:

> If we advise someone not to go ahead obstinately with what he deems to be in itself the best but to adapt himself to the present situation, we shall borrow a likeness from the wise shipman, who does not always steer his vessel along the straight route he would long to take, but frequently adjusts himself to the tempest, frequently to the winds. He "flexes" his sails not toward the harbour he had set out to reach, but to the one made accessible by the present weather.[100]

A text from Colet, which Erasmus probably never read, throws light on why the fiery dean tempered his own instinctive directness. It bears on Saint Paul's flexibility in the presence of so many different audiences encountered in the Hellenic world alone:

> Prudence, then, and caution were part of the agenda, with due rating of persons, places and times. By taking these into account, Paul was for sure the most considerate of all men; having an end-purpose in view, he knew how to adapt the means toward that end in such a way that, although he sought nothing else than the glory of Jesus Christ on earth, and the increase of faith and love, he used a superhuman shrewdness, neither doing nor omitting anything toward anybody which might hinder or delay the achieving of his purpose.[101]

Being addressed to all, even to the outlandish Scots and the miscreant Turks, the Christian revelation is not Hermetic. It is open, yet it calls for continued opening. Its very universality demands a refined hermeneutics in exploring it, and a broad rhetoric in formulating and proclaiming it. The way

[96] Allen 4: Ep. 1202, lines 56–57.
[97] CW 8:248.
[98] ASD 1–2:467.
[99] CW 4:98, 102: "obliquus ductus."
[100] ASD 1–2:237.
[101] Paul is "unus omnium consideratissimus." My "superhuman" is an attempt to render "divina." See another translation, facing the Latin text, in *John Colet's Commentary on First Corinthians*, ed. Bernard O'Kelly and Catherine A. L. Jarrot (Binghamton: Medieval and Renaissance Texts and Studies, 1985), 74–75.

Elizabeth McCutcheon analyzes More's distinction between *mentiri* and *mendacium dicere* in *Utopia*,[102] the most Erasmian of More's books, provides some clues, by way of literary parallels, to the idea of pastoral accommodation and to its practical embodiment in creative writing. The laws of persuasive and stimulating communication can govern Erasmus' classical *paideia* as applied to his priestly office. Like the *paterfamilias* of Matt. 20:1, he draws from his treasure new things and old, adorning theology with the spoils of Egypt, baiting and luring the young to accept the good news as truly new and truly good.

Moria and *Utopia* were written by Christians for Christians in a climate of reformist fervor. Why then should they bristle with hurdles and cruxes? Because their authors are poets: neither of them denies the label even when it is meant to make them less credible.[103] Especially blurred is the boundary between the serious and the humorous: "many times men doubt whether ye speak in sport when ye mean good earnest," a puzzled young man says to More.[104] Colet in similar suspense peered into Erasmus' eyes to try and guess whether it was "in earnest or in sport" that he had spoken well of Saint Thomas Aquinas.[105] Is irony excluded from Erasmus' statement that Colet was hostile or at least unfair to Saint Augustine? Many interpreters offered to read *iniquus* as *partial*, but Erasmus' usage, however elastic, will not authorize such an evasion. The only way out, I believe, is to remember that Erasmus is a poet, and letter-writing is literature, not science. Just as we need not believe that his letter of June 1521 to Jonas is a response to Jonas' own request, although he says so in the opening sentence, just so we need not believe that Colet was hostile to Augustine. As Colet was apt to overstate his mind, a mind also liable to moods of irritation, he provided a perfect voice for crying "Wolf!" in Erasmus' attempt to warn the Lutherans against an excessive cult of Saint Augustine.[106]

---

[102] Elizabeth McCutcheon, *My Dear Peter: The Ars Poetica and Hermeneutics for More's "Utopia"* (Angers: Moreanum, 1983), 44–55. Peter Bietenholz, "'Simulatio': Erasme et les interprétations controversées de Galates 2:11–14," in *Actes du Colloque international Erasme*, ed. Jacques Chomarat, André Godin, and Jean-Claude Margolin (Geneva: Droz, 1990), 161–69, uses the confrontation between Saint Peter and Saint Paul, with Erasmus' commentary thereon, as a prism for the ethics of pretending.

[103] Allen: 4, Ep. 1196, line 450: "Contemnite quantum voletis 'poetriam'." For Tyndale and Joye, both Erasmus and More are liars simply because they are poets. Even Colet is accused of being a poet (Godin, lines 541–42). See J. B. Trapp's note on this charge of "feigning" in CW 9:329–30.

[104] CW 6:69.

[105] Godin, lines 417–18.

[106] Godin, line 262: "nulli erat iniquior Augustino." Lupton explains this "iniquior" with another: "Augustinus ex colluctatione cum Pelagio factus est iniquior libero arbitrio quam fuerat ante" (22): striving with Pelagius has made Augustine more unfair, more unfavorable to free will than he had been. This bias influenced Luther, of whom More has heard, perhaps via Erasmus, that as a loyal Augustinian he holds doggedly to the teaching of Augustine: "Augustini doctrinam mordicus tenens." See *The Correspondence of Sir Thomas More*, ed. E. F. Rogers (Princeton: Princeton University Press, 1947), 171 and CW 15:214.

Coupling a negative with a comparative, *iniquior* is doubly characteristic of Erasmus' elusive way of "denying the contrary."[107] In *apologia* after *apologia*, he keeps denying constructions put on his writings by the bad faith or the ignorance of readers. In not a few letters he does the same. Thus Vincentius Theodorici has interpreted *in totum* as meaning "totally," whereas it means "on the whole, generally speaking," the result being that, in a sentence concerning the Eucharist, he has read "a monstrous falsehood."[108] Erasmus chides him for this poor command of Latin, but he is himself taken to task by the Valladolid theologians for not using the vocabulary of the profession when he writes theology. It is no doubt in protest against their excessive use of a specialized jargon that he chooses common parlance in matters of the Christian revelation, which are common to all the people of God.

Erasmus recognizes, however, that he should have imitated Vitrier and Colet in their care not to cause scandal by an overfree expression of criticism. In 1530, he evokes the quieter times when he underestimated the tenderness of some consciences. Now, he "takes care to give nobody any offence, especially in devotional writings."[109]

As the *Ciceronianus* proves, Erasmus would not allow a concern for the purity of Latin to degenerate into a superstitious cult. Meanwhile, however, that concern had affected his own translation of the New Testament to a point which caused alarm (or delight) and raised protests. Thomas More fought by his friend's side on two fronts. In 1515–1520, he told the rearguard scholastics that it was no sin to substitute a native Latin word like *verriculum* where the Vulgate had merely transliterated the Greek *sagena*.[110] In 1529–1532, he urged that, as a Latin writer, Erasmus had a sound reason for preferring *congregatio* to the Greek *ecclesia*, whereas Tyndale had no such reason for discarding "church," a well-established English word. His substituting the neologism "congregation" could only betoken a "malicious intent." More went on to vindicate Erasmus' orthodoxy with a defiant vigor which is impressive, coming from the champion of the old faith and Erasmus' closest friend for now thirty-three years. Erasmus, More writes, "detesteth and abhorreth the errors and heresies that Tyndale plainly teacheth and abideth by," and that he "meant none heresy" in his occasional change of words "appeareth by his writing

---

[107] This echoes Elizabeth McCutcheon's essay "Denying the Contrary: More's Use of Litotes in *Utopia*," *Moreana* 31–32 (November 1971), reprinted in *Essential Articles for the Study of Thomas More*, ed. R. S. Sylvester and G. P. Marc'hadour (Hamden, Connecticut: Archon, 1977), 263–74.
[108] Allen 4: Ep. 1196, lines 71–80.
[109] Allen 8: Ep. 2315, line 302.
[110] CW 15: 230.

against heretics." More adds that "the infection" of heresy has "so sore poi-
soned" the atmosphere that he himself would with both hands burn some
innocent writings of his friend's and of his own.[111] He insists that "*Moria* doth
in deed but jest upon the abuses of such things, after the manner of a disour's
part in a play."[112] The word "disour" fits the glib "facundity" of Dame Folly
while the word "play," in the sense of drama, covers Erasmus' colloquies.
These share with the *Moria* (and *Utopia*) that ludic, dialogic, teasing quality
which still draws avid readers, brave translators, and busy commentators. Yet,
under that guise, they convey the same "philosophy of Christ" as the *Enchiridion*, and they call to the same combat.[113]

On April 8, 1556, the Council of Trent condemned the improper use of
Holy Scripture for secular purposes, and Erasmus was censured for thus
offending when he quoted from the Bible in his *Adagia*. Yet he had carried this
practice less far than many popular preachers of his day, and he himself
inveighs against the blasphemous habit of using the Word of God in vain.[114]

ERASMUS' ENDURING UBIQUITY

Traduttore traditore: "translator means traitor," the Italians say. Erasmus
is frequently betrayed in translation or paraphrase, and a J. A. Froude, for
instance, was a notorious *traditore*.[115] Recourse to the Latin original is imper-
ative for any important statement. The Toronto edition itself, although excellent on the whole, can be misleading. Since nowhere else does Erasmus
express his idea of the priesthood so fully as in his epistle on Colet and Vitrier,
I have read its latest translation in volume 8 of the *Collected Works of Erasmus*.
There Erasmus is made to write: "I myself was sometimes invited to go with
Colet on pilgrimage."[116] I concluded hastily that these two priests visited more
shrines together than the Walsingham and Canterbury which are the subject

---

[111] CW 8: 177, 178–79.
[112] CW 8: 178. See Walter M. Gordon, *Humanist Play and Belief: The Seriocomic Art of Desiderius Erasmus* (Toronto: University of Toronto Press, 1990), 81–254.
[113] Allen 2: Ep. 337, lines 91–92.
[114] Skelton, whom Erasmus had encountered at court during his first visit, played the priest
by stuffing his verse with scraps from the Latin liturgy. Even a grave prelate such as Warham links
the purgation of Erasmus' kidneys with the feast of Our Lady's Purification (Allen 1: Ep. 286, lines
3–4). The section "Pastiche and Parodie" in my *Thomas More et la Bible* (Paris: Vrin, 1969), 478–
483, includes Erasmian references.
[115] See J. A. Froude, *Life and Letters of Erasmus* (London: Longmans, 1895).
[116] CWE 8: Ep. 1211, line 358.

of the colloquy *Peregrinatio religionis ergo*. Thus, I mused, for all their flippant comments on disgusting abuses, they were habitual pilgrims. Does not "sometimes" imply "more than twice"? But the original has neither "sometimes" nor indeed the pilgrimage. Lupton had been more accurate: "Occasionally he took me with him for company on a journey."[117]

The Eucharist being the chief treasure committed to a priest, Erasmus' attitude towards it is the litmus test of his faith and piety. The European context is lucidly exposed by James Tracy.[118] The British context is of special significance, because nowhere in Christendom was devotion to the Blessed Sacrament more visible than in England, as if the nation would make amends for Wyclif's anathematized challenges. Both universities had a Corpus Christi College, that of Oxford being founded by Erasmus' own friend Bishop Fox of Winchester. Every city of some size had a Corpus Christi cycle of pageants and plays, with a procession during which the guilds vied with each other in paying homage to the monstrance. Even swearwords like "Godbody" and "By the Mass" are witnesses to the fascination exercised by the Eucharist. The London goldsmiths reserved their masterpieces for the sacred vessels which were to contain the Lord's body and blood, hence the complaint, uttered by both Fisher and Colet, that in earlier days golden priests had celebrated in wooden chalices, whereas now golden chalices were being used by wooden priests.[119]

One aberration lay in the fact that a holy voyeurism had replaced active participation. Christ's command "Do this in memory of me" was obeyed only by the officiating priest. The royal family set the fashion of "hearing" Mass each and every day, and their better subjects emulated the practice, not truly "partaking of the table of the Lord," since they seldom went to Holy Communion. Pastors had come to terms with this anomaly. In 1509, preaching the funeral oration of the Lady Margaret, his spiritual child, John Fisher praised her devotion to Mass, and thought her exemplary because she received Holy Communion once a month. Catherine of Aragon caused some surprise by receiving it each Sunday. By dint of reading the Fathers for polemical purposes, Fisher became aware that a frequent Mass-goer should be a frequent communicant.[120]

[117] Lupton, 20.

[118] James D. Tracy, *Erasmus: The Growth of a Mind* (Geneva: Droz, 1972). In *Moreana* 46 (May 1975): 92, I take issue with Tracy's endorsement of Marie Delcourt's thesis of an "estrangement" between Erasmus and More.

[119] The comparison, attributed to Saint Boniface, is found also in Savonarola. See commentary on CW 6:40, lines 26–27, at CW 6:608.

[120] Another sign of Margaret Beaufort's devotion to the Eucharist is her translation "out of French into English" of bk. 4 of the *Imitatio Christi*, "which treateth most specially of the Sacrament of the Altar." The Latin title is *De sacramento*.

One popular superstition connected with the raising of the host was that "seeing God" made one's eyes proof against blindness. When the *Sanctus* bell rang, people would flock to church in order to view the white host above the priest's tonsured head, and then would go out again. Nor did physical presence betoken active participation. Vives tells Erasmus that Henry VIII sampled the *De libero arbitrio* "during Mass."[121] The presence of Christ has become more important than the drama of his sacrifice or the invitation to his wedding-feast. His very presence is slighted when a hymn to the Virgin Mary is sung during consecration, or when a relic of her milk is shown to pilgrims with such zest that they forget about her divine son in the tabernacle.[122]

Erasmus has taught the baptized laity to exercise their priesthood by turning their whole life into one continued Eucharist, a sacrifice of praise and thanksgiving united with the self-giving sacrifice of Christ. That universal call to holiness and militance is now quite explicit in such official documents as Vatican II's *Lumen gentium*, John Paul II's *Christifideles laici* of 1989, and the 1992 *Catechism of the Catholic Church*.

Priests of Erasmus' kind, yet without his genius, have graced, and bothered, every generation of the church's life. By temperament and education they feel less need than most for the Sacraments. Their piety is less demonstrative, and they are easily put off by too much corporal expression or by overinsistence on ritual. A modern priest of this type will, for instance, attend Mass from the pew whenever saying it on his own would entail some bother: locating a sacristan, finding a chalice, dressing an altar, etc. Concelebration, an uncomplicated procedure which stresses ecclesial *concordia*, is one blessing of the new liturgy which would appeal to Erasmus. The rubrics have gone his way by considerably reducing the gestures of the priest at the altar and by simplifying the ritual of all Sacraments.

In October 1536, Pope Paul III, who had offered Erasmus the cardinalate, instituted a commission *De emendanda ecclesia*, "for the amendment of the church." The document which resulted was Erasmian in more than one feature, for instance the suggestion that a moratorium be placed on the recruitment of mendicant orders, since the horde of friars were considered an obstacle to reform. The new institute which had meanwhile come into

---

[121] Allen 5: Ep. 1513, line 5: "inter sacra." O. B. Hardison, *Christian Rite and Christian Drama in the Middle Ages* (Baltimore: Johns Hopkins University Press, 1965), 35–79, draws on Dürer and other artists to illustrate the civic dimension of Eucharistic piety.

[122] In the colloquy "A Pilgrimage for Religion's Sake," Erasmus records an exception to the danger of Mary's standing in the shadow of Jesus. The larger church at Walsingham is reserved for Christ: "in honor of her son she yields that to him." See Thompson, *Colloquies of Erasmus*, 292.

existence, the Society of Jesus, was committed to *pietas litterata*. Its founder was a knight who had gone back to school. On November 1, 1536, Ignatius' companions, on their way from Paris to Rome, paused at Basel to visit the tomb of Erasmus, and the Jesuit *ratio studiorum* would one day implement the essence of his educational program. These men were religious by profession, yet not monks, and teaching was to prove the principal form of their ministry.

Erasmus' emphasis on the importance of instruction makes all the more sense when one remembers that most prelates, even the pious Archbishop Warham, never gave a sermon. And the professional preachers, namely the friars, often neglected to prepare their minds and hearts the way Colet and Vitrier did, by long rumination of Holy Scripture. "It is a heinous offence if a man partakes unworthily of the Lord's body, but greater disaster results for many people if a man adulterates the words of the Gospel," wrote Erasmus.[123] More agreed, to witness his stern letter to the reverend heads of his *alma mater oxoniensis* after a Lenten preacher had inveighed against liberal studies from the pulpit, thus desecrating "the majesty of the preacher's hallowed office which won the world over for Christ."[124] The more learned clerics and monks, knowing the Latin Vulgate by heart, were tempted to draw on it in season and out of season. Both Erasmus and More denounced this taking of the Lord's Word in vain; More satirized that "most inexcusable game" by writing parodies of it.[125]

While the Sacraments—including baptism, the Eucharist, anointing the sick, and reconciling the sinners—occupy a priest off and on, "his teaching office is perpetual," Erasmus writes in *Ecclesiastes*, "and without it all his other functions are useless."[126] The priest has to be more perfect than the lay person because it is "to him that the sword of the Spirit, which is the Word of God, has been entrusted."[127] Insufficiently versed in the languages of the countries where he resided and, it seems, not gifted with a strong voice, Erasmus cannot have preached much. But he wrote model sermons, one of which, composed for Colet's schoolboys, soon received the honor of translation.[128]

---

[123] CWE 8: Ep. 1164, lines 36–38.
[124] CW 15:134.
[125] On the game, see CW 15:272–73. Commenting on "scurrilitas" (Eph. 5:4), Erasmus denounces the insipid or aggressive jokes couched in scriptural terms. See *Erasmus' Annotations on the New Testament: Galatians to Apocalypse*, ed. Anne Reeve (Leiden: E. J. Brill, 1993), 611.
[126] ASD 5–4:202.
[127] ASD 5–4:54
[128] On the early Spanish translation of *Concio de puero Jesu* into *Sermón del niño Jesús* see Marcel Bataillon, *Erasme et l'Espagne*, ed. Daniel Devoto and Charles Amiel, rev. ed., 3 vols. (Geneva: Droz, 1991), 1:222, 2:81–82.

If Vitrier, who was apt to preach as often as seven times in one day, and Colet, who occasionally skipped Mass in order to have more time for preparing his sermons, were exemplary in this respect, we must not forget John Fisher, who was the lodestar of pulpit oratory in England, and to whose insistence we owe Erasmus' *Ecclesiastes*. Fisher was the official preacher for royal funerals and for anti-Lutheran demonstrations. Seventeen sermons by him survive in printed books of his day, and his sequence of ten sermons on the Penitential Psalms went through at least seven editions. He funneled the Lady Margaret's bequests into the endowment of university preacherships.[129]

This trait more than any other endeared Fisher to Erasmus. The posthumous words, addressed to another bishop, by which he praises Fisher for using a unique pattern of pastoral care in teaching the people,[130] sum up similar compliments in earlier letters. Though alarmed by the vagueness and ambiguity of Erasmus in phrasing his rejection of Oecolampadius' doctrine, the good bishop never ceased to be Erasmus' *discipulus*.[131] He proved his confidence in him by giving him a chair in Cambridge and by inviting him to be his escort at the Fifth Lateran Council.[132] No Catholic apologist, to my knowledge, invoked Erasmus' authority more frequently. Fisher quoted him against Lefèvre to reject as spurious the correspondence between Seneca and Saint Paul; then against Luther to point out that in Acts 13:2 the verb *leitourgein* refers to the Eucharistic sacrifice; then against Oecolampadius, giving him first place, even before Cochlaeus, among the German champions of the Catholic church.[133] Fisher's support was reciprocated. Erasmus in 1519 calls Fisher his *unicum praeceptorem*,[134] and his *De libero arbitrio* was written with Fisher's *Assertionis Lutheranae confutatio* at hand. This osmosis between the two theologians is the best proof of their profound unity in the faith. The greatness of the bishop lies in the heroic energy with which he did his homework. Erasmus assumed Oecolampadius to be in honest error, and found fault only with his insolence in challenging the Eucharistic faith of the whole

---

[129] In the prefatory letter to *Ecclesiastes*, Erasmus devotes a full page to Fisher's achievements in this regard, ASD 5–4: 31–32.

[130] ASD 5–4: 142.

[131] He signs himself "Discipulus tuus Io. Roffensis" in a letter of 1517. See Allen 2: Ep. 592, line 25.

[132] Circumstances prevented John Fisher from actually taking part. Nor was Erasmus sure, afterwards, that the Council had been truly ecumenical: "De conciliis non ausim aliquid dicere, nisi forte proximum Concilium Lateranense concilium non fuit" (Allen 5: Ep. 1268, lines 35–36).

[133] "Erasmus imprimis, qui partes Ecclesiae catholicae . . . inuictissime docet," in preface to the *De veritate corporis* (Cologne: Quentel, 1527), fol. BB4, or Fisher's *Opera Omnia* (Würzburg, 1597), col. 748.

[134] Allen 3: Ep. 996, lines 63–64.

church, whereas Fisher's scrutiny enabled him to lay his finger on truncations and omissions which cumulatively amounted to a betrayal of patristic testimonies.[135]

Paradox as a literary device is not unfitting for Christian theology, since the very substance of the Gospel is a paradox, a "folly to the Gentiles" (1 Cor. 1:23) who survive in baptized Christians. Yet Erasmus avoids extremes even in formulation. Luther's petulant equations, such as "the pope is Antichrist" and "the Mass is a blasphemy," or Colet's dictum that "the wisdom of the pagans comes from the devil,"[136] have no counterparts in Erasmus' works. His earliest and best-known formula, that "Monkhood is not piety,"[137] is comparatively mild, thanks to its negative form. It is a far cry from "Monkhood is impiety," as he himself explained. It belongs with older sayings such as *L'habit ne fait pas le moine*: "the habit does not make the monk."

In brief, the believer Erasmus agrees with the artist in treading a via media between the complications of allegorical exegesis or scholastic distinctions on the one hand, and on the other the mighty simplifications, which for instance resolve the mystery of predestination by robbing man of his free will and moral responsibility.

Multiple exposure begets some experience and engenders caution. I knew from personal encounter many of our brave ancestors in *Erasmophilia*: Marcel Bataillon, Henry de Vocht, Pierre Mesnard, Marie Delcourt, Henri de Lubac, Roland Bainton, E. E. Reynolds, Marcel Nauwelaerts, Gordon Rupp, Margaret Mann Phillips. They were all proof against spellbinding. Erasmus was for them a quiet, comradely presence, a professor of patience and of hoping against hope that truth will have the last word.

Phillips goes furthest of them all when in her last paper she calls him the "guide of her soul."[138] She watched her mentor Augustin Renaudet undergo a

---

[135] Rex, in *Theology of John Fisher*, 137, gives three examples of deliberate tampering with sources in Oecolampadius' treatise.

[136] *John Colet's Commentary on First Corinthians*, 218.

[137] *Enchiridion*, Holborn, 135.

[138] Margaret Mann Phillips, "Visages d'Erasme," *Colloque Erasmien de Liège*, ed. Jean-Pierre Massaut (Paris: Société d'Editions "Les Belles Lettres," 1987), 17–29.

conversion from viewing Erasmus as a rationalist emancipated from Christian dogma to labeling him a Catholic theologian tinged with modernism, a judgment not all that far from the charge of Pelagianism made by Luther and Tyndale. As for the sentence from which Renaudet inferred that Erasmus dreamt of a third church, better than either Rome or Wittenberg, she thanks John Olin and Jean-Claude Margolin for convincing her that it means something much more realistic as well as touchingly humble.[139] She endorses Screech's conclusion that Erasmus, as elucidator of the Psalms and other inspired books, was no mere philologist; he was also a prophet, and opened the Silenus of the Old Testament in a way that should lead his readers to Christ as life everlasting, not just as a model. From Halkin's essay "La piété d'Erasme," she cites a passage ending with the phrase "christianisme critique," the subtitle of Mesnard's book on Erasmus. She winds up her survey by pointing out with joyful pride that this half-century has been privileged to perceive "la vocation religieuse d'Erasme."[140]

Erasmus' canonical title for the priesthood was his being already a professed member of a religious community. Ordination added nothing to his obligations as a professed canon. It empowered him to teach, to absolve, and to consecrate. He fulfilled the first of these mandates with exemplary talent and zeal, paying the full price in strenuous study, and accepting buffets from left and right. He was the *miles christianus* of his early treatise, and Luther is unjust when he accuses him of not fighting as a doctor should.[141]

Yet, as teaching is less hieratic than the sacramental ministry, because it is exercised mostly outside of the liturgical context, Erasmus the preceptor and catechist will never convey a sacerdotal image; the less so because, like thousands of priest-teachers after him, he refused to divorce religion from culture, theology from the humanities. To a younger layman like More, he may have been the "soul's guide" mentioned by Phillips, but hardly the "reverend Father in God," an address More uses for other priests. In the two letters appealing to Erasmus' Christian soul, More says nothing that suggests a layman writing to a priest. "You sweat for Christ, expect from him your

---

[139] "Fero igitur hanc Ecclesiam donec video meliorem, et eadem me ferre cogitur donec ipse fiam melior." See a fuller treatment in *Moreana* 98–99 (Dec. 1988): 216, and C. Augustijn, "The Ecclesiology of Erasmus," *Scrinium Erasmianum*, 2: 154–55.

[140] Phillips, "Visages d'Erasme," 29. *Erasme, ou le christianisme critique* (Paris: Seghers, 1969) was the swan song of Pierre Mesnard, who defined the other side of Erasmus' Christianity as "mystique légère," a light dose of mysticism.

[141] "Ad doctorem pertinet docere et pugnare, lehren und wehren: Erasmus neutrum facit." Quoted in C. Augustijn, "Erasmus und seine Theologie: hatte Luther recht?," in *Colloque Erasmien de Liège*, 55.

reward," he says in April 1520, and in 1526 he almost chides him for procrastination in finishing *Hyperaspistes*.[142]

The church, as we have seen, is for Erasmus not a neutral "it," nor a distant "they," but the maternal and bridal mystery of Christ's continued presence on earth. She awaits the conversion of her children. She alone knows the mind of the Bridegroom; she alone interprets it with full authority. In the *Enchiridion*, Erasmus appropriates "the bold saying of Paul" in Rom. 8:38–39: "Who shall separate us from the love of God ? ... Neither death nor life shall or may separate us from the love of God which is in Christ Jesus." That is the challenging tone he adopts, using the same words to express his attachment to the church: "As for me, neither death nor life will wrench me from the fellowship of the Catholic church."[143]

In the days of unchecked clerical dominance, Erasmus accused the friars of being tyrants in beggars' disguise, but when the wind turned against them, and the "beggar-tyrants" were threatened by the physical violence of tyrannical knights, such as Hutten, he shielded them. These assaults on the Dominicans, he writes, may escalate to "savage attacks against priests of every kind of cloth," and he refers to the precedent of Hussite Bohemia, as More was to do. The wealth taken from the clergy will not be spent on relieving the poor, because the equestrian class, after impiously robbing the priests, will put the spoils to worse uses.[144]

The duty of praying is not much stressed at the ordination, since the daily load of the breviary has already been accepted at profession or subdiaconate. Yet praying is the prime function of a priest, as Erasmus points out via Plutarch: "A city honours its priests because they pray to the gods for the common good of all men."[145] Despite the anticlerical mood of the period, the world of priests provided a prestigious social model. They ruled the academic roost and held enviable sway in government. England's chancellors had all been churchmen for two centuries till in 1529 More received the Great Seal of the realm. The way the laity cultivated a clerical image was by two visible practices: reciting the canonical hours and hearing Mass every day. Erasmus angered Béda of the Sorbonne by saying that such devotions, even done with a sincere heart, were not "perfect religion and the height of piety," and that a lay prince renders God a more agreeable sacrifice if he strives to eliminate war

---

[142] Allen 4: Ep. 1090, lines 25–27; Allen 6: Ep. 1770, lines 12–48.
[143] Allen 5: Ep. 1273, line 27.
[144] Allen 4: Ep. 1129, lines 22–25.
[145] CWE 23:193.

and famine, to foster peace, to respect civil liberties, and to check corruption among public servants.[146] This firm statement of priorities tallies with Jesus' vigorous denunciation of smug pharisaic formalism (Matt. 23:13–29) and with Saint James' equally accusatory reminder of what true religion entails (James 1:27–4:17).

Erasmus' downplaying of his priestly character in order to stress the vocation he shared with all Christians through their baptism was meant as a corrective to the clerical emphases of his day's spirituality. The eggs he thus laid were not for Luther alone to hatch. Some are to be found in the basket of the Catholic Reformation: in the life and writings of Saint Francis de Sales and Fénelon; in the *Reducciones* of Paraguay; in the papal encyclicals which from *Rerum Novarum* (1891) to *Centesimus Annus* (1991) have enriched the church's moral theology with a social wing, and inspired a host of generous initiatives. Several labels of modern charities sound Erasmian in their supranational Latinity—*Caritas, Misereor, Pax Christi*, and so forth. He would—from heaven he does—applaud the secular institutes which have mushroomed over the last decades, and the lay, sometimes interdenominational, movements which in various countries are responding to the call for this millennium to end with a decade of evangelization. Most of these organizations wish to implement Vatican II and John Paul II's *Christifideles laici*, by making justice and peace their cornerstones and asserting a predilection for the poor.

John Henry Newman deserves special mention, because he was born in the London which became Erasmus' second home, and in which English editions of Erasmus' works have continued to appear—over thirty different works before 1700. Newman was Erasmus' heir most visibly when he laid stress "on consulting the faithful in matters of doctrine," instead of letting Rome dictate every word and control every step taken by Catholics all over the planet. Like Erasmus, he made foes on both sides of the ecclesial spectrum, becoming a *persona grata* with the pope only at the end of his life. Leo XIII's bestowal of the red hat touched him deeply, and permission to remain on his island home enabled him to accept. Although Erasmus declined the honor, he circulated copies of the pope's letter offering it. If a cardinal is first and foremost a papal counsellor, Erasmus had played the part ever since the election of Leo X. His loyalty to the Holy See is attested by long letters to the Medici popes, then to Adrian VI and Paul III. These contain plenty of firm advice, and the spice of flattery is itself an oblique form of exhortation.

[146] Erasmus says it most insistently in his letter dedicating the *Paraphrase on John's Gospel* to King Ferdinand, the emperor's brother (Allen 5: Ep. 1333, lines 280–91).

In calling the pope *pontifex*, not *papa*, Erasmus is simply using humanist Latin, as also in adopting the expression *philosophia Christi*. Scripture has little regard for "philosophy," but tradition has enobled the term. If *sophia*, "wisdom," expresses the ideal, the prefix *philo* humbly acknowledges that one claims, not to be wise, but to be wisdom's friend and client.

John Colet "looked up to the wonderful majesty of Christ."[147] His contemplation blended Platonic enthusiasm with feudal loyalty to his Lord. Yet, as early as 1499, Erasmus had warned Colet against dehumanizing Christ by placing him above the reach of our mortal frailties. Jesus, he urged, "did not so much want to be admirable as to be lovable."[148] Erasmus emulates his Master in craving to be *amabilis*—such is the meaning of *erasmios*—rather than *mirabilis*. He is even admired by his foes for his genius and learning and versatility; he was beloved by the people nearest to him. Several students of his Paris days remained his lifelong friends; one of them, Mountjoy, insisted on sharing him with his family. Colet's mother, Dame Christian, would remember his stay with her at Stepney "cheerfully and with pleasure."[149] More, who knew him best, endorsed the program of his name by exclaiming *Erasme mi erasmiotate*,[150] a phrase he translated fifteen years later into "Erasmus my darling never so dear."[151] More assures us that his "vehement affection" is prompted by the labors through which Erasmus has won the heart of all of Christendom.[152] No wonder, then, if Boniface Amerbach, the witness of Erasmus' last years, the confidant with whom he exchanged more letters than with anyone else, concludes his farewell to Erasmus by saying: "Most holy was his living, and most holy his dying."[153]

Are we tempted to say *Sancte Erasme, ora pro nobis*, as Nephalius in *Convivium religiosum* could hardly help exclaiming *Sancte Socrates*?[154] Shall we canonize him privately as he did for Vitrier and Colet?[155] He himself would beg us not to. He wants to be loved as a "weak and sick Christian."[156] Vitrier "aspired

---

[147] Godin, line 486.

[148] Allen 1: Ep. 109, line 116.

[149] Allen 2: Ep. 423, line 65.

[150] The superlative, meaning "amabilissime," is printed in Greek (Allen 3: Ep. 683, line 13). In 1532 More will innovate by using Erasmus' first name "Desideri dulcissime" (Allen 10: Ep. 2659, line 2).

[151] CW 8:178.

[152] *Correspondence of Sir Thomas More*, 141; CW 15:158.

[153] Quoted in Gordon Rupp's entry "Erasmus," *Encyclopaedia Britannica*, which I read in the 1968 edition.

[154] ASD 1–3:254.

[155] Godin, lines 604–6.

[156] Allen 5: Ep. 1342, line 999: "Si quis Erasmum non potest amare ut Christianum infirmum, sumat in eum quem volet affectum: ego alius quam sum esse non possum," I render "infirmum" with two epithets because it can simultaneously connote lack of health and lack of strength.

to the glorious palm of martyrdom," Erasmus says; "it is an honor I find myself unworthy of."[157] Let Thomas More and his family be "not only content, but also glad" of heaven's visitation when the fire devours their Chelsea estate; let More repeat Job's proverbial "the Lord gave, the Lord has taken away, blessed be the Lord's name"; Erasmus confesses that he cannot— he cannot yet—apply that formula by thanking God for the discomforts of his life at Freiburg, away from the amenities of Basel.[158] If not quite a saint, then, he is, as Beatus Rhenanus says to the emperor, "on all counts *erasmios*, that is lovable."[159] Nor is Bernard Levin the only person in 1992 who could publicly hail him as "the man I love more than any human being from all the centuries of humanity: Desiderius Erasmus of Rotterdam and Basle."[160]

What is the secret of this lasting appeal? No doubt a deep humanity rooted in the love of God, itself a source of joy and peace. Alacrity, a characteristic mood of that perfect priest, Vitrier, is also a refrain of the debate with Colet, in which Erasmus probes the heart of Jesus in his death-agony, full of "holy joy" even while he "sweated drops of blood."[161] This cheerfulness born of Christian optimism is amalgamated in the writer with a deliberate imitation of Socrates' jocose approach. Horace's question, "what is it that keeps the laugher from telling the truth?" supports Erasmus' claim that "the *Moria* does nothing else under its playful guise than was done by the *Enchiridion*."[162] In his *Apology*, More paraphrases the Roman dictum as "a man may sometime say full sooth in game" and proceeds to justify his own "sports and merry tales" by saying that for "one that is but a layman as I am, it may better haply become him merrily to tell his mind, than seriously and solemnly to preach."[163]

"Ay, there's the rub," no doubt. Erasmus is not a layman. As a priest, it "becomes" him to preach, and as a don, to make pronouncements. Yet this he will not do, so eager is he to shun the style of his fellow theologians, the self-conscious pontificating *magistri nostri* of Louvain and Paris. So, to Sepúlveda as well as to Luther, he appeared as a sceptic, another Lucian. But to Colet he

---

[157] Godin, lines 70–74.

[158] More's letter to his wife Alice, dated from court September 3, 1529, is an anthology piece. See *Correspondence of Sir Thomas More*, 422–23. Erasmus did not know of it when he wrote to Botzheim: "Quantum adhuc absumus a formula beati Iobi!" (Allen 8: Ep. 2205, line 30). The adverb "adhuc" implies that he has not given up trying to attain the grateful abandon to God's loving plan exemplified by "the blessed Job" (1:21).

[159] Allen 1: Ep. IV, line 546.

[160] *The Times Saturday Review*, February 1, 1992.

[161] Godin, lines 26, 41, 95, 112; Allen 1: Ep. 109, lines 67–127.

[162] "Ridentem dicere verum / Quid vetat?" (Sat 1, 1, 24–25, quoted in Allen 2: Ep. 337, lines 99–100); Allen 2: Ep. 337, lines 91–92.

[163] CW 9:170–71.

was the gracious exponent of the Gospel as *eu-angelium*, glad tidings; the *schola catechizationis* that Saint Paul's was would have Erasmus for its catechist, to express the creed in easily memorable and altogether unequivocal Latin verse, and for its preacher, whose sermon would lead the boys to the child Jesus as model, but also as the source of light and life.

Chapter 17 of Saint John's Gospel is traditionally called "the priestly prayer" of Jesus. It stresses knowledge through the Word and the resulting *agapè*, the end fruit being such union between humans as emulates the unity of the three divine Persons. That fairly sums up Erasmus' own priestly program. He informs in the hope of inflaming. Two treatises, separated by ten years, are characteristic of his accents: one, on God's mercy, *De immensa Dei misericordia*, translated into English by Gentian Hervet, at the request of Blessed Margaret Pole, and the other *De amabili ecclesiae concordia*. The keyword in each title contains the root *cor*, which invites a "heart to heart" relationship between the sinful creature and a merciful God, and between the members of the church, through a shared "love and imitation of Christ."[164]

---

[164] This echoes a letter from Colet (Allen 2: Ep. 593, lines 15–19) about the sterility of knowledge which does not lead to "fervent love and imitation of Christ," words cited by J. B. Trapp in *Erasmus, Colet and More* (London: The British Library, 1991), 132. To P. A. Sawada we owe the information that a statue of Erasmus, now preserved in the Museum of Ueno, Tokyo, came to Japan as the figurehead of a Dutch vessel named *De Liefde*, "Love" (the theological virtue of charity) and has been in Japan since 1598. See its reproduction as cover of *Moreana* 64 (March 1980), with explanation on 5–6.

BIBLIOGRAPHY

~

WORKS OF ERASMUS USED IN THIS VOLUME

Ad fratres inferioris Germaniae. ASD (*q.v.*).

"Ad Spiritum Sanctum," *Precationes aliquot novae.* LB (*q.v.*).

Adversus febricitantis cuiusdam libellum responsio. LB (*q.v.*).

Allen = *Opus epistolarum Des. Erasmi Roterodami.* Ed. P. S. Allen, H. M. Allen, and H. W. Garrod. 12 vols. Oxford: Clarendon Press, 1906–1958.

Apologia adversus Petrum Sutorem. LB (*q.v.*).

Appendix respondens ad quaedam antapologiae Petri Sutoris. LB (*q.v.*).

ASD = *Opera Omnia Desiderii Erasmi Roterodami.* Ed. C. Reedijk et al. Amsterdam: North Holland Publishing Co., 1969–.

Christiani matrimonii institutio (1526). LB (*q.v.*).

Colloquies of Erasmus. Trans. Craig R. Thompson. Chicago: University of Chicago Press, 1965.

Concio de puero Jesu. 1511/1514. CWE (*q.v.*).

Concionalis interpretatio in Psalmum LXXXV. 1528. ASD (*q.v.*).

Consilium cuiusdam ex animo cupientis esse consultum et romani pontificis dignitati et christianae religionis tranquillitati. 1520.

Contra pseudoevangelicos. 1530. ASD (*q.v.*).

CW = *Complete Works of Sir Thomas More.* New Haven: Yale University Press, 1963–.

CWE = *Collected Works of Erasmus.* Toronto: University of Toronto Press, 1974–.

De conscribendis epistolis. Cambridge: Siberth, 1521.

De puritate tabernaculi sive ecclesiae christianae. 1536. ASD (*q.v.*).

De sarcienda ecclesiae concordia. 1533.

De veritate corporis et sanguinis Dominici in Eucharistia. Freiburg: Emmeus, 1530.

Declamatio de pueris statim ac liberaliter instituendis. Ed. Jean-Claude Margolin. Geneva: Droz, 1966.

Declarationes adversus censuras theologorum parisiensium. LB (*q.v.*).

A Dialogue concerning Heresies. 1529. CW (*q.v.*).

Dulce bellum inexpertis. 1515.

Ecclesiastes. LB (*q.v.*).

Enchiridion. LB (*q.v.*).

Epistola ad fratres inferioris Germaniae. ASD (*q.v.*).

Epistola contra eos qui se falso iactant evangelicos. 1529. ASD (*q.v.*).

Exomologesis. 1524. LB (*q.v.*).

Explanatio symboli (1533), ASD (*q.v.*).

The Funeral. In Craig R. Thompson, trans. *The Colloquies of Erasmus*. Chicago: University of Chicago Press, 1965.

Hyperaspistes I and *II*. LB (*q.v.*).

In Psalmum XXII Enarratio Triplex. 1530. ASD (*q.v.*).

Institutio principis christianis. 1516.

LB = *Desiderii Erasmi Roterodami Opera Omnia*. Ed. J. Leclerc, 10 vols. Leiden: 1703–1706.

Lupton = Desiderius Erasmus. *The Lives of Jehan Vitrier, Warden of the Franciscan Convent of Saint-Omer, and John Colet, Dean of St. Paul's*. Trans. J. H. Lupton. London: G. Bell, and Sons, 1883.

Methodus. In Holborn (*q.v.*).

Opera Omnia Desiderii Erasmi Roterodami. Ed. C. Reedijk et al. Amsterdam: North Holland Publishing Co., 1969—.

Paraphrase on Acts. 1524. LB (*q.v.*).

Paraphrase on 1 Corinthians. 1519. LB (*q.v.*).

Precatio ad Dominum Jesum pro pace ecclesiae. 1532.

Precationes aliquot novae. 1535. LB (*q.v.*).

Querela Pacis. LB (*q.v.*).

Ratio verae theologiae. Holborn (*q.v.*).

Responsio ad Petri Cursii defensionem.LB (*q.v.*).

Sacri sacerdotii defensio contra Lutherum. 1525.

Spongia adversus aspergines Hutteni, ASD (*q.v.*).

WORKS OF OTHERS.

Amiel, Charles. *See under* Bataillon, Marcel.

Auer, Alfons. *Die vollkommene Frömmigkeit eines Christen*. Düsseldorf: Patmos, 1954.

Augustijn, C. "The Ecclesiology of Erasmus," in *Scrinium Erasmianum*, 2 vols. Ed. J. Coppens. Leiden: E. J. Brill, 1969.

——. "Erasmus und seine Theologie: hatte Luther recht?," in Jean-Pierre Massaut. Ed. *Colloque Erasmien de Liège*. Paris: Société d'Editions "Les Belles Lettres," 1987.

——. *Erasmus von Rotterdam: Leben-Werk-Wirkung*. Munich: C. H. Beck, 1986.

——. *Erasmus: His Life, Works, and Influence*. Trans. J. C. Grayson. Toronto: University of Toronto Press, 1991).

Backus, Irena. "Deux cas d'évolution théologique dans les 'Paraphrases' d'Erasme," in *Actes du Colloque international Erasme*. Ed. Jacques Chomarat, André Godin, and Jean-Claude Margolin. Geneva: Droz, 1990.

——. *Lectures humanistes de Basile de Césarée: traductions latines (1439–1618)*. Paris: Institut d'Etudes Augustiniennes, 1990.

Bainton, Roland H. "The *Querela Pacis* of Erasmus: Classical and Christian Sources," *Archiv für Reformationsgeschichte* 42 (1951): 32–47.

Barland, Adriaan. *Enarrationes in quattuor primos libros Aeneidos*. Antwerp: Hillen, 1544.

Bartlett, Kenneth R. See Eisenbichler, Konrad.

Bataillon, Marcel. *Erasme et l'Espagne*. Ed. Daniel Devoto and Charles Amiel. Rev. ed., 3 vols. Geneva: Droz, 1991.

Bedouelle, Guy. *e Quincuplex Psalterium de Lefèvre d'Etaples*. Geneva: Droz, 1979.

Béné, Charles. *Erasme et Saint Augustin*. Geneva: Droz, 1969.

Bietenholtz, Peter G. "*Simulatio*: Erasme et les interprétations controversées de Galates 2:11–14," in *Actes du Colloque international Erasme*. Ed. Jacques Chomarat, André Godin, and Jean-Claude Margolin. Geneva: Droz, 1990.

——, and Thomas Brian Deutscher, eds. *Contemporaries of Erasmus: A Biographical register of the Renaissance and Reformation*. Toronto: University of Toronto Press, 1985-1987. Intended to accompany: *Collected Works of Erasmus*, 1974.

Boman, Thorleif. *Hebrew Thought Compared with Greek*. Philadelphia: Westminister Press, 1960.

Bot, P. J. M. *Humanisme en Onderwijs in Nederland*. Utrecht: Het Spectrum, 1955.

Bourdieu, Pierre. *Distinction: A Social Critique of the Judgment of Taste*. Cambridge: Harvard University Press, 1984.

Boyle, Marjorie O'Rourke. *Rhetoric and Reform: Erasmus' Civil Dispute with Luther*. Cambridge: Harvard University Press, 1983.

Bruford, W. H. *Culture and Society in Classical Weimar*. Cambridge: Cambridge University Press, 1975.

Budé, Guillaume. *De transitu Hellenismi ad Christianismum*. Paris: R. Estienne, 1535.

Byron, Brian. "From Essence to Presence: A Shift in Eucharistic Expression Illustrated from the Apologetic of Saint Thomas More." In *Miscellanea Moreana*, 429–44.

van Caenegem, R. C. *Geschiedenis van het Strafrecht in Vlaanderen van de Xie tot de XIVe Eeuw*. Brussels: Paleis der Akademien, 1954.

Caprariis, Francesco di. "Conversione alla Storia," part 2 of *Francesco Guicciardini: Dalla Politica alla Storia*. Bari: Laterza, 1950.

Carrington, Laurel. "The Writer and His Style: Erasmus' Clash with Guillaume Budé." *Erasmus of Rotterdam Society Yearbook* 10 (1990): 61–84.

Carvajal, Luis. *Apologia monasticae religionis*. Salamanca, 1528.

——. *Dulcoratio amarulentiarum Erasmicae responsionis*. Paris: Simon Colinaeus, 1530.

The Catechism of the Catholic Church. Rome: Libreria Editrice Vaticana, and Washington: United States Catholic Conference, 1994.

Chabod, Federico. "The Concept of the Renaissance." In *Machiavelli and the Renaissance*. Trans. David Moore. Cambridge: Harvard University Press, 1965.

Chantraine, Georges. *"Mystère" et "Philosophie du Christ" selon Erasme*. Gembloux: Editions J. Duculot, 1971.

———. *Erasme et Luther: Libre et serf arbitre?* Paris: Lethielleux, 1981.

Chomarat, Jacques. *Grammaire et rhétorique chez Erasme*. 2 vols. Paris: Société d'Edition "Les belles lettres," 1981.

———, André Godin, and Jean-Claude Margloin, eds. *Actes du Colloque international Erasme*. Geneva: Droz, 1990.

Clenardus, *De modo docendi pueros analphabetos*. Cologne, 1550.

Colet, John. *John Colet's Commentary on First Corinthians*. Ed. Bernard O'Kelly and Catherine A. L. Jarrot. Binghamton: Medieval and Renaissance Texts and Studies, 1985.

Congar, Yves. *L'Eglise de saint Augustin à l'époque moderne*. Paris: Les Editions du Cerf, 1970.

Coppens, J. ed. *Scrinium Erasmianum*. 2 vols. Leiden: Brill, 1969.

———. *Apologia pro pietate in Erasmi Roterodami Enchiridion cano-nem quintum*, by Eustachius Sichem. Brussel: Paleis der Academiën, 1975.

Dealy, Ross. "The Dynamics of Erasmus' Thought on War." *Erasmus of Rotterdam Society Yearbook* 4 (1984): 53–67.

Della Casa, Giovanni. *Il "Galateo."* Milan: n. p., 1910.

———. *Galateo*. Trans. Konrad Eisenbichler and Kenneth R. Bartlett. Toronto: Centre for Reformation and Renaissance Studies, 1986.

Delumeau, Jean. *Le péché et la peur: Culpabilisation en occident*. Paris: Fayard, 1983. Trans. Eric Nicholson, *Sin and Fear: The Creation of a Guilt Culture in the West*. New York: St. Martin's, 1990.

Derrida, Jacques. *De la grammatologie*. Paris: Editions de Minuit, 1967.

Deutscher, Thomas Brian. *See* Bietenholz, Peter G.

D'Souza, Dinesh. *Illiberal Education*. New York: Free Press, 1991.

Devoto, Daniel. *See* Bataillon, Marcel.

Eisenbichler, Konrad, and Kenneth R. Bartlett, trans. *Galateo* by Giovanni della Casa. Toronto: Centre for Reformation and Renaissance Studies, 1986.

Elias, Norbert. *Über den Prozess der Zivilisation*, 2 vols. Bern and Munich: Francke, 1969.

Enriques, Anna M. "La Vendetta nella Vita e nella Legislazione Fiorentina," *Archivo Storico Italiano*, series 7, 19 (1933): 85–146, 181–223.

Ferguson, Wallace K. ed. *Erasmi Opuscula: A Supplement to the Opera Omnia*. The Hague: Martinus Nijhoff, 1933.

Fernandez-Santamaria, J. A. "Erasmus on the Just War," *Journal of the History of Ideas* 34 (1973): 209–26.

Fish, Stanley. Interview. In D'Souza, Dinesh (*q.v.*).

Fisher, John. *Opera Omnia*. Würzburg, 1597.

Froude, J. A. *Life and Letters of Erasmus*. London: Longmans, 1895.

Gadamer, Hans-Georg. *Truth and Method*. Trans. Joel Weinsheimer and Donald G. Marshall. 2d rev. ed. New York: Crossroad, 1989.

Gebhardt, Georg. *Die Stellung des Erasmus von Rotterdam zur römischen Kirche*. Marburg an der Lahn: Oekumenischer Verlag Dr. R. F. Edel, 1966.

Gerl, Hanna-Barbara. *Rhetorik als Philosophie: Lorenzo Valla*. Munich: W. Fink, 1974.

Godin, André, ed. Desiderius Erasmus. *Vies de Jean Vitrier et de John Colet*. Angers: Editions Moreana, 1982.

———. *See also* Chormarat, Jacques, et al.

Gleason, John B. "The Birth Dates of John Colet and Erasmus of Rotterdam: Fresh Documentary Evidence," *Renaissance Quarterly* 32 (1979):73–76.

———. "The Earliest Evidence for Ecclesiastical Censorship of Printed Books in England," *The Library*, 6th ser., 4 (June 1982):137.

Gogan, Brian. *The Common Corps of Christendom: Ecclesiological Themes in the Writings of Sir Thomas More*. Leiden: E. J. Brill, 1982.

Gordon, Walter M. *Humanist Play and Belief: The Seriocomic Art of Desiderius Erasmus*. Toronto. University of Toronto Press, 1990.

Grafton, Anthony, and Lisa Jardine. *From Humanism to the Humanities*. Cambridge: Harvard University Press, 1986.

Grayson, J. C., trans. *Erasmus: His Life, Works, and Influence* by C. Augustijn. Toronto: University of Toronto Press, 1991.

Guarnaschelli, John S. "Erasmus' Concept of the Church, 1499–1524: An Essay Concerning the Ecclesiological Conflict of the Reformation." Ph.D. dissertation, Yale University, 1966.

Halkin, Léon-E. "La piété d'Erasme," *Revue d'histoire ecclésiastique* 79 (1984).

———. "Erasme contre la liturgie?" in *Miscellanea Moreana: Essays for Germain Marc'hadour*. Ed. Clare M. Murphy, Henri Gibaud, and Mario A. Di Cesare. Binghamton: Medieval and Renaissance Texts and Studies, 1989.

———. "Erasme pèlerin," *Scrinium Erasmianum*. 2 vols. Ed. J. Coppens. Leiden: Brill, 1969.

———. *Erasmus ex Erasmo: Erasme éditeur de sa correspondance*. Aubel, Belgium: P. M. Gason, 1983.

———. *Erasme parmi nous*. Paris: Fayard, 1987.

Hardison, O. B. *Christian Rite and Christian Drama in the Middle Ages*. Baltimore: Johns Hopkins University Press, 1965.

Harlan, David. "Intellectual History and the Return of Literature," *American Historical Review* 94 (1989):600 ff.

Harth, Dietrich. *Philologie und praktische Philosophie: Untersuchungen zum Sprach– und Traditionsverständnis des Erasmus von Rotterdam*. Munich: W. Fink, 1970.

Henderson, John, ed. *See under* Verdon, Timothy.

Hentze, Willi. *Kirche und kirchliche Einheit bei Desiderius Erasmus von Rotterdam*. Paderborn: Verlag Bonifacius-Druckerei, 1974.

Herding, Otto. "Erasmus—Frieden und Krieg," In *Erasmus und Europa*. Ed. August Buck. Wiesbaden: Otto Harrassowitz, 1988.

Heredia, V. Beltran de. *Cartulario de la Universidad de Salamanca VI*. Salamanca: Publicaciones de la Universidad, 1973.

Himelick, Raympnd. trans. *Erasmus and the Seamless Coat of Jesus*. Lafayette, Indiana: Purdue University Press, 1971.

Hoffmann, Manfred. "Erasmus on Church and Ministry," *Erasmus of Rotterdam Society Yearbook* 6 (1986): 30.

——. "Erasmus on Free Will: An Issue Revisited," *Erasmus of Rotterdam Society Yearbook* 10 (1990): 119–20.

Holborn, Hajo, and Annemarie Holbhorn, eds. *Desiderius Erasmus Roterodamus: Ausgewählte Werke*. Munich: C. H. Beck'she Verlagsbuchhandlung, 1933.

Holdcroft, David. *Saussure: Signs, System, and Arbitrariness*. Cambridge: Cambridge University Press, 1991.

House, Seymour B. "Sir Thomas More as Church Patron," *Journal of Ecclesiastical History* 40 (1989): 217.

Hughes, John Jay. *The Stewards of the Lord*. London: Sheed and Ward, 1970.

Jaeger, Werner. *Paideia: The Ideal of Greek Culture*. 3 vols. Oxford: Blackwell, 1939–1944.

Jardine, Lisa. *See* Grafton, Anthony.

Jarrot, Catherine A. L., ed. *See* Colet, John.

Jay, Martin. *The Dialectical Imagination: The Frankfurt School and the Institute of Social Research, 1923–1950*. Boston: Little, Brown, 1973.

Jortin, John. *The Life of Erasmus*. 2 vols. London: J. Whitsun and B. White, 1758–1760.

King, Margaret L. "Book-Lined Cells: Women and Humanism in the Early Italian Renaissance." In Rabil, *Renaissance Humanism* (*q.v.*), 1: 434–53.

Kisch, Guido. *Erasmus' Stellung zu Juden und Judentum*. Tübingen: J. C. B Mohr [Paul Siebeck], 1969.

Kohls, Ernst-Wilhelm. *Die Theologie des Erasmus*. 2 vols. Basel: Helbing & Lichtenhahn/Friedrich Reinhart Verlag, 1966.

Kors, Alan Charles. *Atheism in France, 1650–1729*. Princeton: Princeton University Press, 1990.

Kristeller, P. O. "The Humanist Movement." In *Renaissance Thought*. New York: Harper, 1961.

van Leijenhorst, C. G. "Adrianus Barlandus." In Beitenholz, *Contemporaries of Erasmus*, (*q.v.*), 1: 95–96.

Liu, Alan. "Local Transcendence: Cultural Criticism, Postmodernism, and the Romanticism of Detail," *Representations* 32 (Fall 1990): 97ff.

Lortz, Joseph. *Die Reformation in Deutschland*. 2 vols., 4th ed. Freiburg im Breisgau: Herder, 1962.

Luther, Martin. *D. Martin Luthers Werke*. 61 vols. in 76. Weimar: Böhlau, 1909–1983.

——. *D. Martin Luthers Werke: Briefwechsel*. 15 vols. Weimar: Herrmann Böhlaus Nachfolger, 1930–1978.

——. *Luther's Works*. Ed. Jaroslav Pelikan and Helmut T. Lehman. 55 vols. Philadelphia: Muhlenberg Press, Fortress, 1958–1986.

McConica, James K. "Erasmus and the Grammar of Consent." In *Scrinium Erasmianum*. Ed. J. Coppens. 2 vols. Leiden: Brill, 1969.

——. "Erasmus and the *Julius*: A Humanist Reflects on the Church." In *The Pursuit of Holiness in Late Medieval and Renaissance Religion*. Ed. Charles Trinkaus and Heiko A. Oberman. Leiden: E. J. Brill, 1974.

——. *English Humanists and Reformation Politics under Henry VIII and Edward VI*. Oxford: Clarendon Press, 1965.

McCutcheon, Elizabeth. "Denying the Contrary: More's Use of Litotes in *Utopia*," *Moreana* 31–32 (November 1971). Reprinted in *Essential Articles for the Study of Thomas More*, ed. R. S. Sylvester and G. P. Marc'hadour. Hamden, Connecticut: Archon, 1977.

——. *My Dear Peter: The Ars Poetica and Hermeneutics for More's "Utopia."* Angers: Moreanum, 1983.

McKeon, Richard. "Renaissance and Method in Philosophy," *Studies in the History of Ideas* 3 (1933): 33–101.

McSorley, Harry J. "Free Will, Unfree Will, and Neo-Semipelagianism in Late Scholasticism." Chap. 7 of *Luther, Right or Wrong? An Ecumenical-Theological Study of Luther's Major Work, "The Bondage of the Will."* New York: Newman Press, 1969.

——. "Erasmus and the Primacy of the Roman Pontiff: Between Conciliarism and Papalism," *Archiv für Reformationsgeschichte* 65 (1974): 49–54.

Mansfield, Bruce. *Erasmus: Phoenix of His Age*. Toronto: University of Toronto Press, 1979.

Marc'hadour, Germain. "Pastiche and Parodie." In *Thomas More et la Bible*. Paris: Vrin, 1969.

——. *The Bible in the Works of St. Thomas More*. Nieuwkoop: B. de Graaf, 1970.

——. "Thomas More's Spirituality." In *St Thomas More: Action and Contemplation*. Ed. R. S. Sylvester. New Haven: Yale University Press, 1972.

Margolin, Jean-Claude. *See* Chormarat, Jacques, et al.

Massaut, Jean-Pierre. "Erasme, la Sorbonne et la nature de l'Eglise." In *Colloquium Erasmianum*. Mons: Centre universitaire de l'Etat, 1968.

——, ed. *Colloque Erasmien de Liège*. Paris: Société d'Editions "Les Belles Lettres," 1987.

Megill, Alan. "Nietzsche and the Aesthetic," Chap. 1 of *Prophets of Extremity*. Berkeley: University of California Press, 1987.

Meinecke, Fredrich. *Cosmopolitanism and the National State*. Trans. Robert B. Kimber. Princeton: Princeton University Press, 1970.

Mestwerdt, Paul. *Die Anfänge des Erasmus*. Leipzig: R. Haupt, 1917.

Miller, Clarence H, ed. *Moriae Encomium*. In ASD (*q.v.*).

Monfasani, John. "Humanism and Rhetoric." In Rabil, *Renaissance Humanism: Foundations, Forms and Legacy* (*q.v.*).

More, Thomas. *English Works of Sir Thomas More*. London: Cawood et al., 1557.

——. *The Correspondence of Sir Thomas More*. Ed. E. F. Rogers. Princeton: Princeton University Press, 1947.

Nauert, Charles G., Jr. "Renaissance Humanism: An Emergent Consensus and Its Critics," *Indiana Social Studies Quarterly* 33 (1980): 5–20.

Nicholson, Eric. *Sin and Fear: The Creation of a Guilt Culture in the West*. New York: St. Martin's, 1990.

Oberman, Heiko A. Review of Delumeau, *Sin and Fear (q.v.)*. *Sixteenth Century Journal* 23 (1992): 149–50,.

———. *The Roots of Antisemitism in the Age of Renaissance and Reformation*. Trans. James I. Porter. Philadelphia: Fortress, 1984.

———. *See also* Trinkhaus, Charles.

O'Donnell, Anne M., ed. *Erasmus' Enchiridion Militis Christiani: An English Version*. Oxford: Oxford University Press, 1981.

Oehler, Klaus. "Der Consensus omnium als Kriterium der Wahrheit in der antiken Philosophie und der Patristik," *Antike und Abendland* 10 (1961): 105–16.

Oelrich, Karl Heinz. *Der späte Erasmus und die Reformation*. Münster: Aschendorffische Verlagsbuchhandlung, 1961.

O'Kelly, Bernard, ed. *See* Colet, John.

Olin, John C. "Erasmus and the Church Fathers." In Olin, *Six Essays on Erasmus*. New York: Fordham University Press, 1979.

———, trans. *Thomas More: A Portrait in Words by His Friend Erasmus*. New York: Fordham University Press, 1977.

———, ed. *Christian Humanism and the Reformation*. 3d ed. New York: Fordham University Press, 1987.

O'Malley, John W. "Erasmus and Luther, Continuity and Discontinuity as Key to their Conflict," *Sixteenth Century Journal* 5, no. 2 (1974): 55.

———. *The First Jesuits*. Cambridge: Harvard University Press, 1993.

O'Rourke Boyle, Marjorie. *See* Boyle, Marjorie O'Rourke.

Ozment, Steven. *The Age of Reform: 1250–1550*. New Haven: Yale University Press, 1980.

Padberg, Rudolf. "Erasmus contra Augustinum: Das Problem des bellum justum in der erasmischen Friedensethik,." In *Colloque Erasmien de Liège*, ed. Jean-Pierre Massaut. Paris: Société d'Edition "Les Belles Lettres," 1987), 278–96.

Payne, John B. "Erasmus and Lefèvre d'Etaples as Interpreters of Paul," *Archiv für Reformationsgeschichte* 65 (1974): 54–83.

Peristiany, J. G., ed. *Honour and Shame: The Values of Mediterranean Society*. London: Weidenfeld and Nicholson, 1965.

Peters, Robert. "Erasmus and the Fathers: Their Practical Value," *Church History* 36 (1967): 254–61.

Phillips, Margaret Mann. "Visages d'Erasme," *Colloque Erasmien de Liège*. Ed. Jean-Pierre Massaut. Paris: Société d'Editions "Les Belles Lettres," 1987.

———. *The "Adages" of Erasmus: A Study with Translations*. Cambridge: Cambridge University Press, 1964.

Piers, Gerhardt, and Milton B. Singer. *Shame and Guilt: A Psychoanalytical and a Cultural Study*. Springfield, Ill.: Thomas, 1953.

Pio, Alberto. *Tres et viginiti libri in locos lucubrationum variarum Erasmi Roterodami*. Paris: Josse Bade, 1531.

Popkin, Richard. *Skepticism from Erasmus to Descartes*. Assen: Van Gorcum, 1960.

Post, R. R. *The Modern Devotion*. Leiden: E. J. Brill, 1969.

Quintilian. *Institutionis oratoris libri XII*.

Rabil, Albert, Jr., ed. *Renaissance Humanism: Foundations, Forms and Legacy*, 3 vols. Philadelphia: University of Pennsylvania Press, 1988.

Ranke, Leopold von. "Vorrede." In *Deutsche Geschichte im Zeitalter der Reformation*, eEd. Willy Andreas, 2 vols. Wiesbaden and Berlin: Vollmer, 1957.

Reeve, Anne, ed. *Erasmus' Annotations on the New Testament: The Gospels*. London: Duckworth, 1986.

———, ed. *Erasmus' Annotations on the New Testament: Galatians to Apocalypse*. Leiden: E. J. Brill, 1993.

———, and M. A. Screech, eds. *Novum Testamentum*: Erasmus' Annotations on the New Testament: Acts—Romans—I and II Corinthians. Leiden: E. J. Brill, 1990.

Rex, Richard. *The Theology of John Fisher*. Cambridge: Cambridge University Press.

Reynolde, William. *A Treatise Containing the True Catholic and Apostolic Faith of the Holy Sacrifice and Sacrament Ordained by Christ at His Last Supper.* Antwerp: J. Trognesius, 1593; Menston: Scolar Press, 1970.

Rogers, E. F., ed. *See* More, Thomas.

Rummel, Erika. *Erasmus' Annotations on the New Testament: From Philologist to Theologian*. Toronto: University of Toronto Press, 1986.

———. *Erasmus and His Catholic Critics*, 2 vols. Nieuwkoop: De Graaf, 1989.

———. "*Nihil actum est sine authoritate maiorum*: New Evidence Concerning an Erasmian Letter Rejecting the Accusation of Apostasy," *Bibliothèque d'Huma-nisme et Renaissance* 54 (1992): 725–31.

Rupp, E. Gordon, and Philip S. Watson, trans. and eds. *Luther and Erasmus: Free Will and Salvation*. London: SCM Press, 1969.

Ryan, Michael. *Marxism and Deconstruction*. Baltimore: Johns Hopkins University Press, 1983.

Schilling, Heinz. "Calvinism and the Making of the Modern Mind: Ecclesiastical Discipline of Public and Private Sin from the Sixteenth to the Nineteenth Century." In *Civic Calvinism*. Kirksville, Mo.: Sixteenth Century Essays and Studies, 1991.

Schindling, Anton. *Humanistische Hochschule und Freie Reichsstadt*. Wiesbaden: Steiner, 1971.

Schoeck, R. J. *Erasmus of Europe: The Making of a Humanist*. Edinburgh: Edinburgh University Press, 1990.

Schoengen, M., ed. *Narratio de Inchoatione Domus Clericorum in Zwollis*, by Jacobus de Voecht. Amsterdam: Mueller, 1908.

Schottenloher, Otto. "Erasmus und die Respublica Christiana," *Historische Zeitschrift* 210 (1970): 313.

———. *Erasmus im Ringen um die humanistische Bildungsform*. Münster: Aschendorff, 1933.

Screech, M. A. *Ecstasy and the Praise of Folly*. London: Duckworth, 1980. .

———. *See also* Reeve, Anne.

Sichem, Eustachius.*Apologia pro pietate in Erasmi Roterodami Enchiridion canonem quintum*. Antwerp: Vorsterman, 1531.

Slater, Phil. *Origin and Significance of the Frankfurt School: A Marxist Perspective*. London: Routledge and K. Paul, 1977.

Stadtwald, Kurt."'When O Rome Will You Cease to Hiss?' The Image of the Pope in the Politics of German Humanism." Ph.D. dissertation. University of Minnesota, 1991.

Steiner, George. *Real Presences: Is There Anything in What We Say?* Chicago: University of Chicago Press, 1989.

Sowards, J. Kelley. Review of *Erasmus of Rotterdam Society Yearbook* 1 (1981) in *Moreana*, 75–76 (1982): 64.

Thompson, Craig R. ed. *Inquisitio de fide: A Colloquy by Desiderius Erasmus Roterodamus*. New Haven: Yale University Press, 1950.

———, trans. *The Colloquies of Erasmus*. Chicago: University of Chicago Press, 1965.

Tracy, James D. "Erasmus Becomes a German," *Renaissance Quarterly* 21 (1968): 281–88.

———. "Against the 'Barbarians': the Young Erasmus and His Humanist Contemporaries," *Sixteenth Century Journal* 11 (1980): 7–8.

———. "Two Erasmuses, Two Luthers: Erasmus' Strategy in Defense of *De Libero Arbitrio*," *Archiv für Reformationsgeschichte* 78 (1987): 37–60.

———. "From Humanism to the Humanities: A Critique of Grafton and Jardine," *Modern Language Quarterly* 51 (1990): 122–43.

———. *Erasmus: The Growth of a Mind*. Geneva: Droz, 1972.

———. *The Politics of Erasmus: A Pacifist Intellectual and His Political Milieu*. Toronto: University of Toronto Press, 1978.

———. *Holland under Habsburg Rule, 1506–1566: The Formation of a Body Politic*. Berkeley: University of California Press, 1990.

Trapp, J. B. In *Erasmus, Colet and More*. London: The British Library, 1991.

Trinkaus, Charles. "Erasmus, Augustine, and the Nominalists," *Archiv für Reformationsgeschichte* 67 (1976): 5–32.

———, and Heiko A. Oberman, eds. *The Pursuit of Holiness in Late Medieval and Renaissance Religion*. Leiden: E. J. Brill, 1974.

Verdon, Timothy, and John Henderson, eds. *Christianity and the Renaissance: Image and Religious Imagination in the Quattrocento*.Syracuse: Syracuse University Press, 1990.

de Vocht, Henri. *History of the Foundation and Rise of the Collegium Trilingue Lovaniese: 1517–1550*. 4 vols. Louvain: Libraire Universitaire, 1951–1955.

de Voecht, Jacobus. *Narratio de Inchoatione Domus Clericorum in Zwollis*. Ed. M. Schoengen. Amsterdam: Mueller, 1908.

Vredeveld, Harry. "The Ages of Erasmus and the Year of His Birth," *Renaissance Quarterly* 46 (1993): 754–809.

Walter, Peter, *Theologie aus dem Geist der Rhetorik zur Schriftauslegung des Erasmus von Rotterdam*. Mainz: Matthias-Grunewald-Verlag, 1991.

Watson,Philip S. *See* Rupp, E. Gordon.

Welti, Manfred. "Ennio Filionardi." In Bietenholz, *Contemporaries of Erasmus* (*q.v.*), 2:34–35.

Welzig , Werner, ed., *Erasmus von Rotterdam: Ausgewählte Schriften*. 8 vols. Darmstadt: Wissenschaftliche Buchgesellschaft, 1967–1980.

Williams, Raymond. *Culture and Society: 1780–1950*. 1958; reprint, New York: Columbia University Press, 1983.

Woodward, W. H. *Vittorino da Feltre and Other Humanist Educators*. 1897; reprint, New York: Teachers College, Columbia University, 1964.

Worstbrock, F. J., ed. *J. Wimpfelingi Opera Selecta*. Munich: W. Fink, 1965.

Scripture References

INDEX

Continued next page

Continued next page

DATE DUE			